Gone Beaver
and
My Girlfriend's Girlfriend

Sticking Place Books 2026
© Jim McBride
Introduction © James Kenney

www.stickingplacebooks.com

ISBN 979-8-89976-066-2

Gone Beaver
and
My Girlfriend's Girlfriend

Jim McBride's
Lost Screenplays of the 1970s

Sticking Place Books
New York

Jim McBride, early 1980s.

Rediscovering Jim McBride
By James Kenney

Underground Beginnings: *David Holzman's Diary* (1967)

In the late 1960s, Jim McBride burst onto the scene as a bold young auteur with *David Holzman's Diary* (1967), today now widely regarded as one of the great independent works in American film history. Made on a shoestring budget (a mere $2,500) and shot guerrilla-style on the streets of New York, *David Holzman's Diary* is a faux documentary presented as the filmed diary of an aspiring filmmaker. At once an intimate character study and a sly satire of cinéma vérité, the film felt so authentic that early audiences were fooled—some viewers were "outraged" to discover in the end credits that David Holzman was fictional.

Yet this ingenious experiment was more than a "meta" cinematic prank. It was, in the words of critic Dave Kehr, an "ingenious puzzle movie" that probed the very nature of truth on film. McBride's protagonist sets out to capture the essence of his life by turning the camera on himself, only to discover that the very act of filming distorts what he hopes to preserve, exposing how observation reshapes experience and how the search for truth on film inevitably creates its own kind of fiction.

What makes the film all the more remarkable is how indirectly McBride arrived at it. He didn't come out of film school steeped in underground cinema or the French New Wave. "I did like watching movies," McBride explains, "but it's a longer story than it needs to be." As a college student, he spent a junior year in Brazil, where movies became both refuge and education. "Besides not speaking the language very well and not really getting a lot out of my classes, I went to the movies because everything was subtitled. I could understand Portuguese better by reading subtitles than by listening to it." It was there that he encountered his first art film—*La Dolce Vita*—"which made a big impression."

When McBride returned to the United States, he ended up at New York University largely by circumstance: "It was the only place that would accept my credits." Film, at first, was simply an elective. "Somebody told me, 'Take this movie course because all you do is watch movies!'" It sounded like a good idea, and in that class McBride encountered something that had never occurred to him before: "There were all these people who were planning to work in the movies. It never occurred to me that regular people could do that."

Among those classmates was Martin Scorsese. "Marty," recalls McBride, "was this guy who had seen every movie ever made and could quote them shot by shot. He was somebody I'd never met before—somebody who was really obsessed with the movies." That obsession proved contagious. Still, McBride insists that his formal education at NYU was relatively traditional. "There was no awareness of the Nouvelle Vague, underground movies or cinéma vérité that I recall. That all came just a little bit after. Jean-Luc Godard's *Breathless* in 1962 really was the start for many of us." It was only after graduating and while working what he describes as "lowly jobs like sweeping up editing rooms" that McBride felt the ground shift beneath him. "That's when all this exciting stuff was happening. Suddenly there were underground movies. I went to see them all."

David Holzman's Diary.

The genesis of *David Holzman's Diary* remains elusive, even to McBride. "It's a fair question," he told me when I asked how the idea came together. "I can't really remember in great detail." He recalls working for a company that made promotional films selling land in Florida when he had the idea "to make a diary movie. I don't really know where the idea came from." McBride found a cameraman and an actor and shot some footage—only to be fired from his job soon after. He stored the film in the trunk of his beat-up Volkswagen while searching for an editing room. When he finally found one, the film was gone. "It was stolen," he said. "God knows why anybody would, but in those days I guess people thought 16mm film must be porn."

The project might have ended there, but a year or two later McBride found himself working with Michael Wadleigh (later to direct *Woodstock*) at Paradigm Films. Wadleigh, he recalls, was "a handheld cinéma vérité cameraman for hire—which was a very rare thing in those days." McBride was doing basic work—syncing dailies, occasional sound—when he mentioned the diary-film idea. "Wadleigh said, 'Well, let's do it.' And we did." (Wadleigh gets a producer credit on the film.) The production was as improvised as the film itself: equipment that was rented for paid jobs would be quietly kept over the weekend, allowing McBride and his collaborators to shoot when no one was looking.

At the same time, McBride was immersing himself in the ethos of documentary cinema. "I was now passionate about cinéma vérité," he said. Working with Kit Carson, who played David Holzman, McBride became involved in interviewing the movement's central figures—Albert and David Maysles, Ricky Leacock, D.A. Pennebaker—for a commissioned monograph for the Museum of Modern Art. "We spent a good amount of time hanging out with them," he recalls. In his memory, some of that research came after *David Holzman's Diary* was shot, some before. The chronology, like the film itself, resists tidy ordering.

Despite, or perhaps because of this loose, almost accidental genesis, *David Holzman's Diary* struck a nerve. Despite its limited release, it quickly became a cause célèbre among cinephiles and critics. Chuck Kraemer predicted it would be remembered as "the underground autobiographical cinema verité film of the sixties." Much later, Richard Brody wrote in *The New Yorker* that the film is "an extraordinary portrait, through sharp and sentimental inventions, of the moods and tones of the era." And filmmakers took notice. Brian De Palma recalled in *Film Comment* that seeing *David Holzman's Diary* inspired him and his peers to pick up cameras: "My friends and I had cameras all the time… I filmed a whole section of my life… And it all came from *David Holzman's Diary*."

With its mix of wit and vérité grit, the film stands as an underground classic that anticipated today's selfie-documentary culture and announced, almost inadvertently, the arrival of a filmmaker uniquely attuned to the paradoxes of truth, performance, and self-exposure on film.

New Hollywood Experiments and Lost Visions (1969–1970s)

McBride followed up his groundbreaking debut with a pair of unconventional semi-documentaries that further blurred the line between life and art. *My Girlfriend's Wedding* (1969) was an intensely personal project, a real portrait of McBride's English girlfriend, Clarissa, marrying another man (a Yippie radical) just to stay in the country. Initially conceived as a short companion piece to *David Holzman*, it evolved into a feature-length vérité confession. In it, Clarissa speaks frankly about her life (past loves, a child given up for adoption, even an abortion) while McBride's camera captures the raw truth of her situation. The film opens with Clarissa literally holding up a mirror to the camera, symbolizing the self-reflection at play. If *David Holzman's Diary* was fiction posing as fact, *My Girlfriend's Wedding* was, as Jonathan Rosenbaum put it, "true autobiography offered as spectacle," turning McBride and his partner into actors in their own real-life drama.

He continued this experiment with *Pictures from Life's Other Side* (1971), a film whose origins are inseparable from the life McBride was living at the time. He, a pregnant Clarissa, and her ten-year-old son, Joe, left New York and headed west. "We took a trip across the country," he recalls, "thinking we were going to find—I don't know—another place to live. It was kind of the idea of getting back to the earth, and that kind of thing. We were very much hippies." The journey itself became the film. "We ended up in this little town in Northern California, living in a really remote place in the middle of nowhere, where Clarissa had the baby. We got into the life of living kind of in the wilderness, in the woods." Shot with the same diaristic openness that defined his earlier work, *Pictures from Life's Other Side* documents a family in motion—geographically, emotionally, and ideologically, and captures a way of life shaped by countercultural ideals and lived uncertainty.

As a "sequel-of-a-sort" to *My Girlfriend's Wedding*, the film pushed McBride's methods even further, featuring an extraordinarily candid depiction of free-love-era mores; the trio's casual nudity, intimacy, and domestic closeness can still startle modern viewers. Taken together, *David Holzman's Diary*, *My Girlfriend's Wedding* and *Pictures from Life's Other Side* form a loose trilogy of diary films, united by McBride's sustained inquiry into the unstable boundary between truth and performance. As he later reflected, he was "obsessed" at the time with questions of what was real and what was "honest" on camera. Few filmmakers of the period were as formally daring—or as personally exposed—in probing the intersection of lived experience and cinema during this fertile moment in New York underground film.

Amid these documentaries, McBride ventured into more narrative filmmaking under the banner of the emerging New Hollywood movement. His next feature, *Glen and Randa* (1971), began as a screenplay he wrote with Lorenzo Mans thanks to a grant from the American Film Institute, which had plans to produce feature films. In McBride's recollection, AFI held onto the project "for more than a year," and when they ultimately couldn't make it happen, they returned the rights along with "a small grant—$15,000, as a kind of booby prize" (money he used to make *Pictures from Life's Other Side*). Years later, during pre-production, McBride adds that Rudy Wurlitzer—"a friend of ours"—came in and "wrote some additional stuff" for the film. On-screen, the result retains the intimacy of McBride's earlier work: shot in an up-close, quasi-documentary style, *Glen and Randa* follows two naïve young survivors wandering a wasteland after civilization's collapse, with the same vérité naturalism McBride had applied to contemporary life. The film's oddness paid dividends with critics—*Time* named it one of the ten best films of 1971 and praised McBride's "distinctive cinematic flair," but its X rating and limited release kept it from the wider audience it deserved. In retrospect, it stands as a fascinating early-'70s artifact—an offbeat, daring blend of science-fiction premise and countercultural temperament. Film historian Kenneth Godwin later called it "one of the most convincing visions of the collapse of civilization ever put on screen," achieved through the same loose, vérité-inspired techniques that define McBride's earliest films.

In 1974, McBride took what might look, from a distance, like an unexpected detour when he directed a bawdy teen sex comedy called *Hot Times* (originally title: *A Hard Day for Archie*). But McBride is quick to correct the assumption that this was a reluctant or purely expedient assignment. "I very much wanted to make *Hot Times*," he says, explaining that the project came about after he ran into Lewis Mishkin, "a guy I'd attended third grade with" who had since become a producer of soft-core pornography. Mishkin agreed to finance the film on two conditions: "teenagers and sex," recalls McBride, adding that the characters "had to be either doing it or talking about it in every scene." McBride wrote the script, directed and edited the film himself, all for $5,000—and, as he puts it, "was, and still am, pretty proud of the result."

Stylistically and tonally, *Hot Times*—a raunchy spoof loosely inspired by *Archie* comics rather than cinéma vérité or post-apocalyptic allegory— was far removed from McBride's earlier, more formally adventurous work. The finished film was further compromised by distributor interference and censorship, and it quickly vanished into grindhouse obscurity. More importantly, it marked a turning point. After *Hot Times*, McBride didn't direct another movie for nearly a decade. Hollywood's doors remained hard to pry open and several passion projects he developed in this period fell apart, leaving the rightfully celebrated wunderkind of the '60s on the outside looking in. It was a frustrating era in which McBride nearly had to abandon filmmaking altogether; at one point in the early '70s he drove a taxi in New York to make ends meet.

Yet it was precisely during this difficult interlude that McBride wrote two of his most intriguing works—bold screenplays that, had they been produced, might today be hailed as cult classics of 1970s cinema. These "lost" projects, *Gone Beaver* and *My Girlfriend's Girlfriend*, form a revealing bridge between McBride's seminal work of the late 1960s and his eventual Hollywood resurgence in the 1980s.

The more outward-facing and ambitious of the two is *Gone Beaver*. Co-written with Lorenzo Mans, the project was McBride's audacious attempt to reinvent the Western. Set in the 1840s Rocky Mountains, the story is about an unlikely group of figures: a French-Canadian trapper (Coops Cooper), a cultured European artist wandering the frontier, a young Native American on a vision quest, and a stranded Englishwoman. In McBride and Mans's hands, this familiar terrain became something utterly singular. "We didn't invent the way the characters talked," says McBride. "It was all based on a lot of research into the culture of mountain men." Rather than a whimsical or stylized conceit, the screenplay's distinctive frontier argot grew out of historical immersion, grounding its hallucinatory qualities in lived vernacular. As a result, *Gone Beaver* brims with the hallmarks of the Acid Western subgenre (as later defined by critics like Pauline Kael): existential drift, spiritual ambiguity, and a subversive, dreamlike interrogation of American frontier mythology. Jonathan Rosenbaum, who reviewed the script, called it a "visionary" piece of work, and the project attracted serious talent. Vanessa Redgrave and Bruce Dern were attached to star, and Oscar-winning cinematographer Néstor Almendros was slated to shoot it. For a moment, *Gone Beaver* seemed poised to become McBride's magnum opus, an ambitious Western associated with BBS, the company behind *Easy Rider, The Last Picture Show,* and *Five Easy Pieces.*

But pre-production was troubled by a convergence of issues—visa problems, budget pressures, growing tensions with producers. McBride is also frank about his own role in the breakup. "I'm not sure that my departure from the project was completely high-minded," he adds. *Gone Beaver* ultimately never reached the screen, becoming another casualty of a rapidly changing industry, but its status as an unmade film has only deepened its mystique, a visionary script whose absence continues to haunt the margins of 1970s American cinema.

If *Gone Beaver* represents McBride's most expansive unrealized vision of the decade, *My Girlfriend's Girlfriend,* also unproduced, marks a decisive turn inward. Written after *Gone Beaver* stalled, the script is a raw, unfiltered relationship drama, unapologetic in its frank treatment of sexuality, power, and emotional vulnerability. Had it been filmed, it would have fit seamlessly into the most intimate strain of New Hollywood cinema. Reading it today, one is struck by how it walks a tightrope between realism and provocation, as if daring its characters to speak with unvarnished honesty even when it is messy or uncomfortable. Scenes don't feel conventionally written so much as caught in the moment. The dialogue has an almost improvised verisimilitude; we witness fumbling gestures of intimacy and affection that ring painfully true. McBride is decentering the typical male ego of the period's relationship dramas, embracing a *personal is political* ethos that examines gender and desire with a candor reminiscent of contemporaries like Paul Mazursky or John Cassavetes. It's a quieter, more intimate "what if" than *Gone Beaver,* surely—but no less revealing of McBride's range and sensitivity as a writer.

Taken together, *My Girlfriend's Girlfriend* and *Gone Beaver* show-case the remarkable range of McBride's imagination in the 1970s. One is an unflinchingly intimate, contemporary tale; the other a grand, mythic period piece. Tonally, they could not be further apart—yet they are kindred in their boldness. Each in its own way embodies the daring spirit of New Hollywood's golden years, when young filmmakers briefly had the freedom to chase idiosyncratic, noncommercial visions. In a sense, they represent the extremes of landscape and psyche that Jim McBride was exploring in that era, from the messy bedrooms of modern relation-ships to the wide-open mysticism of the Old West. While the films were never made, the scripts survive as vivid evidence of McBride's uncom-promising artistry during a period of transition, both for himself and for Hollywood at large.

Hollywood Reinvention: The 1980s Resurgence

After nearly a decade in the wilderness, McBride found a path back into filmmaking in the 1980s—but not because opportunity suddenly knocked. When he came to Hollywood, he says, "It was *My Girlfriend's Girlfriend* that I was trying to hawk." After being "rejected all over town," McBride was given blunt advice: "Someone told me I had to attach myself to a known quantity, like a book or a play, to get any traction." His response was strategic rather than opportunistic. "I came up with the idea of remaking *Breathless*," he said. "There were five years between conceiving it and actually making the film, and I had a lot of help, but it was my idea."

McBride's *Breathless* (1983) was not a studio assignment but a project he shepherded across years of stalled development, false starts, and near collapses. When the idea was first taken to Universal—through a friend of Kit Carson's—the studio responded enthusiastically. "Universal said, 'Oh, that's a great idea—let's do it,'" recalls McBride. The studio agreed to fund the script, which had not yet been written. It was at this early stage that casting entered the conversation, prematurely and problematically. "The guy at Universal said to me, 'By the way, I have this neighbor out in Malibu who I think might be really good for this movie. What do you think of Richard Gere?' I said, 'That's a terrible idea.'"

McBride and Carson wrote the script, Universal liked it, and atten-tion shifted to casting. The first serious candidate was Robert De Niro, who liked the script but remained elusive. "I'd call him every two weeks," says McBride. "He wouldn't commit, but he wouldn't say no either." Universal refused to move on. "They said, 'If De Niro's interested, we're interested.'" The stalemate dragged on for months until McBride called old schoolmate Martin Scorsese, who explained that De Niro was deeply-embedded in another role—*Raging Bull*—and physically transformed to the point of exhaustion. At McBride's request, Scorsese asked De Niro to

Valérie Kaprisky and Richard Gere in *Breathless.*

definitively say no so McBride could move on. De Niro did that—and Universal promptly dropped the project.

After a years-long slog through other studios and stars, the project eventually landed at Orion. Many actors were approached, and responses were consistent: they liked the script, then met McBride and said no. "They didn't want to do it with me directing," he says. "I was an unknown quantity." His agent finally urged him to step aside as director and retain only a writing credit. Reluctantly, McBride agreed and the film moved forward without him. A new director, Frank (*Quadrophenia*) Roddam came on and brought Richard Gere into the project. Pre-production began, then Roddam left to pursue another film. Gere refused to work with McBride. A new director was courted: Michael Mann, then primarily known for *Thief*. Mann rewrote the script in ways McBride "didn't particularly appreciate," entered pre-production, then left to pursue another project. Once again, the film was adrift. "They went back to Gere and said, 'How about McBride?' He said no." Desperate, McBride reached out to Paul Schrader, whom he knew loosely through Scorsese and who had directed Gere in *American Gigolo*. Schrader agreed to intervene. Gere agreed to meet.

Those meetings did not go well—at first. "I'm really not good at this kind of stuff—pitching people or impressing people with my brilliance," admits McBride. Between meetings, McBride wandered into a bookstore and found a book of photographs of Jerry Lee Lewis, the hero of the *Breathless* protagonist, in performance. He brought the book to the next meeting with Gere. "Something clicked in his head," says McBride.

"I think whatever idea of the character he had was the Michael Mann character. Somehow, when he saw these photos, me and my approach made sense to him." Gere and McBride pulled the project back to his original conception. Finally McBride had the job.

Seen in this light, *Breathless* reads less as a gift from the system than as a hard-won act of survival. There is still a poetic irony at work: the filmmaker who launched his career quoting Jean-Luc Godard in *David Holzman's Diary* now found himself officially remaking Godard's signature film. In McBride's transposition of the French New Wave classic ("*Breathless* was the thing that made me want to make movies," he once remarked) to sun-drenched 1980s Los Angeles, Gere plays a volatile, impulsive American, drawn into a charged relationship with a French student. The film sizzles with neon color and playful homage: comic-book imagery, rock-and-roll propulsion, jump cuts filtering Godard's spirit through American pop gloss.

Jim McBride and Richard Gere.

Directing Gere was its own education. "I was a wreck," admits McBride. As shooting began, he told Gere, "I've never directed real actors before. I know what to do with the camera, and I know what I want the character to be like—but you have to help me." Gere did. He insisted on protecting rehearsal space, eliminating distractions, and making the area in front of the camera feel safe. After a few tentative days, something shifted. Their ideas of the character initially differed; their instincts often clashed. But the collaboration took hold. "He liked the way I staged things," recalls McBride, "and it became a really wonderful relationship."

Critical reaction to *Breathless* was divided. Some found it brash and exhilarating, others saw a Hollywood remake of Godard as sacrilege. McBride himself approached the film with characteristic self-awareness, jokingly calling it "an exploitation of the Godard movie" and acknowledging that he took the job, in part, simply "to get a chance to direct a movie" after years on the sidelines. In hindsight, *Breathless* stands as an audacious collision of European art-film legacy and 1980s American excess, as well as proof that McBride could survive inside the studio system without surrendering his instincts. It was not a capitulation but a recalibration.

Looking back, McBride is acutely aware of how improbable this comeback really was. When I asked whether he had felt similar anxiety years earlier—reading *Gone Beaver* again now, with its buffalo stampedes, sprawling landscapes, and demanding physical production, he surprised me by saying no. At the time, he recalls, the scale didn't intimidate him. "Funny thing is, no—I had lots of great images in my mind." What changed was perspective. "When I reread the script now, before I sent it to you," he said, "my thought was: this is unmakeable. It's ridiculous."

This admission reframes *Gone Beaver* as a measure of how far McBride's imagination once ranged, and how the industry around him ultimately narrowed. In the early 1970s he could conceive of a film that moved freely between myth, history, and spectacle without doubting his ability to direct it. By the early 1980s, after years of stalled projects and professional exile, survival itself had become the achievement. *Breathless* may have been smaller, more strategic, and born of necessity, but it carried with it the hard-earned discipline of a filmmaker who had learned what could and could not be made, and under what conditions.

That tension between the unmakeable and the merely difficult would define McBride's second act. If *Gone Beaver* represents the outer limit of his unrestrained 1970s imagination, *Breathless* marks the moment when that imagination learned how to adapt without disappearing. The films that followed would benefit from both impulses: the visual audacity of the earlier scripts and the practical clarity forged in Hollywood's crucible.

McBride's next film, *The Big Easy* (1986), marked the moment when his hard-won Hollywood education finally paid off. A sexy neo-noir thriller

Ellen Barkin and Dennis Quaid in *The Big Easy.*

set in the humid, jazz-soaked environs of New Orleans, the film became both a critical and commercial hit. McBride directed and co-wrote the picture, infusing what might have been a fairly standard crime story—cops, mobsters, political corruption—with a rowdy sense of place and character that lifted it far above the typical 1980s thriller.

The project came to him without ceremony. "I really couldn't get arrested," says McBride. "A lot of it's my own fault—I'm not really good at selling myself." His agent sent him a script originally set amid police corruption in Chicago. McBride saw potential, but only if it were rewritten. "I said: 'I think you should move it to New Orleans.' There's plenty of corruption there and it's much more organic." The suggestion wasn't arbitrary. Years earlier, McBride had spent time in the city while attempting to adapt Walker Percy's *The Moviegoer.* "We had gone to New Orleans to explore and learn a bit about the culture, and it seemed a great place to set *The Big Easy,*" he recalls. "The producer agreed, and that's really how I got the gig."

What followed was a perfect alignment of material, cast, and temperament. Dennis Quaid, who had recently starred in *The Right Stuff,* playing a genial, mildly corrupt New Orleans cop, brings an easy swagger that never curdles into cynicism. When the producer suggested Quaid, McBride was thrilled. The two connected quickly—helped, McBride suspects, by the fact that Quaid had seen and liked *Breathless.* Ellen Barkin gives a funny, sensual performance as a repressed district attorney determined to root out corruption. Her steely resolve collides with Quaid's insouciant charm in scenes that crackle with humor, friction, and carnality.

Critics responded enthusiastically. Roger Ebert placed *The Big Easy* on his list of the ten best films of 1987, calling it "one of the most definitely regional American films ever made," soaked in the music, dialect, and atmosphere of Louisiana. He praised McBride and his actors for "put[ting] a new spin on everything," noting that neither the romance nor the suspense "seem familiar" because the film pulses with offbeat life and local flavor. After years in the wilderness, McBride had delivered a stylish, crowd-pleasing film that still bore his unmistakable stamp—proof that his feel for character and environment could flourish inside a commercial framework.

Riding on *The Big Easy*'s success, McBride next tackled a high-profile biopic: *Great Balls of Fire!* (1989), the story of rock 'n' roll wild man Jerry Lee Lewis. Quaid threw himself into the role of the flamboyant, piano-pounding Lewis, and McBride delivered a film as frenetic and larger-than-life as its subject. *Great Balls of Fire!* further showcased McBride's versatility and his ongoing fascination with the tension between persona and truth (a theme running back to *David Holzman's Diary*). In capturing Lewis's outrageous public antics and private follies, McBride once again explored the performance of self—albeit this time on the grand stage of rock stardom.

Legacy and Rediscovery

By the end of the 1980s, Jim McBride had experienced the full spectrum of an artist's life in film: underground innovator, frustrated outsider, Hollywood craftsman. In the decades that followed, he continued to work steadily, often in forms and venues that reflected the changing realities of the industry. Like many filmmakers of his generation, McBride found that by the 1990s, serious adult films were increasingly unlikely to receive traditional theatrical releases, instead premiering on cable or circulating quietly.

Not every project landed where he hoped. In the mid-1990s he directed *Uncovered*, a European production starring Kate Beckinsale based on a novel by Arturo Pérez-Reverte. Looking back, McBride is unsparing about the experience. "It was one of the really bad decisions that I made," he acknowledges. Enticed by the opportunity to work in Europe and offered "more money than I'd ever made before," he agreed to the project, rewrote the script, and pressed ahead. "It just didn't work," he says, "and I have nothing but painful memories about it."

McBride's later period includes work he clearly remains fond of. *The Wrong Man* stands out. Made for Showtime and starring John Lithgow and Rosanna Arquette, it's a tight little noir that sneaks up on you. What looks at first like a simple man-on-the-run story turns into something more observant and offbeat, a drifting study of uneasy personalities rubbing against one another in sun-bleached ports and back roads. McBride lets

Dennis Quaid in *Great Balls of Fire.*

the scenes play out without fuss, trusting small looks, shifts in tone, and sudden turns of behavior to generate tension, and the oddball trio at the center gives the film a nervous, unpredictable pulse. It's modestly scaled but confident, closer in spirit to classic fatalistic noir than many slicker higher profile neo noirs of the period. For McBride, it's certainly his favorite among his later projects.

For cinephiles, McBride's legacy remains defined by the extraordinary bookends of his career. At one end stands *David Holzman's Diary*, his scrappy, brilliant debut and still one of the sharpest dissections of how cinema distorts even as it seeks truth. At the other, twenty years later, is *The Big Easy*, a film that proved McBride could translate his personal vision into mainstream genre filmmaking without losing its texture or soul. Bridging those poles are the fascinating, volatile projects of the 1970s — films made, unmade, or only imagined. This volume finally shines a light on two of the bravest and boldest of those unseen works and offers readers a chance to explore the missing chapters of McBride's creative life and his imagination at its most unleashed. *My Girlfriend's Girlfriend* and *Gone Beaver* capture a crucial moment of transition, the point where the freewheeling promise of the late 1960s collided with the harsher economic and institutional realities of the film industry. They show an artist unwilling to abandon bold ideas, even as the conditions for realizing them evaporated. On the page, both are brimming with the same vitality, intelligence, and audacity that define McBride's finest films. Together they reveal a storyteller of remarkable range, one who could imagine works as disparate as

Jim McBride, 1990s.

a faux-documentary, a poetic post-apocalypse, a raunchy teen comedy, a neon New Wave remake, a sultry Southern noir, a rock-and-roll biopic, and an acid Western.

For students of 1970s cinema and fans of McBride's work from the '60s and '80s, these scripts are more than just archival curiosities. They are engrossing works of art and key pieces of the McBride puzzle. Reading them, we gain new insight into how the daring spirit of the '60s flowed into the experiments of the '70s and how those experiments, in turn, laid the groundwork for McBride's 1980s reinvention. In short, *My Girlfriend's Girlfriend* and *Gone Beaver* invite us to rediscover Jim McBride as the risk-taker and storyteller he has always been—a director who gave us one of the greatest indie films of the 1960s, and who still, even in the projects that got away, speaks to what cinema can be at its most passionately personal and bracingly original.

GONE BEAVER

(Second draft screenplay)

Mans/McBride

May 22, 1972.

Hyampom, California

1. EXT. DAY. BEAVER STREAM

The sun is setting behind a mountain ridge. Beams of
orange light cast long shadows across a mountain meadow
below.

There is a stream, blocked at intervals by beaver dams.
On either bank are stumps of young trees. Grass and
flowers grow atop the dams. Frogs are chirruping along
the stream. A beaver drags a sapling into the stream.
Just beside where he enters the stream, there is a long
pole stuck in the ground, securing a metal chain which
leads into the water. There is a willow branch with a
white substance at its tip, arched above the water. The
beaver slips into the stream. The beaver's nose appears
above the water, sniffing. He swims toward the tip of
the willow branch. He scrambles up the bank of the stream,
trying to get closer, to get a better whiff.

2. EXT. DAY. BEAVER STREAM (UNDERWATER)

There is a large steel trap, planted on a ledge in the bank,
just below the surface of the water. We see the beaver's
hind leg step into the trap, and the great jaws clamp
down. The beaver plunges into the water, pulling the trap
off its ledge. On the floor of the stream the beaver
struggles desperately. Now he tries to swim up for air,
but the heavy trap, resting on the bottom, holds him
there. The beaver tries to chew the trap, then his own
leg. Finally, he drowns.

3. EXT. DAY. BEAVER STREAM

We see the meadow and the mountains beyond. We watch the
sun fall behind the mountains (TIME LAPSE PHOTOGRAPHY).

4. EXT. DAY. BEAVER STREAM

We watch the sun rise from behind the eastern mountains
(TIME LAPSE PHOTOGRAPHY).

A lone rider comes slowly towards the camera. He leads
a pack mule behind him, carrying trapper paraphernalia
and packs of beaver pelts. He is playing the fiddle and
we can hear it faintly. From time to time, he hums along
with the tune, and when he comes to the chorus, he sings
the line, "The sun comes up, the sun goes down". That's
the only part of the song that he can remember. This is
COUPS COOPER. He is tall and lean, about thirty, with long
red hair and a bushy red beard. He wears grease-stained
fringed buckskin, and an extravagant beaver hat, decorated
with feathers and elk's teeth. He has a Hawken rifle slung
across the pommel of his saddle. He plays the song over
and over punctuating it with little shouts. The camera
follows him across the meadow to the beaver stream.

4. CONTINUED

He slips off his horse by the edge of the stream. The
"float stick" marks his catch. He pulls it from the
water by the trap chain. He removes the beaver from the
trap and skins it. With his Green River knife (a fancy
butcher knife), he slits the beaver all the way up the
middle, and proceeds to peel and slice the hide from
the body. He removes a gland from the beaver's groin,
then the beaver's tail. He throws the rest of the body
away. He packs his trap and pelt away and mounts his
horse.

He rides off into the chapparal. A coyote appears. She
sniffs the beaver's remains, then gobbles them up.

5. EXT. DAY. COUPS' CAMP

The sun is setting. Coups is camping in a clearing by
a stream. Upstream and downstream, there are high bluffs.
Behind Coups is a long sloping meadow. He makes his camp
by a big rock along the water's edge. His horse is
grazing, picketed to a braided twenty-five foot rope,
called a riata. The mule, just relieved of its packs,
is rolling on its back, kicking its legs in the air.
He, too, is picketed on a riata.

He lays a small handful of punk on a rock, and strikes
sparks into it with his flints. It smolders. He takes
a handful of dried grass, and forms a little nest of it
around the punk. He waves the nest in the air. It flames
up. He lays it on the ground and adds twigs.

6. EXT. NIGHT. COUPS' CAMP

The fire is blazing now. Coups carries in an armload of
driftwood. He dumps the wood by the fire. The beaver
tail sizzles over the fire, skewered on the wiping stick
of his gun. Several beaver skins, stitched onto circular
willow hoops, lie on rocks to dry by the fire. His buffalo
robes lie by the fire, encircled by a rope to ward off
snakes. All this while, a great din of frogs has been
building up along the stream. The sun is down now. Coups
lights his pipe with a taper from the fire. A coyote howls,
far off. Another coyote, closer by, takes up the call.
Coups blows a puff of smoke to each of the four directions.
Soon we can hear all of the coyotes in the vicinity howling
and yipping to one another. This is something like a
musical concert. ("The music of the coyote - part bark,
whine, yelp, and occasionally a spasmodic laugh - now tenor,
now basso, now treble solo." Lewis H. Garrard)

Coups looks up at the sky. It is filled with stars. He
adds a piece of wood to the fire. He watches it catch
alight and burn. He looks closer and closer into the fire
until he can only see the grain of the red hot coals,
looking like pulsating, symmetrical caves in the side of
a glowing red mountain, and can only hear the hissing of
the hot air deep down in the coals.

7. <u>EXT. DAY. COUPS' CAMP</u>

The fire is just down to glowing embers. It is just
before dawn. Coups is asleep. His horse snorts. The
coyotes are silent. Coups wakes, picks up his gun, and
crosses to his horse. He can see the moon going down in
the pale sky. He walks in a circle around his camp.
he goes up a little rise. He looks out. Everything is
still. He walks a little farther. Here, it is pitch
dark. A breeze wafts by. He sniffs the breeze. He
hears a twig crack, and whirls around, pulling his rifle
to his shoulder. He listens for a moment, then continues
walking his circle. He does a couple of cartwheels. He
has practically come full circle. He looks toward the
moon. He sees, very faintly, a figure, silhouetted against
the moon, far away. He drops to his hands and knees, and
puts his ear to the ground. He runs to the fire and begins
to kick the burning coals in the river, which snap and
spit as they hit the water. Coups smothers the remaining
coals with dirt, and covers them with brush and leaves.
He unpickets his horse and mule and leads them back to
camp. He hurriedly packs his gear, constantly glancing
back at the steadily approaching figure.

We begin to hear snatches of Indian singing. The song
keeps breaking off abruptly in grunts, there is silence,
and then it begins again.

Coups takes a large piece of brush and, using it like a
broom, sweeps away every foot- and hoof-print from the area.

The sound of the singing gets closer. Now we can also
hear gasps and grunts. The singer sounds like he is in
great pain.

Coups drives his horse ahead of him into the stream,
brushing away their trail as they go. He leads the horse
upstream and under an overhanging ledge, where they are
shaded from the moonlight.

The singing figure passes close by the abandoned campsite.
It is a young Indian, named LOOKS FOR HIS HORSES. He is
about seventeen years old. He is naked, except for a
coyote skin loincloth. His body is painted white, except
for his forearms and hands, ankles and feet, and face and
neck, which are painted red. Two pieces of bone are
skewered into the flesh of his back. Attached to the
skewers is a cord, and attached to the cord is a buffalo
skull, which drags on the ground. Blood trickles from the
wounds on his back. His feet are bare and bloody. He is
in a trance. He staggers forward, almost without control.
His eyes are glazed. He keeps falling, picking himself up,
and staggering on. He keeps trying to sing, but doesn't
always manage to get it out. He stumbles into the stream.
He drags himself and his burden across the stream and up
the hill on the far side. He begins to sing again, his
medicine song.

7. CONTINUED

Coups rides warily out of his hiding place.

The Indian has disappeared over the top of the hill. One can still hear him singing. Suddenly the singing stops. There is no other sound.

Coups covers the horse's nose with his hand and leads his two animals across the stream and up the far hill. He crawls to the top of the hill and looks down.

8. <u>EXT. DAWN. MOUNTAIN LEDGE</u>

Fifty feet below him there is a small ledge that overlooks the plains to the East, where the sun is rising. On the ground there, a circle has been etched with a knife. There is a black line painted across the north-south axis of the circle, and a red line across the east-west axis. Four poles are planted in the ground at the four spots where the lines touch the circle. There is a fifth pole in the center, where the two lines cross. Feathers, strips of leather, and animal skins adorn the tops of each pole, with the buffalo skull hanging from the center one. There are footprints inside the circle where Looks has been dancing.

Looks For His Horses is in a trance, sitting beside the center pole, bent over his left hand, with a knife in his right hand. He amputates the top joint of the fourth finger of his left hand. He lifts up his dismembered fingertip and offers it to the sky, singing a medicine song. He places his fingertip on the red line, halfway between the center pole and the eastern pole. Then he faints.

A gust of wind comes up for a moment. A hawk swoops overhead, his movement seemingly synchronized with the gust of wind. As the shadow of the hawk crosses over the Indian's body, he rolls over onto his side with a moan, as if propelled by the wind. Looks For His Horses, eyes still closed, begins to talk urgently. He remains inert.

On the hill above, Coups laughs to himself and slaps his thigh. He turns and leads his animals away through the brush.

Down below, there is suddenly a coyote bitch, sitting on her haunches by the eastern pole, staring at the young Indian. The boy sits up with a start, sees the coyote, but doesn't move. The coyote advances toward the boy's severed fingertip. She eats it. The Indian faints again. The coyote begins to talk. That is to say, she makes strange, insistent noises in her throat, as though she were trying to bark without opening her mouth. The Indian replies in his trance. They seem to have a conversation.

7. CONTINUED

Suddenly, there is a whoop. The coyote ducks into the
brush. Below the Indian, on the plain, emerges a bizarre
sight. It is Coups. He is naked, except for his loincloth. His body is pale white, from lack of exposure to
the sun, except for his forearms and hands, ankles and
feet, and face and neck, which are sunburned. His body
is festooned with hundreds of spots of clay. He is
standing on his horse's back, playing his fiddle, singing
a raucus song, and doing a little dance.

Looks For His Horses leans forward, straining to hear
the song, trying to repeat the tune.

Coups' horse makes a wide circle on the prairie, then
disappears back into the brush.

A flock of Canadian geese fly by overhead.

8. EXT. DAY. BY A RIVER

The ducks fly by overhead. RUDOLPH FRIEDERICH KURZ, a
Swiss painter, watches them. He is perched on a stool,
sketching at an easel. He is sketching the open vista
of the prairie and the mountains beyond. He is in his
twenties, short, chubby, slightly effeminate. He wears
a cape, a floppy felt "Werther" hat, and wears a scarf
around his neck. His nose is red, and he coughs and
sniffles a great deal. Nearby, in the background, there
is an extremely large Indian woman, MRS. DOLORES, and her
two children, a five year old boy, and an infant. She is
setting up camp.

The river is covered with a thin blanket of dead leaves.
A beautiful woman's head appears from underwater. This
is ANNIE. She lifts her hand out of the water. It holds
a turtle. Annie's character combines wordly sophistication
with a chaotic sense of her own life.

Kurz turns his head from the ducks to Annie.

                    KURZ
                 (coughs)
What is a duck in front of a duck; a duck behind a duck;
and a duck between two ducks?

                    ANNIE
                 (sighs)
I'm sure I don't know.

                    KURZ
Three ducks on the river.

Annie strokes the belly of the turtle, trying to get it
to stick its head out of its shell.

8. CONTINUED

                    ANNIE

You have the most pathetic sense of humor, Mr. Kurz.

                    KURZ

It's an Indian riddle. You said you wanted to know
everything about the Indians around here.

Annie sets the turtle down on the bank.

                    ANNIE

There you are, little one.

She slides back into the water, making a very pretty
picture. Kurz has a beautifully fashioned rawhide case
beside him, called a <u>parflesche.</u> He coughs, rifles through
it, and pulls out a medicine bottle. He takes a sip.

                    ANNIE

I wish you wouldn't stare at me like that.

                    KURZ

Purely professional, my dear, I assure you.

                    ANNIE

Ha!

Kurt fumbles in his parflesche again. He pulls out a silk
shawl with Spanish embroidery. He holds it open to Annie.
She emerges from the water, nude. She shivers. She has a
heart-shaped gold locket around her neck.
                    ANNIE

Brrrr.

                    KURZ

Ah, the impetuous Diana.

Instead of letting Kurz wrap her in the shawl, Annie takes
it from him and wraps it around herself. Kurz persistently
makes these advances toward Annie, and she persistently
rejects them.

                    ANNIE

Bugger, it's cold.

                    KURZ

That used to belong to Zephir's squaw; the one that got
scalped? Her daughter traded it with a Cheyenne sister-in-
law for a three pound sack of New Orleans sugar. That's
not a bad deal around here.

He takes another sip from his medicine bottle.

                    ANNIE

Well, how did <u>you</u> come by such an exquisite thing?

She clutches the shawl to her body. Most of her shows
through the wet silk. She jumps back and forth from one
foot to the other, shivers, and chatters her teeth.

8. CONTINUED

Kurz' eyes glaze over, and his eyelids drop to halfmast.

                    KURZ
                  (dreamy)
It...floated down to me. Indians don't like to keep dead
relatives' possessions.

                    ANNIE
What is that stuff you're always drinking? (blasé) Oh,
Laudanum. I should have realized. In a couple of weeks
you'll be just like Harry. (sarcastic) Wonderful company
for a girl.

Kurz snaps himself out of his stupor.

                    KURZ
No, no, it's just for my cough.

He coughs again for emphasis. Annie comes up behind him
and looks at his sketch. In the upper right hand corner
is a drawing of Annie, nude, kneeling by the water in the
pose of the White Rock girl. His sketch of the prairie
is in the middleground of the paper.

                    ANNIE
Oh, Rudolph. Look what you've done to me!

He is quite mellow from the Laudanum by now. Laudanum was
a commercial brand of opium - a cough medicine.

                    KURZ
Whatever do you mean, my dear?

                    ANNIE
I don't look at all like that. You've made my legs so
skinny.

Kurz has become absorbed in his sketch of the prairie.

                    KURZ
I must finish this before the buffalo come.

Annie walks around to a spot in the sun, in front of Kurz.
She stretches languidly and lets the shawl fall open a bit.

                    ANNIE
Don't you like me as I am, Rudolph?

Kurz looks up and his sketch is forgotten.

                    KURZ
Don't move. I must have you like that.

He begins to sketch furiously. Annie closes her shawl and
turns her back.

                    KURZ
Annie, please.

8. CONTINUED

He is sweating now.

                    ANNIE
I don't like the way you draw me, Rudolph.

                    KURZ
It's your essence I want, Annie. It is the ideal within
you that I wish to bring out. My vision of man in the
perfect state is embodied in the nude. But, nudity
without any suggestion of sensuous appeal.

                    ANNIE
Ha!

                    KURZ
Really, Annie, you insult me.

                    ANNIE
No, you insult me.

She watches Mrs. Dolores setting up camp.

                    KURZ
All my life it has been my ambition to study the antique
from real life. I always had a passion for the classics,
the culture of the ancient Greeks. That's why I've come
to this wilderness. People who are accustomed to being
nude assume postures different from those who are habitually
clothed. Clothes are even a sign of shame. That's why
I've come to America, in quest of Indians who could serve
as my models. Aboriginal man! Primeval world! But you.
You have the classical face. The noble demeanor, the
cultivated dignity. Most of the models in Europe are
slatterns, all full of false modesty, but you, you are
like these people here. You have no sense of shame.

He has a coughing fit. He reaches into his bag again and
drinks some more Laudanum.

                    ANNIE
So, then, you paint my face and attach it to another's
body.

                    KURZ
No, no, no, no.

She reaches out for the Laudanum.

                    ANNIE
Give us a sip, luv.

He hesitates.

                    KURZ
Don't take too much, will you? I've only a limited supply.

He coughs again. Annie takes a sip and hands the bottle
back.

8. CONTINUED

                    KURZ

You don't think there might be some Laudanum left in
Sir Harry's belongings, do you? I'd make you a good
trade.

                    ANNIE

I can't sell anything of his. Oh, I say...!

She swoons against a tree and slides to the ground. She
shakes her head and blinks her eyes. The Laudanum has
just hit her.

                    ANNIE

Good stuff.

                    KURZ

Why not?

                    ANNIE

Huh?

                    KURZ

Why can't you sell it?

                    ANNIE

Your charming employer, Mr. James...

                    KURZ

What do you mean?

                    ANNIE

He has decided to impound all of Harry's "goods and
chattels", as he calls them, and ship them to Harry's
estate "for disposition". Self righteous little bastard.

                    KURZ

My, my, such language. But....he can't be impounding
the wine?

                    ANNIE

Everything.

                    KURZ

All of those potted foods? The cheeses?

Annie watches a tiny spider crawling on her leg.

                    KURZ

All of those sardines and imported vegetables? All?
And his clothes? I had my eye on that silk smoking
jacket of his... Such a pity. Well, at least eventually
you should come into some money, when the will is read in
Scotland.

                    ANNIE

Don't be a fool. Women like me don't figure in gentlemen's
wills. We are for the present.

8. CONTINUED

                    KURZ

Yes, well, I see.

Annie suddenly begins to cry with rage.

                    ANNIE

I bought him that bloody jacket! He hardly ever used it.
Now no one will use it. Do you think his wife will use it?
Ha!

Kurz approaches her and strokes her hair. The shawl has
fallen open now. Tears are falling from her cheeks to her
breasts, and running down her abdomen and into her navel.

                    ANNIE

Wretched swine. Knowing him, he probably arranged it all
that way.

Kurz becomes bolder: he puts an arm on her shoulder, and
sinks to his knees beside her.

                    KURZ

                    ANNIE
                   (bitter)

His Lordship. Who else?

                    KURZ

Sir Harry? But he was killed.

                    ANNIE

Yes. You see?

                    KURZ

Be reasonable, Annie.

He drops his hand to her waist. She ignores his embrace.
She just cries, her hand in her lap, not bothering to
wipe her tears.

                    ANNIE

Oh, you didn't know how it was with Harry and me.

                    KURZ

There, there. This won't do.

He slips his arm around her waist, brushing her breast with
his wrist. She gets up abruptly and walks away a few paces,
staring at the prairie.

                    ANNIE

Do you think we might miss the buffalo?

                    KURZ

Look here, Annie, you came here with Sir Harry, even though
you wanted to leave Sir Harry. Then Sir Harry was killed.

8. CONTINUED

                              KURZ
                             (cont.)
All right. In a way this makes things more clear. Don't
worry. I will provide for your wants. In a few days the
pack train will be taking us on the journey back to St. Louis.
And who knows? Perhaps we shall become close. We could
have many adventures together. Have you ever been to Panamá?

She turns and faces him, silhouetted against the bright
afternoon sun. Her tears are dry, and her face is composed,
even cheerful.

                              ANNIE
You needn't trouble yourself. I shall manage quite well.

Kurz is staring at her through half lidded eyes. Annie
wanders down to the river.

                              ANNIE
You know, when the Blackfeet attacked us, and I was running
for my life, I felt I had finally left Europe, and I thought:
"My life has become quite complicated, but I shall cry no
more." I hid in a thicket for the longest time. And then,
suddenly, they were searching all around, searching for me,
I suppose. And a young brave rode up and stopped, no
farther from me than you are now, holding Harry's rifle.
I recognized it - it was a very special rifle that they
all talked about. He was very fierce and handsome, this
boy. And he wore a necklace made entirely of human fingers.

                              KURZ
Mein Gott!

                              ANNIE
I thought that my heart would fly out of my mouth. And
he turned and looked straight at me. And I thought: "What
will happen? Torture? Rape? Slavery? Will he eat my
flesh? Hang my fingers around his neck?"

She stops.

                              KURZ
Mein Gott. What happened?

                              ANNIE
He stared at me for the longest time. And then he just
rode away. When Stump and Gouge Eye found me that evening,
I was sleeping like a baby.

                              KURZ
Oh, Annie!

She looks out toward the prairie again.

8. CONTINUED

                    ANNIE

You don't suppose we'll be disappointed do you? I did so
hope to see this chase.

                    KURZ

No, no, I've seen it before. You see, the buffalo always
quarter downwind when they are being chased. That way
they can smell their pursuers as they run away. They will
come out just between those two hills. You'll see. Gouge
Eye worked it out for me. We're at the perfect spot for
viewing it.

Annie is jumping from one foot to the other again. Kurz
looks at her puzzled.

                    KURZ

Why don't you put your clothes on? Aren't you cold?

                    ANNIE

Turn around, Rudolph; and stand over there.

He starts to do it, while protesting.

                    KURZ

What is this?

                    ANNIE

Just do as I say. Now hold out your arms, holding the
ends of your cape.

In the background, Mrs. Dolores looks over at them.

                    KURZ

Annie, what are you doing? Mrs. Dolores thinks I am
signalling her.

                    ANNIE:

I don't want her to see me.

                    KURZ

But what are you doing?

Annie is squatting on the gro und, holding her shawl up
around her waist. In the background, Mrs. Dolores calls
out to Kurz.

Kurz says, in Crow, "It's alright!" He waves his cape

She calls back.

Kurz shouts louder, "It's alright!" He waves his cape.

Mrs. Dolores shrugs and goes back to work.

                    ANNIE

But you don't suppose he meant what he said....

                    KURZ

- Who?

8. CONTINUED

                    ANNIE

Little Mr. Stump. About killing us a buffalo right beside
the camp.

She pees.

                    ANNIE

That was just one of his tall tales, wasn't it?

Kurz hears her pee, and turns red.

                    KURZ

Well, we'll see. These mountain men...

                    A VOICE
                    (off camera)

Wal, marm. ef Stump McGlaughlin tells you he aims ter
do somethin', ye oughten' ter disbelieve him.

Annie turns around and screams somewhere in the middle of
this. What she sees is Coups, sitting on his horse, holding
the rein of his mule, in the middle of the river, watching
her pee. She leaps up, pulls the shawl around her, and runs
to hide behind Kurz. Kurz wheels around, so surprised that
he forgets to let his arms down. Coups gives Annie a big
smile, pulls off his hat, and bursts into song. He sings
a bawdy song of the period. As he sings, he rides across
the river, up the bank, and in a circle around and around
Annie and Kurz. Completing his song, he breaks into a
monologue.

                    COUPS

Marm, me name's Coups Cooper, the one as got rubbed out
on the Heely, the very same as seed the putrefied forest,
what's taken topknot off'n every kind of red nigger north
of the Wah-To-Yah, and counted coup on his own mother the
very day he was borned! Beaver's a cunnin' crittur, but this
chile's trapped a heap. At throwin' meat when meat's a-
running, he'll shine in the biggest kind of crowd! At deer
or buffler or darn red Injuns either, he's some! He knows
the signs of Injuns slick: Blackfoot or Sioux, Pawnee or
Burntwood, Zeton, Rapaho, Shian, or Shoshonee; Yutah,
Piyutah, Ricaree or Yamahareek; Absarokee, Minitaree, Gros
Ventres, Mandan, Hunkpapa, Nez Percey, Assiniboine or
Hicarilly Apach -- their trails as plain as writin' ter
this ol' hoss. Yaaaahhhheeeee!!! I'm the carcagne: wolf
from nose to shoulder, and ba'r from shoulder down! Waugh!

He hands Annie the reins to his mule. Stupefied, she
takes them. He reaches into a pouch by his side, pulls
out a couple of musket balls, and pops them in his mouth.
He cocks his rifle and starts off.

8. CONTINUED

                        COUPS

Hold onto ol' Sal for me, will ye, marm? Now, which way'd
you say them buffler war, guv'ner? Nary mind: this niggur
can smell 'em.

He is already riding off.

                        COUPS

Shore war _some_ talkin' to you. Well, it war. This beaver
ain't seen a white face in three or four moons.

He is still talking as his voice fades away. Annie and
Kurz watch him ride off toward the foothills, too stunned
to speak.

9. EXT. DAY. ON THE PRAIRIE

Coups is riding toward the foothills, just in the direction
that Kurz pointed out earlier. He can hear faint rumbling
sounds. They get louder very quickly: gunshots, yells,
bellows, and the din of stampeding animals. He kicks his
horse into a gallop. Suddenly, the buffalo come charging
across his field of vision, from between the two hills.
The noise is deafening. The dust billows up and obscures
the landscape. In the foreground, Coups can see one rider
almost caught up to his quarry, straining forward in his
saddle, guiding his horse with only his knees, using his
arms to aim his rifle. Suddenly, the horse stumbles into
a gopher hole, and horse and rider go flying. Several
other buffalo are bearing down from behind, about to
trample the fallen rider. Coups cuts them off, riding
on a collision course with them, and firing his rifle at
the last minute. At the rifle shot, the herd swerves
sharply and away, followed by several Crow hunters. Coups
reins his horse around and heads for the fallen rider.
There is another horseman heading for him too. The two
ride up on either side, and lift him up between them, by
the armpits. The other rider is an old wizened trapper
named GOUGE EYE. His left eye has no pupil, having been
gouged out in a fight many years before. He grins at Coups.
He has very few teeth.

                     GOUGE EYE
                      (shouts)

What! Coups, ol' hoss. Not gone under yet?

The fallen rider is his partner, STUMP. He is of mixed
white and Indian blood. He has a wooden leg. He is quite
old, too. He looks up dazed, still hanging between the
two galloping horses. Coups grins at him.

                       STUMP
                      (shouts)

Cuss me for a Kioway!

Coups and Gouge Eye hoist him up behind Gouge Eye. Coups
lets out a yell.

9. CONTINUED

                              COUPS

Ayyyyyayyyyyaayyyyyeeeeeee!!!!!

He takes off after another buffalo. Gouge Eye reins his
horse around to retrieve Stump's horse.

Coups tears after the buffalo and the other hunters who are
way ahead of him. He passes a dead buffalo. Dust is everywhere. Riding at full gallop, Coups uncorks his powder horn,
pours a new charge down the barrel of his gun, recorks the
powder horn, spits a musket ball from his mouth down the
barrel, and pounds the buttplate on his saddle to set the
bullet home. He comes up to the moving cloud of dust and
charges in. He can make out only dark charging shapes in
the murk. There is a confusion of noises. He spots an
animal that he wants. He strains to overtake it. The
buffalo's hooves throw great clods of dirt in his face. He
comes up upon the buffalo. The great wild eyed beast is
overwhelming in its enormity. Coups is drunk with the chase.
He is urging his horse forward, aiming his gun, shouting
insensibly at the top of his lungs. He keeps swerving
against the giant bull, trying to guide its direction. The
bull, in turn, tries to gore Coups' horse. They charge along
like this, in tandem, for a long way, over hills and crashing
through underbrush, sometimes the buffalo seeming to pull
away, only for Coups to come up on him again. Finally,
Coups fires. The animal crashes to the ground. Coups and
his horse keep charging along with the momentum. Then they
rein around.

Suddenly, there is silence. The herd and the hunters recede
in the distance. An occasional shot is fired. Here and
there across the plain are other carcasses. Coups' horse
is snorting for breath, and bathed with foam. Coups is
beatific, breathless, and wringing with sweat.

The dust clears. The buffalo lies just beside camp. Annie
and Kurz stand in the background, agape, their faces flushed
with excitement.

                              KURZ

Mein Gott!

The buffalo is still alive. It tries and tries to lift
itself up. Finally it succeeds and stands there swaying
from side to side, blood spurting from its nose, bellowing
and shaking its head. Coups rides up to face it, gasping
for breath. In the background, one can see several Indian
women riding out with travois-laden horses toward another
fallen buffalo. Coups leaps off his horse, brandishing
his knife. The animal bellows once more. Then, suddenly
a convulsive tremor seizes his body and, with a low, sobbing
gasp, he falls over on his side, limbs extended, stiff and
motionless.

Off in the distance, Stump and Gouge Eye, now on their own
horses, ride toward camp. Coups leaps up on the buffalo
carcass and lets out a war whoop. Stump and Gouge Eye
whoop back. Kurz is hurrying toward Coups, carrying his
sketching equipment. In the background, Annie is hiding

9. CONTINUED

in a thicket, trying to get into her clothes.

Gouge Eye rides up to Coups and drops to the ground in a crouch. He growls. Coups rears back and snarls like a coyote. They circle each other, snarling and growling. They clasp right hands, and each lines up his right foot alongside the other's. They try to throw each other off balance -- Indian wrestling. But the rules of this version permit hitting, gouging, hair-pulling, and whatever else the opponents can do with their free hands. Still no words, just animal sounds, they strain mightily against one another. In the background Stump is picketing his horse, and Annie is doing up her buttons.

                    KURZ

Egad, sir! That was bully. Very bully.

Gouge Eye, a giant of a man, but quite old, falls to his knees under Coups' strength. He yields with a sigh.

                    GOUGE EYE

Great Jehosaphat, Pocahontis and John Smith!

                    COUPS

Yore on the way out, ol' hoss.

Gouge Eye can't believe that he's been beat. He looks at his hand, flexes it, looks back at Coups. Kurz is looking the buffalo over, considering it from various angles. Stump is seen in the background, limping toward them. He is posturing with exaggerated discomfort, as if each step were his last. He carries a jug of liquor, and stops every few steps to take a swig. Gouge Eye looks at his hand again.

                    GOUGE EYE

Must of slipped a grease ball upside muh moksin. If this waren't some, I wouldn't say so.

                    COUPS

Well, it are! Ye looks white as a peeled onion, hoss. Ye got hair in yore ears....

He bends down to help Gouge Eye up, mockingly. Gouge Eye Shakes him off, and begins to spread the buffalo's legs out, front and back, in preparation for rolling it over.

                    COUPS

...an' yore on the way out. Downhill all the way for ye now, I reckon.

                    GOUGE EYE
                    (grouchy)

Quit fiddle-footin around an' give a niggur a hand with this crittur.

Stump staggers up. Coups goes to embrace him. Stump holds up the jug in self- defense.

9. CONTINUED

                    STUMP

.Don't touch boy. I'll crawl yore hump.

.Coups grabs the jug and hoists it over his shoulder. From
.this point on the jug and others are constantly going the
rounds. Gouge Eye calls to them.

                    GOUGE EYE

Hump them asses, boys!

The four men, Coups, Stump, Gouge Eye, and Kurz, line up
  with some effort, roll the buffalo over onto its stomach,
.braced up by its legs, spread out on either side. Coups
pulls out his knife, and makes the first incision, into the
hump, and drawing it all the way down along the backbone.
Gouge Eye at one end, and Stump at the other, each make a
vertical slit, from the backbone down to the ground, along
the insides of the legs. Gouge Eye has a long stiletto knife,

                    KURZ

Is that a European knife, Mr. Gouge Eye?

                    GOUGE EYE

This hyar, hoss? We calls this a Arkansas Toothpick.

He and Stump slice the skin away from the body, peeling it
down like a flap and laying it, fat side up, on the ground,
like a picnic tablecloth.

                    STUMP

Cain't beat old Green River though.

                    GOUGE EYE

Shet yore leaky mouth, an git to workin'.

Coups kneels down by the buffalo's head and proceeds to cut
out the tongue. Kurz finds himself a spot on the far side
of the carcass, and sets about sketching it. Stump and
Gouge Eye continue working and griping.

                    COUPS
                    (to Kurz)

Say, guvner, be ye the medicine painter them Absarokee
is always jawin' about?

                    KURZ

I suppose I must be. There aren't any other painters
west of St. Louis that I know about.

Coups brandishes the enormous, bloody tongue, and starts
walking toward the other end of the bull. He stops midway
and turns to Kurz, blocking his view.

9. CONTINUED

                              COUPS

Seen a purty fair eagle pitcher o' yor'n hanging ou
a Hidatsa chief's medicine lodge, down the Muscle sh

                              KURZ

Ah, yes. Rottentail. My first customer.

                              COUPS

He sure was proud of that thing. Said it helped him
battles.

                              KURZ

What do you mean "was"? Has it been destroyed?

Kurz cranes his neck to see around Coups. Coups turn
and heads for the tail end of the carcass.

                              COUPS

Heered ol' Rottentail got rubbed out by a young Shian
pipeholder out of Little Wolf's band, a while back. M
likely hangin on his medicine pole now.

He stoops down by the buffalo's tail end. He grips the
buffalo tongue between his teeth in order to free both
hands. He cuts off the bull's balls.

In the background, Annie has finished dressing, and is
at the campsite, gesticulating to Mrs. Dolores.

Coups jerks his head in her direction and takes the tor
from his teeth.

                              COUPS

~ Say, guvner, what's the price of the fancy white meat?

                              KURZ
                            (laughs)

Annie? I wish I knew? Love or whim, I suppose.

Coups sticks the tongue back between his teeth and, kni
in one hand, bleeding scrotum in the other, proceeds tc
camp. Meanwhile, Stump and Gouge Eye have got into an
argument about how to butcher a buffalo.

                            GOUGE EYE

Ti-yah! Do ye hyar, now, ye damned greenhorn? Do ye sp
fat bull like that whar you was raised? Them doins won
shine in this crowd, boy! Do ye hyar, damn ye!

                              STUMP

What! Butcher meat across the grain! Why, whar'll the
blood be goin' to, ye precious Ned? Down the grain, I
and let yer flaps be long, or out the juice'll run slic
Do ye hyar, now?

10. EXT. DAY. CAMPSITE

Mrs. Dolores has prepared an elaborate campsite. There

10. CONTINUED

three large fires, laid out in a triangle, with scaffolding
of sticks for roasting some of the meat. There are two
other fires off to the side, one burning on top of an old
buffalo skin and the other beside a pit, lined with another
buffalo skin and filled with boiling water. There are also
piles of firewood, a large bladder filled with drinking water
suspended from a tree branch, several buffalo robes, packs,
and open parfleches.

Mrs. Dolores' five year old boy is peeing into one of the
fires. Her infant baby is asleep in a cradleboard, hanging
from another branch. She and Annie are engaged in a struggle
to understand each other, having no common language.

                    MRS. DOLORES

Espanol? Yo habla espagnol mucho bien.

                    ANNIE

No, pas Spagnol. Francais? Parlez-vous Francais?

Annie looks up and gives a frightening yelp as Coups walks
up. Mrs. Dolores laughs. Coups takes the tongue out of his
mouth and drops it into a fire, shoveling coals over it with
his knife.

                    COUPS

How do again, marm? (tips his hat to Mrs. Dolores)
How do, Miz Dolores?

                    ANNIE
                (a bit haughty)

Would you mind asking Mrs. Dolores how I might help her?

                    COUPS

Shoot, marm. White gals ain't much for this kind of work.
You'd best set back and look purty. And that ye be, or I'm
a niggur.

                    ANNIE

I don't believe I asked for your advice. Or your racialist
remarks.

Coups looks puzzled. He holds up the bull's balls, and
hangs them on a stick over the fire.

                    COUPS

Ever try Rocky Mountain oysters, marm? Grow Ha'r on yer
chest.

Annie looks at hime with cold fury.

                    COUPS

Alright, alright.

He turns to Mrs. Dolores and lets her know Annie's wishes
in sign language. Mrs. Dolores looks at Annie, just as perplexed as Coups.

10. CONTINUED

Stump comes hobbling up, carrying the buffalo's hump and hump ribs. Mrs. Dolores motions for Annie to help her. Stump drops the hump into the pit of boiling water. In the fire beside the pit, there are rocks being heated. Stump kicks several of them into the water. It boils more rapidly. Mrs. Dolores and Annie to the fire burning on the buffalo robe. They carefully pull the robe aside, revealing another pit, smoke pouring out of it. Very hot coals lie on the bottom. Mrs. Dolores helps Stump deposit the hump ribs in the pit. Then, she lays several green branches on top of the meat, and she and Annie replace the fire on top of the pit. The conversation goes all through it. Coups stares at Annie all through Stump's monologue. This makes her self-conscious and angry.

                    STUMP

Cuss me for a Kioway, ef it ain't Coups Cooper, the mountains' own! Heered ye were gone beaver on the Heely, hoss.

                    COUPS

Rubbed out, putrefied, and re-surrected, sartian, ol' coon.

Stump backs up to Annie, and rubs his ass against hers. She turns around and gives him a big smile.

                    STUMP

Has ye set eyes on muh new pardner, hyar?

                    COUPS

Well, I has!

Annie walks off in a huff to help Mrs. Dolores.

                    STUMP

She's some, she is. Wuth her weight in beaver. Come out with an English dude, Sir Harry somethin' or other. We meets up with em just tother side of Three Forks, and hitches up -- seein as we's all bound for Absarokee Fort. That ar Englishman, Sir Harry: he had a norwest capote on, and a two shot gun rifled. Well, them English are darned fools -- the men that is, marm -- but that one did shoot some. Least-wise he made it throw plum center. He made the buffler come, he did. He war no trader, nor a trapper, and flung his dollars right smart. Anyways, we wakes up in the mornin, just afore day, the devil's screechin'. Blackfoots, they was, Bug's Boys, The Devil's own. I grabs my knife, keels one, ol' Gouge Eye grabs tother by the ha'r, and makes meat of him, too. Waugh! ef we didn't, and give an ogwh-ogwh long-side of that yellin, or I'm a grease hungry hivverano. This chile don't le t an Injun count coup on his cayyard always. Miss Annie, she makes tracks for timbe first whack. And Sir Harry, who had a rank leaky mouth that morning and war booze blind. Sir Harry, he stands up and turns out to the first Blackfoot arrers as was a-comin'. That limey wore beef

10. CONTINUED

                    STUMP
                   (cont.)

plumb to the hocks, but he war hard to sit! He cussed his
way to the misty beyond awhiles three of thar cussed arrers
tickled his meatbag -- but not afore he drops two of them
with that ol' two shoot. Thar was grit in him, and a ha'r
of the black b'ar at that. And he had the best powder as
ever I flashed through life, and his gun was handsome,
that's a fact, and this niggur wouldn't lie, 'cause :
folks on his momma's side, they wore moksins, and ye
knows a red niggur's tongue is straight!

Stump is wearing a rather odd, hairy shirt. It is, in
fact, a shirt made entirely of scalps. He shows Coups
three relatively fresh ones on the hem. They turn and
head back toward the fallen buffalo. Coups keeps glancing
back at Annie.

                    COUPS

Shoot, hoss, you got enough scalps thar to roof a cabin.

                    STUMP

Thar's a heap o' history in the hyar shirt, ol' coon.

Annie and Mrs. Dolores pull the fire laden epishamore
(untanned buffalo hide) over the roasting pit. A rider
comes into camp -- JOE DOLORES. He is a big, fat Mexican,
equal in size and proportions to his wife. His two
front teeth are made of gold. They shine when he smiles,
which is often. His five year old boy takes his horse's
reins. He shouts at the boy in Spanish. When he turns
around, the boy makes a face at him, and walks off with
the horse. His wife starts yelling at him. The baby
starts crying. Annie goes to comfort the baby. As his
wife yells at him, Joe cranes his neck over toward the
other trappers around the buffalo. He sees Coups. He
takes off his hat, rubs his hands on it, breaks into a
smile, and starts running toward Coups with astonishing
speed, whooping.

11. EXT. DAY. BY THE DEAD BUFFALO.

Gouge Eye looks up from his work and see Joe Dolores
barrelling toward them.

                    GOUGE EYE

Uh-oh, hell's about to pop.

Coups looks around.

                    COUPS

Joe Dolores, you ol' greaser! Give me yore paw!

Joe Dolores leaps into Coups' arms, grabbing him by the
ears, and riding him like a bucking bronco.

                    JOE DOLORES

Ay! Coos, carajo! Muchacho, dat I heer joo was go under

11. CONTINUED

> JOE DOLORES
> (cont.)

in de Rio Gila!

Coups staggers under his immense weight, and the two of them go toppling. Annie comes up.

> ANNIE

Oh, I say!

Coups and Joe Dolores have landed in the midst of the fatty "tablecloth", where all of the buffalo's internal organs have been arrayed. This side of the bull has been completely cut up. Large chunks and strips of red meat are everywhere. Gouge Eye is just now engaged in butchering out the bull's thigh bone.

Stump salvages the liver, pulls out his knife, cuts himself a slice, douses it with gunpowder, and lets it slither down his throat.

Coups and Joe Dolores are having a difficult time getting up, slipping and sliding all over the fat, trying to get purchase. They are laughing and pushing each other around. The trappers AD LIB remarks. Stump holds up the liver to Annie, who is somewhat disconcerted by this sudden display of gore.

> STUMP

Care for an appetizer, Missy?

Behind him Kurz is sketching. Far out on the prairie, other people gather around other carcasses. Several coyotes lurk about. Mrs. Dolores arrives. Gouge Eye begins loading her up with cuts of meat, draping them across her arms, over her shoulders, anywhere there is room. Coups and Joe Dolores finally stagger to their feet, laughing and out of breath, and find themselves face to face with Annie. Joe Dolores is terribly embarrased. He stutters for something to say.

> ANNIE

I say!

Joe and Coups are completely covered in grease. Coups looks at Annie with a sly grin. He lifts up the hem of his buckskin shirt, and the buffalo's heart falls out, onto the ground.

> JOE DOLORES

Coos, I present you Miss Annie. She widow-woman. Jou see her ebryday all black foofurraw (waves at her black velvet dress). Her husband, Meester Sir Harry, he get go under by the puta madre Blackfeets.

> ANNIE

I am not .. widow.

> COUPS
> (brightens up)

11. CONTINUED

                    ANNIE
No. I just like to wear black.

Coups picks up a kidney, pokes a hole in it and lets the
fat drip into his mouth.

                    COUPS
Cousin? Niece? Daughter? Cook?

                    ANNIE
                  (smiles)
You're wondering about my virtue, Mr. Cooper?

                    COUPS
                  (smiles)
Shoot, no, marm, virtue don't fetch half the price out
hyar as it will back in the States.

Annie taps Mrs. Dolores on the shoulders.

                    ANNIE
May I be of any help, Mrs. Dolores?

Mrs. Dolores turns and hands Annie a steaming mass of
intestines. She begins gesticulating. She points to
Joe.

                    MRS. DOLORES
Heema....lodgepole....

She makes the motions of beating someone with a stick.

                    MRS. DOLORES
...lodgepole...lodgepole...

She spits on the ground, shrugs and turns away toward
camp. Joe Dolores kicks her in the ass.

                    JOE DOLORES
Anda puerca!

She turns around, kicks him back and starts off again.
He follows and kicks her again. She kicks him back.
This goes on all the way to camp. Annie doesn't know
what to do with the intestines she's been given. She
tries to hold them delicately. They keep slipping out
of her grasp. Coups laughs at her. She turns and follows
Mrs. Dolores.

Gouge Eye hands Coups a curved tin flask of whisky. Coups
takes an extremely long guzzle, and hands it to Stump. He
follows after Annie drunkenly imitating her steps, then
dives and starts rolling around in the dirt, cleaning himself of the grease. He sings. "The sun comes up, the sun
goes down".

12. <u>EXT. DAY.   BESIDE THE DEAD BUFFALO</u>

We see the same scene from Kurz' point of view. From his
side, the buffalo is completely intact, and the revelers
on the other side seem to be engaged in some mysterious
ritual. The buffalo is mammoth in relation to the people.
Kurz has come along quite well on his sketch, but his
buffalo looks a good deal more heroic than the actual one.
Coups wanders over to watch Kurz sketch. He is covered
with dust. All the while he talks to Kurz, he keeps
slapping it off, sending out great clouds, some of which
land on Kurz' sketch and his immaculate clothes.

                    COUPS

Say, guvner, this niggur seed a Absarokee boy cuttin'
off his own finger fer cayeute's meat this mornin'.

                    KURZ

Cutting off his finger, you say? Was it the top joint of
this finger?

                    COUPS

Well, it war.

They can see Annie walking toward them, away from camp,
holding her greasy hands in front of her, so as not to
soil her dress.

                    KURZ

Why you must have seen a young brave looking for a vision.

                    COUPS

Most likely looking fer his finger now.

                    KURZ

Did you hear that, Annie? Mr. Cooper here saw an Absaroka
brave having a vision. (to Coups) Would you mind? You're
just in my light.

Coups, sucking on another piece of kidney, moves out of
Kurz' light and smiles at Annie.

                    ANNIE
                  (arriving)

What's that? A vision, you say?

                    KURZ

Yes, you know. Every Indian brave around here...when he
gets to be sixteen or seventeen...goes out alone and fasts
and prays and tries to get a sign from his God to guide
his life.

In the background, Joe Dolores and his wife are yelling
at each other again. He belts her. Their five year old
boy starts to cry. She turns around and belts him. The
boy turns and kicks a dog, who runs off, yowling at two
coyotes who are hanging around the outer perimeter of the
camp. The coyotes snarl and bark back.

12. CONTINUED

                    ANNIE

What s--ort of sign.

                    COUPS

Wal, marm, a varmint'll come and jaw at 'em, or they'll
dream about skulpin' enemies or stealin' hosses.

                    ANNIE

And do they all get these signs?

                    KURZ

Most do, or say they do.

                    COUPS

Elseways, they kin buy that medicine from some coon what's
got more'n he needs.

                    ANNIE
               (ignoring Coups)

And do their dreams come true?

                    KURZ

Well, yes, it's quite extraordinary; most often, they do.

                    ANNIE

Are they all saints then?

This sets Coups off into gales of laughter.

                    COUPS

Saints, is it? More like devils, this niggur'd say.

Some fat from the kidney Coups is eating drops onto Kurz'
sketch. Kurz tries to rub it off.

                    KURZ

They are all Nature's children, in their way.

                    COUPS

Wal, this chile give the boy somethin' to brag about in
the lodges, sartain!

He erupts into laughter again.

                    ANNIE

I gather that you're an Indian hater, too, Mr. Cooper.

                    COUPS

Me, marm? Why I'm just another pore niggur like the rest.

Just then, two Indian women ride by, dragging travois behind
their horses, laden with buffalo meat. When they see Kurz,
they turn their heads and cover their faces with their robes.
Kurz tries to ignore them. Annie wipes her hands on Kurz'
paint rag.

12. CONTINUED

                    KURZ

 Annie! Don't get grease all over it!

                    ANNIE

 It's just a rag.

 Annie sighs. Kurz is sitting on a little camp stool. Annie
 scrunches down beside him and nudges him over, to the edge.

                    ANNIE

 Let me share your stool, Rudolph. I'm bushed.

                    KURZ

 Annie!

 She looks at him, terribly hurt.

                    ANNIE

 You won't share it with me?

 Kurz sighs and tries to adjust himself to painting with one
 cheek on the stool.

                    ANNIE

 Why do those women hide their faces from you?

                    KURZ

 They are afraid I might paint them.

                    ANNIE

 But didn't you tell me that the Indians were all competing
 to be your models?

 Kurz breaks the point of his pencil.

                    KURZ

 Mein Gott!

 He begins to sharpen it with his knife. 'It is practically
 down to the nub.

                    KURZ

 Well, it's a bit difficult to explain. To the Indians,
 it's a religious question, you see. They are astounded
 with the ability to draw a perfect likeness. It seems like
 magic to them, but many of the -- still in the minority, I'm
 happy to say -- many of them believe that when you make such
 a perfect likeness, you actually take away the life of your
 subject. Four Bears, the medicine chief of the Crow, is
 still one of my most ardent supporters. I'm doing his
 portrait back at the fort.

 Coups takes a musketball from his possibles bag. With the
 back of his belt axe, he begins to pound the musket ball,
 first flattening it out and then shaping it into a long
 cylinder, coming to a point at one end. Kurz hasn't
 succeeded in adjusting to half a stool. He stands up to
 continue sketching. Annie moves over to take advantage
 of the full seat.

12. CONTINUED

                         COUPS

They say he's a powerful chief, guv.

                         KURZ

There, you see! I assure you that these Indians are far
more generous patrons than I could find in the salons of
Europe.

                         ANNIE

No doubt.

She looks over Kurz' shoulder at the sketch.

                         ANNIE

You do idealize things, terribly. Rudolph.

Kurz sighs. His feet hurt. He looks up at the sky. The
sun is going down. He begins to pack up his easel and drawing
board. Gouge Eye shouts from the background.

                         GOUGE EYE

Ho, boys! Hyar's the fixin's and hyar's the coon what
knows poor bull from fat cow! Heeeeyaawww! Freeze onto it!

                         COUPS

Wooooôha!

Kurz and Annie start for the camp. Coups hangs behind,
still pounding. In the background, at camp, Joe Dolores
has started playing his guitar.

                         KURZ

Aren't you coming, Mr. Cooper?

                         COUPS

Be thar in a shake, hoss.

                         ANNIE

But Rudolph, why do some of them think your paintings are
bad medicine?

                         KURZ
                       (sighs)

Catlin, the first painter out here, wintered with the
Mandans on the Missouri, and just after he left, there was
a terrible outbreak of small pox, which all but exterminated
the tr   Another painter, Swiss like me - a friend,
actually - named Bodmer, painted the Indians, and soon after
he arrived, the cholera broke out, which had an even more
devastating effect on the Arikara and the Herantsa.

Coups catches up with them.

                         COUPS

This beaver minds them times. Waugh! They was dyin' like
flies under frost!

                    KURZ

So, you can see how superstitions begin. Many
won't even talk to me.

                    ANNIE

I don't blame them.

                    KURZ

Well, anyway, now with influenza appearing among the Crows,
Watson James won't let me paint any more Indians. I have
to hide my paintings. It's outrageous.

                    ANNIE

I dare say.

                    KURZ

What a Philistine that man is. The only paintings he deems
worthy of merit are life-size portraits with eyes that follow
one around the room. And, of course, those wretched eagle
pennants he has me make for his special customers.

Coups hands Kurz the lead cylinder he has fashioned.

                    COUPS

Hyar's a pencil for ye, hoss.

                    KURZ

Look at that! Does it really work?

He searches around for something to test it on.

                    COUPS

It'll work fine for ye, hoss.

Kurz tests it, It works.

                    KURZ

Isn't that amazing. I've been at my wit's end about what
to do when I run out of pencils.

13. EXT. DAY. CAMPSITE

Joe Dolores and his wife are singing and dancing together,
a Spanish song:

                    THE DOLORES

          No la llore, que no!
          No la llore,
          Que fue la gran bandolera,
          Enterrador,
          No la llore.

They dance without moving their feet. They wiggle their
shoulders, shake their hips, and bump bellies.

13. CONTINUED

Stump and Gouge Eye are sitting crosslegged, facing each other across a buffalo robe piled high with the long snake of the bull's intestines. Each man has an end and is wolfing it down, without bothering to chew. They seem to be engaged in a contest to see who can eat the most the fastest.

> THE DOLORES
> (singing)
>
> No la llore más,
> Ni la sienta más,
> Que fué la gran bandolera,
> Enterrador,
> No la llore.
>
> No la llore,
> No la llore,
> Que fué la gran bandolera,
> Enterrador,
> No la llore.
>
> No la llore más,
> Su lengua la mato,
> Que fué la gran bandolera,
> Enterrador,
> No la llore.

> COUPS
> (as they arrive)

Ever try boudins, marm?

Annie turns away.

> ANNIE

Oh, I can't look!

Joe Dolores' son hands her a jug. She closes her eyes, holds her nose, and takes a deep swallow. Coups taps Gouge Eye on the shoulder.

> COUPS

Bacca.

Gouge Eye pulls a purse from inside his shirt. The purse is made of a woman's breast. Coups cuts himself a chew of tobacco from a plug in the purse. He nudges Annie, and holds out the purse.

> COUPS

Care for a chaw, marm?

She turns, screams, and automatically clutches her arms across her own breasts.

> ANNIE

That's horrible. Where did it come from?

13. CONTINUED

                    COUPS

Ol' Gouge Eye, marm.

                    ANNIE

You men are savages!

                    COUPS

Now, don't you be takin' him wrong, marm. He didn't make
meat outen that ol' squaw. He traded it fair and square
offin a Blackfoot medicine man. Wal, meat's meat is what
they say in the mountains.

He shrugs and hands it back to Gouge Eye. Gouge Eye
fondles it lasciviously with his free hand, winks at Annie,
and puts it back in his shirt. Stump bites off the end of
his boudins, smacks his lips and says to Annie:

                    STUMP

Marm, ye fix some tasty boudins!

Gouge Eye takes advantage of Stump's pause.

                    STUMP

Feed fair! Ye alkalied....

He grabs the slippery thing, and with a sudden yank, pulls
several yards out of Gouge Eye's throat, and proceeds to
gobble it up. Annie turns away again. Coups goes over
to the fire.

                    ANNIE

They sound like the most terrifying people, the Blackfeet.

                    COUPS

The Devil's Own is what they calls 'em.

                    ANNIE

You know, I was almost captured by the Blackfeet.

                    COUPS

Ol' Stump war jist a-tellin' me.

                    ANNIE

What do you think they would do with a captured white
woman? Would they think of her as a goddess? Like the
Africans do?

                    COUPS
                  (laughs)

Wal, marm, that ain't hardly never been no white women in
the mountains bafore. 'Cept of course mebbe a preacher's
wife -- believe I recollect one -- but she waren't hardly
no woman a-tall.

                    ANNIE

Perhaps they would have made me Queen of the Blackfeet.

13. CONTINUED

                              COUPS

Hyar's a coon as wouldn't keer to find out.

He takes another swig of booze. He is quite drunk by now.
He begins to dance wildly around Joe and Mrs. Dolores.

                              COUPS

Hooraw for mountain doins! Ai-yi-yi-yi-yi-yi-yi.

Stump comes up, fresh from his hors d'oevres, smacking his
lips and wiping his greasy hands on his beard.

                              STUMP

Waugh! This chile's a heap better and ready for huggin'.

He flourishes his hat to Annie.

                              STUMP

Comme la va? No cary por fandango, sinyorita?

                              ANNIE

Merci beaucoup, M'sieur.

Stump begins to swing her around and around, doing wild
leaps on his peg leg. Coups has pulled out his fiddle, and
is playing madly, dancing around Mrs. Dolores and then Annie.
The trappers dance in an eclectic combination of buck-and-
wing, mixed with Indian steps, war whoops, outrageous twirls
and leaps, and animal imitations.

Kurz is taking a secretive sip of Laudanum. He is setting
up his easel again. In his stupor, he knocks it over. He
picks it up again. One corner of his now overcrowded
sketch has a big splotch of mud on it. Gouge Eye grabs
him by the arm, and drags him off to dance.

                              GOUGE EYE

Nary mind that, hoss.

They all form a circle, dancing, singing and shouting at
each other around the triangle of campfires. Everybody
improvises extravagently, except for Kurz who, under the
influence of the Laudanum, gets quite dizzy. The dogs
join in, barking and snapping at their feet. Annie is
passed to each dancer in turn, including Mrs. Dolores. We
follow Annie. Each successive participant gives a specialized,
virtuoso performance. Gouge Eye shouts to Annie across the
circle.

                              GOUGE EYE

Say, marm, did I ever tell you about my squaw?

                              ANNIE

What happened to her, Mr. Gouge Eye?

                              GOUGE EYE

Why, I sent her to Rome, marm.

13. CONTINUED

                    ANNIE

Rome, Italy?

                    GOUGE EYE

No, marm, to roam on the peraira!

The boys break up at this. Stump begins to twirl like a
dervish on his wooden stump. The others AD LIB encouragement. Kurz reels out of the circle, and staggers away.
Annie pinches Stump's cheeck.

                    ANNIE

And what about you, my poor little blackanoor?

                    STUMP

Wal, this beaver's hell for sign, but a woman's breast
is the hardest kind of rock to me, and leaves no trail
that I can see of. Meanin' no disrespect o' course.

                    ANNIE

And you, Mr. Coups? Have you ever been married?

                    COUPS

Are you wonderin' about my virtue marm?

                    ANNIE

Perhaps.

She is fairly well lit herself, by this time. Coups gets
down on his knees in front of her and, fiddling, sings:

                    COUPS

               Do you carrot all for me?
               My heart red beets for you,
               With your turnip nose
               And your radish clothes,
               You are a peach.
               If we canteloupe,
               Lettice marry;
               We'd make a peach of a pear.

Joe and Mrs. Dolores drift off to uncover the roasting pit.
Smoke comes billowing out. Kurz is sitting off to the sid e
in a stupor, staring at his sketch. Coups, still fiddling,
does a couple of steps over to the fire, breaks for a
moment to pour the now-cooked Rocky Mountain oysters down
his throat. Then he gives a belch of satisfaction and goes
back to fiddling. Gouge Eye carves off hump ribs from a
roast by the fire. Everyone is very, very drunk, by now.
Annie is being silly. She begins to recite a Cockney
verse, very fast, like saying a jawbreaker.

                    ANNIE

A for 'orses, B for mutton, C for yourself, D ferential,
E vangelical, F avescent, G for police, H for 'imself,
I for an eye, J for...can't remember, K for a nibble,

                                        (cont.)

13. CONTINUED

> ANNIE
> (cont.)

L for leather, M phasis, N velope, O ver there, P for relief, Q for...can't remember, R fa mo', S for...S fa... can't remember, T for two, U for me, V fa la France, X for breakfast, Y for mistress, Zed for breezes.

General applause and cheers. Gouge Eye hands her a hump rib.

> GOUGE EYE

Hump ribs, marm. Sweetest meat in the world.

Annie takes a dainty bite.

> ANNIE

My, this is delicious. Is this what you eat all the time?

> GOUGE EYE

Why, marm, only a greenhorn would eat ned when....

> ANNIE

Ned?

> KURZ

Pork.

> GOUGE EYE

....when thar's buffler in the mountains.

He tears off a giant piece of meat and swallows it whole.

> GOUGE EYE

Eeeeeeeyahhhhh!!! Yassir, marm, give a mountain man a leetle 'bacca, ef'n it's a plug a plew.

> COUPS
> (holding up his powderhorn)

....some Dupont and G'lena....

> STUMP
> (holding up his knife)

....an' ol' Green River....

> GOUGE EYE

Waugh! And he makes tracks for the Bayou Salade! Darn the white diggin's anyhow!

By now, everyone is eating with Saturnalian abandon, accompanied by grunts, groans, belches, and wordless expressions of delight.

13. CONTINUED

                    STUMP

Ever et dog, marm?

                    ANNIE

Dog?

                    STUMP

Ef thar's any meat that runs as kin take the shine outen
dog, wal, you kin slide!

Kurz is morosely sketching again, this time seated by the
fire, holding his sketchbook on his knees. There is really
no room on the sheet, what with his drawing of Annie, the
buffalo hunt, the buffalo itself, a stain of mud, finger-
prints, smears of grease and dust. He is trying to squeeze
a little campfire scene into the upper right hand corner.
All of the drawings overlap and run into each other. His
eye lids are at half mast again. His hand is very heavy.
It slips, smudging the sketch. He sighs. He picks up a
piece of stale bread an d tries to rub out the smudge. It
only makes it worse. He looks at the ruin of his work.
Suddenly he perks up. He likes the smudge. He begins
smudging other parts of the picture. Someone hands him a
flask. He takes a long swig. Liquor pours down his neck
and jacket, and some of it spills onto the sketch. He
begins spreading the liquor around the paper. He pours
more on, and hands the flask back.

While this has been going on, the following has occured.

                    GOUGE EYE

Say, marm, did ye ever hyar this 'un?   I went down to the
river,

                    STUMP

Couldn't get across,

                    GOUGE EYE

Jumped on a niggur;,

                    STUMP

Thought he was a hoss;

                    GOUGE EYE

The hoss wouldn't pull;

                    STUMP

Sold him for a bull;

                    GOUGE EYE

The bull wouldn't holler,

                    STUMP

Sold him for a dollar;

                              (cont.)

13. CONTINUED

                    GOUGE EYE
The dollar wouldn't pass,
                    STUMP
Threw it in the grass;
                    GOUGE EYE
The grass wouldn't run,
                    STUMP
Sold it for a gun;
                    GOUGE EYE
The gun wouldn't shoot,
                    STUMP
Sold it for a boot;
                    GOUGE EYE
The boot wouldn't fit,
                    STUMP
So I threw it in the shit;
                    GOUGE EYE
And you slipped in it!"

On the last line, Gouge Eye throws Stump into the mud.
He crashes into Kurz. Kurz' drawing board goes flying,
and lands in the pit of boiling water. Stump dashes to
rescue it, profusely apologetic. Kurz doesn't mind. He
takes another long swig of Laudanum. Stump brings the
drawing board back.

                    KURZ
How's she look?

                    STUMP
Hoss, this beaver's got the smallest kind of heart to tell
ye.

He shows it to Kurz. The drawing paper is still tacked to
the board, soggy, and completely blank.

                    KURZ
                  (drunkenly)
Mr. Stump, do you know what Heraclitus said?

                    STUMP
Don't believe I do, hoss.

                    KURZ
Well, I'm going to tell you. He said...he said ...

He starts reciting in Greek.

13. CONTINUED

                    STUMP

How's that, hoss?

                    KURZ

Sorry, very sorry. "To God all things are fair and good
and right..." How about that? "but men hold some things
wrong and some things right!"

                    STUMP

That's good advice, hoss!

Kurz passes out. Stump lies the drawing board across
Kurz' chest and folds his hands over it. Just behind them
Coups is lying on the ground, leaning back against a tree,
playing a rather melancholy tune on the fiddle. Coups is
staring at Annie again, making her self-conscious. Mrs.
Dolores is also staring at her. Everyone else is arrayed
around the fires, listening to the music. Joe Dolores
begins to snore. Gouge Eye is still eating. The dogs are
asleep. Suddenly, a coyote howls just nearby. It is
night by now. The dogs jump up and begin barking frantically. This sets all of the coyotes in the vicinity
to howling. The baby starts to cry. Mrs. Dolores sticks
her breast in its mouth. One of the dogs jumps up on Kurz'
drawing board. Kurz, in his sleep, brushes the dog away.

                    KURZ

Nein, nein, nein, nein.

The muddy paw prints, brushed around by Kurz' hands, make
a new picture on the sketch paper. Stump snuggles down
beside Annie.

                    STUMP

Say thar, sugar pie, did this beaver ever unpack that
story about how he got his stump?

Gouge Eye curls up in a buffalo robe. He mimics what
stump is going to say.

                    GOUGE EYE

"Mind it was down on the Taos trail..."

He yawns and rolls over with his back to the fire.

                    STUMP

Mind it was down on the Taos trail with Old Gabe. Got
inter a ruction with Jicarilla Apaches - mean bastards,
beggin yer pardon, marm. That thar's another story, but
the long and the short of it is that this chile gets left
behind with a big hole in his leg.

Coups lifts himself up and staggers away from camp. He
takes a very long pee. The sky is filled with stars, and
other campfires dot the horizon.

13. CONTINUED

                    STUMP
                 (voice over)
Wal, time comes when the hole starts aturnin' green,
and I says ter meself, "Hoss, it's off with ye, or
this chile's gone beaver." So, I doesn't have much
trouble hackin away the meat, but when I gets ter that
ol' bone, she jes' won't come. So, I picks up a rock and
snaps her off slick, and throws the ol' leg in the river.
Wal, then, 'twaren't nothin' ter jes' saw off the end
with ol' Green River.

Coups finishes peeing. Two dogs from camp sniff around
his pee. Two pairs of yellow eyes - the coyotes - glint
reflections of the fire.

                    STUMP
              (his voice gets drowsy)
Wal, now, as time goes by, thar's no more meat in muh
possibles bag, done et muh possibles bag, done et muh
moccassins, done stuck muh hands in an anthill and licked
'em off, everything thar was ter eat, this niggur et.
Wal, right thar's when I spies that ol' leg, a-setting
thar in the water.

Coups stumbles around a bit, trips, falls on his ass, tries
to get up, gives up, and passes out. Back at the campfire, everyone has fallen asleep, except Annie, Stump,
and Mrs. Dolores. Mrs. Dolores is still staring at Annie.
Stump's eyelids are drooping. He keeps nodding off in
the middle of sentences.

                    STUMP

Thar she set, jes' as fresh as the day she lef' me. Says
I, "Meat's meat," and sets ter cookin her up. An' darned
ef she waren't sweet an' juicy as a buffler's hump rib...
(yawn)...Course, I et around that green hole fer a while...
but arter some time, that got ter lookin' good too...

He is asleep. Annie is staring into the fire. It is
suddenly very quiet. Annie looks up and sees Mrs. Dolores
staring at her. Mrs. Dolores smiles. Tears start rolling
down Annie's cheecks. Mrs. Dolores wonders if she has done
something wrong.

                    ANNIE

I'm sorry...I'm terribly sorry...I don't mean to cry...
It's not important...

Mrs. Dolores begins to talk to Annie in a soft voice, in
Crow. Neither understands the other. Annie sobs more and
more. She lies down, covers her head with a blanket, and
cries and cries. Mrs. Dolores lies down next to Joe. As
an afterthought, she punches him in the back. She goes to
sleep.

Annie is asleep by now. Coups wakes up. He goes over to
the fire, puts on some more wood, and hangs a slice of meat
over it. Annie rolls over in her sleep, in such a way as

13. CONTINUED

to expose part of her thigh.   Coups stares at Annie's
thigh. He moves up closer for a better look. All of a
sudden, Annie starts to talk in her sleep. She is talking
to someone, but we only hear her half of the conversation.

ANNIE

Oh. What's that? Oh. It's horrible...You couldn't see
it...Because you weren't asleep at that moment. But I could..

She stops talking. Coups takes the meat from the fire and
starts eating it, watching Annie. Annie starts talking again.

ANNIE

I just discovered where they left it...The head...By the
river...It's where they hid it,.I guess...Some kind of
animal. I didn't know you spoke English...It was inside
out...I've got all the information. And there were porcu-
pine quills. I've got all the pieces...I think it was
Leonard...No...Yes...It was a pretty spot, though... a bend
in the river.

14. EXT. DAY. FORT ABSAROKA

Fort Absaroka is a collection of small log buildings, enclosed
by a rectangular stockage of upright logs. It sits in the
middle of a plain by a river. A halfmile downriver is an
encampment of Crow Indians, perhaps twenty tipis. There is
a well-worn trail between the camp and the fort. A group
of Indians are hanging around the gate of the fort. There
is a herd of horses, a cavayard, grazing near the fort.
There is another cavayard near the Crow camp.

The party of Kurz, Annie, Coups, Gouge Eye, Stump and the
Dolores family shoot off their guns and gallop in raggle
taggle fashion toward the gate.

15. EXT. DAY. THE GATE OF THE FORT

Coups arrives first, then Stump and Gouge Eye, and finally
the others. Two Indian girls ride by, dressed in their
best garnished buckskins, with red blankets and silk ker-
chiefs on their heads. Their horses are rigged with
sleighbells that jingle.

COUPS

Ho, gals! Dehorn the awerdenty. Hyar's some coons what's
half froze for likker.

He jumps off his horse and leads it through the gate.
Standing at the gate is an Indian couple, wrapped together
in a blanket which c   their heads and whole bodies.
They sidle up to Coups. The man opens the blanket to
reveal his squaw, a very pretty, very young girl, all
dressed up. She smiles at Coups. Her old man mumbles
something and lifts up the girl's skirt, showing off her
bush. Coups laughs and makes a sign. The blanket closes
up and the couple sidles off to wait again. Annie rides
up, breathless, followed shortly after by the Dolores family.

15. CONTINUED

A boy and an engagée come up to take their horses. The
trappers start to unpack their horses. Inside the fort, a
chaotic scene is in progress. The ground is almost
exclusively mud. Dozens of trappers and Indians are
drinking, gambling and generally carousing. In one corner,
two men are trying to gouge each other's eyes out, urged
on by a small crowd. There is another fellow running
around, screaming, trembling, frothing at the mouth,
rolling in the mud, caught in delerium tremens. He stumbles
into one of several fires arrayed around the courtyard.

Engagées, employees of the fort, are rushing back and
forth carrying and packing things, exceedingly busy. Two
are working a beaver press, pressing loose pelts into bales.
There are several French American trappers playing music
in another corner. Along the near wall are three one-
story, sod covered log houses. Between the Storehouse and
and Toolhouse, there is a huge pile of buffalo heads. There
is a live eagle, in a wooden cage, hanging over the door
of the storeroom. WATSON JAMES, the bourgeois of the fort,
the company trader, is standing by the storeroom door. He
is a young, ambitious Eastener, very properly dressed.
There is a general banter around Coups and the other trappers.

                    A VOICE

Hauw, Coups! Heered ye was rubbed out on the Heely.

Annie gives her horse's reins to the boy and starts for
Kurz' quarters.

                    ANNIE

I've got to get out of these clothes.

Kurz follows after her. Watson James starts across the
courtyard to intercept Annie at Kurz' door. He tips his
silk hat and hands Annie a bunch of wildflowers.

                  WATSON JAMES

....Rather crude, but the best one could procure under
the circumstances. I thought these here bore a striking
resemblance to your English azaleas.

                    ANNIE

Why, Mr. James, does this mean that you've recanted?

                  WATSON JAMES

Just paying my respects, Miss Ainley. Please call me
Watty.

                    ANNIE

Watty!

                  WATSON JAMES

As for Sir Harry's goods and chattels, I fear I must
remain steadfast.

15. CONTINUED

ANNIE

You mean all of his things go to his wife.

WATSON JAMES

Please, don'tt embarrass me; I never discuss business
with ladies.

KURZ

What about that red velvet smoking jacket he had? I can
get a good buffalo runner for it. A magnificent animal.
From Hump, the Arapaho pipeholder? (To Annie) He's the
one who prepares the tobacco and lights the pipe when
they go on raids and hunting parties and such. Do you
know what his medicine is? Buffalo dung. He always carries
a couple of chips of it in his hair.

WATSON JAMES

Mr. Kurz! Please!

Annie laughs.

KURZ

He always mixes a little in with the tobacco. Heh. Heh.
(Turning to Watson James) Anyway, when he heard it was a
smoking jacket....

WATSON JAMES
(smiles)

I'm sorry.

ANNIE

You leave me without means of support, Mr. James.

WATSON JAMES

Watty, please.

ANNIE:

You leave me destitute, Mr. Watty. How shall I earn my
keep? Shall I sell my favors for trinkets like the Indian
girls?

WATSON JAMES

Perish the thought, ma'am! Nothing would give me greater
pleasure than to have the honor to be your patron while
you are here, and to keep you in the style to which you
are accustomed. As much as possible, given our rather
primitive circumstances, of course.

ANNIE

Why, Mr. Watty, whatever do you mean?

WATSON JAMES
(to Kurz)

There are some customers waiting in the storeroom.

15. CONTINUED

                    KURZ
Don't you want me to finish that pennant?
                    WATSON JAMES
Just take care of the customers, and then finish the
pennant.
Kurz shrugs and walks off.
                    WATSON JAMES
Just what I said, ma'am.
                    ANNIE
And what, pray, would be required in exchange for such
generosity?
Watson blushes.
                    WATSON JAMES
Please, you embarrass me again.
                    ANNIE
In my experience, it is always better to make these matters
clear in the beginning.
                    WATSON JAMES
If I may say so, Miss Ainley, it is just that experience
and sophistication of yours which led me to believe you
would prefer a frank proposal to an arch and extenuated
courtship.
                    ANNIE
Are you offering marriage, then?
                    WATSON JAMES
Would that I could, ma'am. nowever I have a family of
my own already in St. Louis. So, you see, the...
                    ANNIE
You desire me. You weesh to mek laahve to me. N'est-ce
pas?
He turns bright red.
                    ANNIE
You dream of my body. You long for my touch. You brush
up against me at every opportunity. You have heard about
me. Everyone talks about me. You know I was Sir Harry's
mistress. You know that I have lived with other men. And
so you think, "Well, perhaps something is possible..."
                    WATSON JAMES
Please, Annie, you make...
                    ANNIE
Miss Ainley!

15 CONTINUED

WATSON JAMES

Please, please, dear lady, you wrong me.

Annie runs the tip of a finger down his chest.

ANNIE

Ohhh, it's alright, Watty. I understand how you feel. I
see you glancing up at my window every day. I see you
coming into poor Rudolph's rooms and sending him on ridiculous errands so that you may sneak a peek at his sketches
of me. You poor thing; it must be torture for you. But
the joke's on you, you see. Poor Rudolph has idealized me
terribly, I'm afraid. Look, I'll show you.

She makes as if to lift her skirt.

WATSON JAMES

Miss Ainley, please! Not in front of all these trappers.

ANNIE

Ahh, there's something you ought to know about me. I
have no shame. Hadn't you heard that, too? I am a free
spirit; not one of your caged animals. I have read all of
Lord Byron, and I don't care a damn for anyone.

She hoists her skirt high above her knees.

ANNIE

Now, look at that.

All of the men in the near vicinity turn and stare.
Conversation stops abruptly.

ANNIE

Do you see how thick and stubby they are? Regardez les
pieds....(showing her feet) So broad. So large! Truly
peasant's feet, wouldn't you say, guv?

She drops her skirt and looks Watson James in the eyes.

ANNIE

I know this will disappoint you terribly, Watty, you poor
dear, but I wasn't born into gentility, I was seduced into
it.
Watson starts to back away under her assualt.

ANNIE

Oh, and you should see my body. Not at all as Rudolph
represents it. Oh, no. I have had a child, you see, and
you know what that does to a poor girl's figure. The tum
goes first, of course -- never really gets back her original
shape. The, there are the titties, poor things. They just
go all to hell. First they fill up, and then they begin
to droop, and the nipples get all wrinkly and brown. A
bit revoltin', ain't it, ducky? And then, there's the
arse   fills out a bit, I'm afraid....

15. CONTINUED

Watson James holds up his hand.

                    WATSON JAMES

Please, no more, Miss Ainley. You have made yourself
perfectly clear. Forgive my presumption.

He turns and starts away. Annie runs up to him and touches
him on the arm. He stops. She takes the flowers from his
hand.

                    ANNIE

Thank you so much for the flowers. I'm really quite fond
of you, you know.

                    WATSON JAMES

I hope you'll reconsider. I'm planning a rather exciting
tour to the Oregon Territory. Making maps. I thought
that you might like to come along. We could chart unknown paths together.

                    ANNIE

Good day, Mr. Watty.

16. EXT. DAY. QUADRANGLE OF FORT

Stump, Gouge Eye and Coups are crossing the quadrangle. Coups
is carrying several packs of beaver. There are lots of
people milling about, drinking and carousing. Old friends
call out to the three trappers as they walk along.

                    FIRST TRAPPER

Hauw! Coups. Heered you was rubbed out down on the
Sweetwater.

                    COUPS

On the Heely, hoss, on the Heely.

They pass three men who are competing to pee on each other
without getting peed on themselves. An old Indian woman
blocks their way, holding up a beautifully decorated buffalo
robe. They brush past her. They reach the storehouse.

17. INT. DAY. STOREHOUSE

There are furs piled all over the place. There are two
counters, at right angles to one another, where the trading
takes place. Behind the far counter is Kurz, trading with
two Crow warriors. He is having a sneezing fit. On the
counters are arrayed a variety of trade goods, mostly
"fofurraw", costume jewellry, ribbons, and bolts of bright
red cloth; and along the walls behind are stacked kegs of
staples, such as coffee, flour, and tobacco, and piles of
three point Hudson's Bay blankets. Hanging from the ceiling
are rows of salted buffalo tongues. There are three or four
eagle pennants in the corner. The three trappers come in.
Watson James comes bustling in after them.

                    GOUGE EYE

Hauw! Watty, meet Coups Cooper, another customer fer ye.

1 7.CONTINUED

                    COUPS

What's the price of beaver, hoss?

                    WATSON JAMES

Aren't you the one that was supposed to have been killed
on the...what river was it?

                    COUPS

Heely, hoss. What's the price of beaver?

In the background, the trade with the Indians goes on in
fierce pantomime, with not a word being said, except for
an occasional consultation in Crow between the two warriors.

                    WATSON JAMES

One dollar.

                    COUPS

One dollar what?

                    WATSON JAMES

One dollar a pelt.

                    COUPS

Ride over that trail again, and chew it finer, hoss.

Stump breaks into a loud, wheezy laugh at the look on Coups'
face. One of the Indians points to Watson James' silk hat.
Kurz shakes his head, and indicates that it's not for sale.

                    WATSON JAMES

You see, Mr. Cooper, they're now making hats out of silk.

                    COUPS

That thar?

He snatches the hat from Watson James' head and puts it on
his own head. Coups struts up and down. His two friends
are in hysterics. The two Indians thrust signs in Kurz'
face.

                    STUMP

Yer look right peart, hoss.

                    COUPS

Yer calls this a hat?

                    WATSON JAMES
                    (affably)

Why, it's the height of elegance, Mr. Cooper. No gentleman in the East would be caught without one.

                    COUPS

Tell me something, Watty. Aren't this stuff made out of
worm spit?

He looks at the hat and wrinkles his face, disgusted.

17. CONTINUED

COUPS

Waugh! It won't shine, Watty.

WATSON JAMES

You know how the whims of fashion are, Mr. Cooper.   They're just not buying beaver hats anymore.

Coups dips the silk hat into a barrel of water.

WATSON JAMES

What are you doing?

While Watson's attention is distracted, Gouge Eye sneaks a handful of coffee grounds from the counter and puts them in his right hand pocket.

COUPS

Shoot, Watty, this hyar stovepipe won't even hold water.

WATSON JAMES

Mr. Kurz, would you look up Mr. Cooper's account? (To Coups - still affable) I'm afraid you're going to have to pay for that.

Coups scrunches the hat down on his head, spilling the water all over himself, and mugs for his friends. Kurz turns his back to open the account book. The Indians steal handfuls of trinkets from the counter.

COUPS

Now she's beginning to feel like a hat!

KURZ

"Powder and balls, twenty dollars; one three point Hudson's Bay Blanket..."

WATSON JAMES

Not the whole list......

Gouge Eye mixes a pinch of sugar and coffee in the palm of his hand, and pops it into his mouth.

WATSON JAMES
(to Kurz)

Just give me a total, Mr. Kurz.

KURZ

Two hundred and seventeen dollars.

WATSON JAMES

Plus twenty dollars for the hat.

KURZ

Two hundred and thirty seven dollars.

WATSON JAMES

How many pelts did you bring?

17. CONTINUED

Coups throws the pile of furs onto the counter.

                    COUPS

Heaps, hoss.

Pause. Watson begins counting the pelts.

                    COUPS

Shoot, Him, this niggur won't have enough ter buy an
outfit and a leetle fuforraw....Wal, the price o' beaver'll
go up next year. I'll jes' have ter borry some from the
Company agin.

Watson is shaking his head and counting.

                    WATSON JAMES

Thirty five...I'm afraid we're not extending any credit
any more.

                    COUPS

Whaaaat?!

                    WATSON JAMES

Have you got any buffalo hides? There's a good market
for them. They're experimenting with making yarn from
the hair.

Coups makes a gesture of disgust.

                    WATSON JAMES

Any scalps? Scalps fetch a good price. No scalps?

                    GOUGE EYE
                    (to Coups)

A plew won't even fetch a plug a bacca.

                    WATSON JAMES

Don't you understand, Mr. Cooper? There is no more beaver
trade. We're closing up the fort.

Stump picks up the jug of whiskey and holds it out to
Coups. Coups ignores it. He takes the soggy silk hat
off his head and puts his fist through the top, dropping it
on the counter. He points his rifle at Watson James.

                    COUPS

Yore a liar.

                    WATSON JAMES
                    (still affable)

Seventy eight...Please Mr. Cooper, save yourself the
trouble. I assure you that there is nothing you can do to
change the way things are. Mr. Jim Bridger held a knife
to my throat this morning. Mr. Joe Meek threw a fit on
the floor, right there, and I can tell you, it was a
horrifying sight to behold. Mr. Moses Harris threatened
to castrate me. But, you see, none of you can alter the
fact that the beaver trade is finished. There is a new

17. CONTINUED

                    WATSON JAMES
                      (CONT.)
era coming...There   - two hundred and forty pelts.

He hands Coups three pelts.

                    WATSON JAMES

Your change, I'm sorry. America is on the verge of a great
western expansion. Settlers will be moving west...

                    COUPS

Waugh! A nation of greenhorns in the mountains? That's
like beaver in the ocean, Watty! It won't shine!

Watson pulls a gold nugget from his pocket and fiddles
with it.

                    WATSON JAMES

We need all of this space for civilization to grow. Right
here on these plains will be cities, surrounded by prosperous
farms. Not even trees that bear no fruits will be per-
mitted by the surge of progress. The forest will become
houses, the rivers will be great avenues of commerce.

Coups picks up his three pelts and prepares to leave. One
of the Indians comes up to him, motions to the hat, and
indicates in signs that he wants to buy it.

                    WATSON JAMES

Be reasonable, Mr. Cooper. I like you. I can help. The
beaver trade is ended, but there are new opportunities for
men with the skills and imagination that you have.... Wagon
trains will need guides and scouts, there will be military
expeditions in need of hunters and experienced Indian
fighters...

Coups puts the hat on the Indian's head.

                    COUPS

Thar ye be, hoss. On the peraira.

                    WATSON JAMES

Ask your friends. I've already engaged them for a little
expedition to Oregon.

                    COUPS
                  (to Gouge Eye)

Expedition?

                    WATSON JAMES

Oh, a little map making scheme of mine. Perhaps you'd be
interested...I'd appreciate it if you'd keep it under your
hat.

Coups grabs Watson James' hair and shows it to the Indians.

17. CONTINUED

                    COUPS

Purty scalp lock.

Watson only smiles. Coups takes his three pelts and walks
out of the door. Stump sneaks a jug of whiskey, and the
two trappers follow Coups out.

18. EXT. NIGHT. OUTSIDE THE STOREROOM

Coups, Stump, and Gouge Eye come out of the storeroom.
Stump hands Coups the jug. Coups takes a swig. Kurz
comes out of the door and starts across the quadrangle.
Five other men are lounging in front of the storeroom,
staring at Kurz' upstairs window across the way. The three
trappers stop to look too.

19. EXT. DAY. KURZ' APARTMENT

Kurz' apartment has an upstairs and a downstairs. There
is a window upstairs, through which Annie can be seen
dressing.

                    SECOND TRAPPER

She's mine.

                    THIRD TRAPPER

This coon seed her fust.

Kurz enters his apartment through a Dutch door downstairs.
Upstairs, one breast pops out of Annie's petticoat. She
tucks it back in.

                    SECOND TRAPPER

Hip, hip....

                    OTHERS

Huuurah!

They repeat it three times. We see Kurz enter Annie's
room, cross to the window and close the shutters.

20. INT. DAY. KURZ' UPSTAIRS ROOM

This is the watchtower of the fort. Kurz has turned it
into a studio, and Annie has turned it into a boudoir. The
room is cluttered. There are many pieces of female clothing
hanging from nails in the log walls. Two rustic tables are
piled with drawings, drawing materials and Indian objects.
A half finished eagle pennant lies in one corner. Several
paintings in progress done on stretched deer hide, are
pinned to the wall. There is a gray fox in a cage made of
branches, and a mynah bird prancing around, speaking German
every once in a while. There is a bed, covered with buffalo
robes, bright red blankets, and improvised fur pillows.
There is a trap door in the floor with a ladder leading downstairs.

20. CONTINUED

                         KURZ

The fire is really going down there. That room is already
quite warm.

Annie starts putting on a dress. She is ignoring Kurz.
Kurz rubs his hands together. He stares at Annie's face
to prevent himself from staring at the rest of her. Annie
looks at the dress, decides against it, and starts taking
it off. Kurz' eyes drop with the dress. Annie turns and
catches him staring. Kurz' eyes go back to her eyes.

                         ANNIE

Go downstairs while I'm dressing.

Kurz climbs down through the trap door

21.   INT. DAY. KURZ' DOWNSTAIRS ROOM

Downstairs is a harness room. All of the paraphernalia
for a caravan of mules and horses is here. In addition,
Kurz has several trunks, spilling over with his collection
of Indian artifacts and clothing. He has made a bed for
himself on the earth floor by the fireplace. There is
also an easel with a half finished portrait of the afore-
mentioned Four Bears, and a lone, straightbacked chair.

                         KURZ

Pity you didn't come here by boat around the Horn.

                         ANNIE

Why?

He follows the sound of her footsteps on the ceiling.

                         KURZ

Because you missed Panamá. I've been thinking of Panamá...
Ah, Panamá.

                         ANNIE

What's in Panamá?

Kurz paces around the little room. Whenever he passes
the ladder, he glances up through the trap door.

                         KURZ

Oh, it's glorious in Panamá, Annie. It's another place
entirely. There is a tribe there that venerates perversion.

                         ANNIE

Oh, I say!

                         KURZ

Can you imagine, obscenity being devotional?

He puts some more wood on the fire.

                         KURZ

These Crows are just horse thieves and dandies compared
to them.

21. CONTINUED

                    ANNIE

Have you seen my hairbrush?

He hears Annie start walking again. He rushes to the trap
door just in time t o get a glimpse of Annie's dress.

                    ANNIE

What sort of perversion?

Kurz looks into the fire.

                    KURZ

Oh...all of them...homosexuality, bestialism, oral perversion.
Of course, they frown on fornication as such.

He rubs his hands together as if he were cold. He finds her
hairbrush and rushes up the ladder with it.

                    KURZ

Yes, and it's warm in Panamá, too.

22. INT. DAY. KURZ' UPSTAIRS ROOM

He comes up through the trap door. Annie is sitting on
the bed, in a new black velvet dress, skirt up over her
thighs, legs akimbo, adjusting her garter.

                    KURZ

I'd love to paint you like that.

She looks at him, glances down at his crotch. There is a
bulge in his pants. She gets furious.

                    ANNIE

I don't want to pose for you anymore! I don't want to be
stared at any more! I don't want to be stuck in this room
any more! I feel like a prisoner. I just want to flee.

                    MYNAH BIRD

Ludwig von Beethoven!

                    KURZ

You can go out whenever you want.

                    ANNIE

Do you want me to be raped? Oh, you have my hairbrush!
She takes it from Kurz and brushes her hair violently.

                    ANNIE

God damned men.

                    KURZ

Mein Gott! What the hell have I done to you?

                    ANNIE

And I don't want to sleep with you, here or in Panamá!
There is a loud knock on a door downstairs. Kurz goes
down the ladder.

23. <u>INT. DAY. DOWNSTAIRS ROOM</u>

He opens the Dutch door, and there is no one there. Someone
knocks again on the big window that looks outside the fort.
He goes to the window and opens it. Outside are Looks For
His Horses and five friends, all teenagers on horseback.
Two brothers ride double on one horse. Looks For His Horses
greets Kurz in Crow and sign talk. Kurz replies in English
and sign talk.

                    KURZ

Hauw, Looks For His Horses; come inside if you want to
talk to me. It's cold.

Looks For His Horses climbs off his horse on to the window-
sill and into the room. Annie is squatting by the trapdoor,
upstairs, curious to find out who it is. Looks spots her.
She backs out of view. Kurz makes an apologetic sign to
the boys outside and closes the wooden window.

Looks For His Horses says, "Is that your squaw?"

One of the Indian brothers pushes the window open a crack
and sticks his head in.

                    KURZ

No. She is a widow. She's leaving soon.

Annie appears at the trapdoor.

                    ANNIE

What are you telling your friend about me? I'm not a
widow.

Seeing Annie, Looks For His Horses covers his mouth with
his right hand.

                    KURZ

It's hard to be subtle in sign talk.

The boy at the window pushes it open. The others crowd
around outside, staring at Annie and covering their mouths.
Annie is dumbfounded by such extravagance. She doubts what
to do for a brief moment, then decides to come downstairs.

                    ANNIE

Look the other way while I come down.

                    KURZ
                  (to Looks)

Don't look at her.

Looks For His Horses smiles and turns around. Kurz closes
the window on the boys. He and Looks For His Horses stand
facing the closed window. Looks For His Horses says to
Kurz, in Crow and signs, "Is something wrong with her?
This is the first white woman I see and no one wants her
for a wife." The boys outside laugh.

                    ANNIE

What did he say?

23. CONTINUED

                         KURZ
He wants to know if there is something wrong with you
that no one will buy you.

Kurz and Looks For His Horses turn around to face Annie.
The mynah bird starts squawking in Kurz' ear. Kurz brushes
it away and goes to sit on the only chair in the room, by
the fire.

                    ANNIE
What does he think? That I'm a common trollop?

Next to Kurz on the floor is a drawing notebook. He
picks it up, takes out Coups' improvised lead pencil.
He points with the pencil to the other two, saying their
names in turn.

                    KURZ
Annie. Looks For His Horses...No, to them women are
property. They buy them from each other. You know that,
didn't you?

Kurz starts sketching Looks For His Horses.

                    ANNIE
You must be mistaken.

Annie looks at the fire.

                    ANNIE
Your fires are too warm, Rudolph. Ask your friend.

Looks For His Horses says to Kurz, "Is this woman real
or did you bring her about with your medicine?"

                    KURZ
He thinks I created you by blowing life into a painting.

                    ANNIE
How sweet! Ask him if he has a girlfriend.

                    KURZ
                 (to himself)
How many times will....

The mynah bird sits on Annie's shoulder. Looks reaches
out the window. A friend passes him two beautiful, freshly
tanned buffalo robes. He flings them to the floor at Kurz'
feet. Looks For His Horses says, "I had a vision. A
coyote came and talked to me."

                    KURZ
He had a vision.

                    ANNIE
Goodness!

23. CONTINUED

                    KURZ

A coyote spoke to him.

Looks For His Horses says, "I ask you now this question:
is my death going to be hot, or is it going to be cold?"

                    KURZ

He wants to know if his death will be hot or cold.

                    ANNIE

How extraordinary.

Looks For His Horses says, "Will I die a wet death, or will
I die a dry death?"

                    KURZ

Wet or dry death?

                    ANNIE

But death is always cold.

Annie goes to the fire and looks over Kurz' shoulder at
the sketch of Looks For His Horses.

                    KURZ

It seems you'll be the sphinx tonight. (To Looks) The
woman says death is always cold.

Looks For His Horses says, "I wish Iron Eyes to paint my
vision on this robe. The other is his."

Kurz starts to protest.

                    KURZ

You know I can't do that, Schatzie.

                    ANNIE

What does he want?

                    KURZ

He wants me to paint his vision on this buffalo robe.

                    ANNIE

Why can't you do it?

                    KURZ

The social hierachies here are more Byzantine than the
Queen's own court. He is just a young brave. (To Looks)
All the chiefs would be angry, Schatzie. You are not
important enough. You are not a Four Bears or a Covers
His Face.

Looks For His Horses says, "But I have had a vision!"

23. CONTINUED

                    KURZ

I know you've had a vision. But that doesn't make you
a warrior. You must live out your vision.

Looks For His Horses says, "But no one understands my
vision. In the village, they say that it is bad medicine.
But it was a powerful vision. I saw a flame haired white
man..."

                    KURZ

Whaaat? You saw a white man...?

                    ANNIE

Whay are you so patronizing, Rudolph? What did he say?

                    KURZ

He saw a white man in his vision. His uncle, the medicine
man, says it's very bad medicine. He (pointing to Looks)
thinks it was a powerful vision. I just can't paint it,
though. Politics.

Annie snatches Kurz' sketch and shows it to Looks For His
Horses.

                    ANNIE

That's you.

                    KURZ

Annie!

He snatches the sketch and throws it in the fire. Looks
For His Horses runs to the fireplace and watches his image
burn away. He begins to chant a distorted imitation of
the song Coups sang in Looks' vision.

                    LOOKS

De sungaza - desungazun

                    KURZ
                  (to Annie)

You see what superstition does?

Looks breaks off his singing and, with one motion, pulls
his knife and jumps in the air with a whoop, arms spread
wide. The window bursts open, and the five Indian boys pour
into the room with weapons drawn.

Annie screams and runs out the Dutch door.

24. EXT. DAY. INSIDE THE FORT

Annie runs out of the door of Kurz' apartment.

                    ANNIE

Help! Help! They're going to kill him!

Two riders bear down on her. At the last moment, they
swerve past on either side, barely avoiding trampling her.

24. CONTINUED

Twenty yards away, she sees Coups with a bunch of trappers.
She stumbles over a trapper and a Crow girl, who are fucking
on the ground. She runs up to Coups and the others. They
are standing around the dead body of the third trapper.
Several trappers are paying off bets in beaver skins to
Coups. Stump, Gouge Eye and Watson James can be seen in
the background, talking. There is an Indian girl behind
Coups - the same girl whose bush was shown to him at the
gate.

                    ANNIE

That man is dead!

Mrs. Dolores and a Chinook woman come up to Annie and
start feeling her soft velvet dress.

                    MRS. DOLORES

Aaahhheeey...

                    CHINOOK WOMAN

Oooooooohhh...

The second trapper is shoving a pistol back in his belt.

                    SECOND TRAPPER

That thar war muh best friend.

                    FOURTH TRAPPER

Ef he warn't some, I wouldn't say so.

                    SECOND TRAPPER

Well, he war.

                    COUPS

Ho, boys, hyar's the deck, an' hyar's the plews; who
dares set his hoss?

                    FOURTH TRAPPER

This chile ain't setting his hoss, but he'll lay to his
beaver.

Coups starts dealing cards, using the third trapper's body
for a table.

                    COUPS

Marm, does ye fancy playing euchre with these hyar coons?

                    ANNIE

You indolent fools! Aren't you going to bury this man?

                    COUPS

We'll interre him, marm...manana. Meat don't spoil in
the mountains.

All the trappers laugh. The Chinook woman pinches Annie's
cheek. Rouge comes off on her fingers. Annie screams and
runs back toward Kurz' quarters. She trips over the fucking
couple again.

25. <u>EXT. DAY. OUTSIDE KURZ' QUARTERS</u>

A very drunk Joe Dolores is standing beneath the upstairs
window, craning his neck to get a glimpse of Annie. The
shadow of an Indian boy crosses the window. Annie comes
running up.

ANNIE

Oh, my God!

Joe Dolores turns, sees Annie, looks back up at the window,
then back at Annie.

JOE DOLORES

Blessed be de seed from come de tree from come de cradle
dat make you go (snores).

His eyes close. He reels against the door. Annie shakes
him.

ANNIE

Quick! Quick! Open the door. I can't bear to look.

She covers her eyes with her hands. Joe Dolores salutes
her and opens the door. At the same moment the door is
pulled open from the inside. Joe Dolores goes crashing
to the ground. Kurz and Looks For His Horses and friends
pour out of the Apartment, over and around Joe Dolores.
Annie peeks through her fingers.

KURZ

Annie! Where have you been? We've been waiting for you.

ANNIE

I've been trying to save your life. No one seems to care
about anyone around here.

KURZ

Oh, that. That was just Indian temperament.

Annie can see the Indian girl come up to Looks and the
two brothers. She shows them a trinket she has been given.
One of the boys opens his robe and shows them a pair of
Annie's bloomers he has stolen.

ANNIE

Oh, I say, Rudolph! That boy has nicked me bloomers...
what cheek!

Two of the Indian boys are trying to sneak Kurz' chair
out of the room behind his back. He sees them.

KURZ

No, no, no... Put that back.

The boys put the chair back inside.

KURZ

It's terrible, Annie. They're so <u>wicked</u>! But...they're
incurable, so what can you do?...Looks For His Horses has
just been telling me about his vision. It's quite amazing.
Remind me to tell you about it some time.

25.   CONTINUED

Behind Annie, the euchre game goes on. The Indian girl
goes back to Coups. Annie follows her with her eyes. We
hear the conversation at the game. Faintly, in the background, we can hear the music of a group of French American
trappers.

                    FOURTH TRAPPER

Thirty year have I been knockin' about these mountains, from
Missoura's head, as far south as the starvin' Gila. I've
trapped a heap, and many hundred pack of beaver I've traded
in my time. Waugh! What has come of it, and whar's the
dollars as ought to be in muh possibles? Whar's the ind o'
this, I say! Is a man to be hunted by Injuns all his days?
Many's the time I said I'd strike for Taos, and trap a squaw,
for this chile's gettin' old and feels like wantin' a
woman's face about his lodge for the balance of his days.

Kurz offers Annie his arm.

                    KURZ

Voulez-vous promener, ma cherie?

Annie takes his arm without replying. They stroll away
from the Indian boys. Kurz leads her very correctly around
the fucking couple.

                    YOUNG TRAPPER
                    (off camera)

Wal, this boy's froze onto the purtiest leetle Nez Percey
punkin. Gonna make her my own and winter with her folks
over by Three Forks.

                    FIFTH TRAPPER
                    (off camera)

For twenty year I packed a squaw along. Not one but many.
First I had a Blackfoot -- darndest slut as ever cried for
fufurraw. My buffalo hoss, and as good as four packs of
beaver I give fer ol' Bull Tail's daughter. Traps wouldn't
buy her all the beads and vermillion she wanted; and in
two years I sold her for one of Jake Hawken's guns -- the
very one I hold in my hands. Then I tried the Sioux, the
Shian, and a Digger from t'other side, who made the best
moksin as I ever wore. Bad was the best, and after she
was gone under, I tried no more.

Kurz introduces Annie to an Indian couple standing along
their way. The man has a crooked nose, and very crooked
teeth. His wife hangs on to him.

                    KURZ

Miss Ainley, may I present Crooked Nose and Teeth, and his
wife, No Toes. This is Miss Ainley.

Crooked Nose and Teeth is the crier of Four Bears' band. A
very respected man. He goes around the camp and calls out
the orders of the chiefs.

                    ANNIE

How fascinating!

25. CONTINUED

Meanwhile the conversation at the euchre game continues, off camera.

                    COUPS
                 (off camera)

Wal, I'll be dipped in horeshit! Put out the hard chink boys, this niggur's hotter than Taos lightnin'!

Annie glances over to the euchre game. The Indian girl is sitting on a pack of beaver pelts, just behind Coups, her feet dangling by his shoulders. Coups turns to the girl and says something. She pulls several beaver pelts from beneath her and hands them to him. He throws them into the pot on the dead man's body. He gives the girl's ankle an affectionate stroke. He sees Annie and gives her a big smile. Annie turns away.

                  SIXTH TRAPPER

Afore I left the settlements, I knowed a white gal. Her name I disremember, but she stands afore me as plain as Chimley Rock on Platte, and five year or more harn't changed a feature on her face to me. Ef ye asks this chile, red blood won't shine any w_ays ye fix it. Leave the Spanish slut to her greasers, and hold on til you take the trail to ol' Missoura, whar white and Christian gals are to be had for axkin'.

                 SECOND TRAPPER

Them white gals is a deal too much like pictures.

Annie and Kurz continue strolling. They come to a group of French American trappers, gathered around a fire, playing instruments and singing. There is a crowd listening. They are playing romantic songs, in primitive three quarter time, singing in a Cajun patois. The conversation at the euchre game has faded into the background. Nearby, Watson James, Stump and Gouge Eye are talking earnestly. Watson James tips his hat when he sees Annie. She gives him a cold look.

                  GOUGE EYE

Ye goes up to the Madison and cuts back east to whar The Firehole runs into it. Foller the Firehole up half a sun from it's mouth and you'll see a little stream that drops into it from the east, hard by a stand of three ponderosas what shoots up outen some rocks. They's taken ter callin that Clyman's Creek, cause a leetle further up thar is whar ol' Jim Clyman lost his ha'r to a bunch of Ricarees outen' ol' Gray Eyes' band.

Kurz is listening in to Gouge Eye. Watson James has his eye on Annie. Annie watches the musicians. The singer sings to her. She smiles and looks away. She sees Coups playing at the euchre game. He looks up and catches Annie's eye again. He gives her a big grin. Just then, the Indian girl bends down and blows in Coups' ear. Coups plays cards very carelessly. He hardly looks at his cards, dividing his attention between the Indian girl and Annie. Sometimes

                                        (cont.)

25. CONTINUED

the players pile loot in front of him. And sometimes they
take it away and ask for more. Earlier in the game, he
had quite a sizeable pile. Now it is rapidly diminishing.
The players AD LIB euchre talk in the background. Annie
puts her arm through Kurz' without taking her eyes from
Coups, Kurz looks around.

                         KURZ

Why, Annie.....,

                         ANNIE

Shhh, Rudolph! Don't speak. And turn your head away.

She is still looking at Coups. Coups reaches up and
strokes the Indian girl's ankle, still staring at Annie.

                       GOUGE EYE

Then ye crosses up through Two Ocean Pass....

                         STUMP

Now, hyar'swhar it starts a-gettin' strange. Thar's a
smell -- faint now, ye knows it, but ye cen't put yore
finger on it.

                       GOUGE EYE

Ye picks yore way through a forest of lodgepole pine...

                         STUMP

...And now and then ye'll come to a clearin' and ye'll
see leetle puffs of smoke risin up hyar and thar above the
trees. And that smell's agittin' strong. And now ye knows
what it is. It's brimstone, by Gawd! Brimstone!

                       GOUGE EYE

And all on a sudden, the stuff is all around you, oozin'
and a bubblin' outen the earth and shootin' straight up
in the air...

                         STUMP

And thar's a putrefied forest thar, full o' putrefied
flowers, and putrefied trees, full o' putrefied birds
singing putrefied songs...

                      WATSON JAMES

Ah, this is the famous Yellowstone you're always talking
about.

                       GOUGE EYE

Right the first whack, Watty. And thar's a mountain of
glass thar...

Meanwhile, Coups and Annie are still staring at each other.
Coups is fondling the Indian girl's thigh. Annie, holding
Kurz' arm, runs a finger down his back. He sighs, not
daring to turn around.

25. CONTINUED

                    KURZ

Annie!

Coups kisses the inside of the Indian girl's thigh and
smiles again at Annie.

                SECOND TRAPPER

Pay up, Coups.

Coups asks the girl to get up. He throws the rest of his
bever pelts onto the dead body. Watson James is watching
Annie with great interest.

                    STUMP

Shore enough, Watty! And ye walks up to the base o' that
mountain, and ye'll be wading through the bones of thousands
o' dead birds what've flew plumb into it without ever
knowin' it was thar.

                GOUGE EYE

Course thar's not a ha'r o' game up thar this time o'
year.

                WATSON JAMES

I'm prepared to supply food and engage men and mules to
transport it.

                    STUMP

They's spooks up thar. An' spirits and goblins and things
folks like you and me don't know nothin' about, Watty.

                GOUGE EYE

Which means we don't have to worry none about Injuns. They's
skeered to go near the place. Big medicine.

                    STUMP

Ceptin o' course the Blackfeets.

Annie crushes her breasts against Kurz' back, still trying
to stare Coups down. Kurz' neck is perspiring.

                FOURTH TRAPPER

Yore down to the blanket ol' coon.

Coups is cleaned out. Coups takes off his blanket and puts
it around the Indian girl. He kisses her and puts his hand
up under her skirt. She smiles at him. He pats her on
the behind and she trots away. Coups is down to the clothes
on his back. Another trapper grabs the Indian girl. Annie
turns away. She breathes into Kurz' ear.

                    ANNIE

Kurz you must take me home quickly.

                    KURZ

Yes, yes. Quickly.

He hurries her off back toward his apartment. Watson
James follows Annie with his eyes.

25. CONTINUED

She can't resist another glance at the euchre game.
Coups is busily stripping down to his breechcloth and then
throwing his clothes into the pot.

                    COUPS

Whooee! Whar's the likker, boys? This beaver's settin'
on a cold deck!

Coups is naked except for a breechcloth, and a pipe pouch
hanging around his neck. We can see black spots all over
his chest and back.

                    KURZ

I'll make you some wonderful tea that I traded from an
old Chinook woman. It's made from the leaves of a plant
that only grows on the northern slopes of the Cascade
range in Oregon Territory. It makes one feel very...
romantic..

By the door to Kurz' rooms, Looks For His Horses' friends
have started a flamboyant Indian gambling game, called
Hands. The five friends sit in a row, facing five others
an assortment of other Indians and trappers, around a
pile of quivers, knives and calico. Looks For His Horses
stands aside among a crowd of onlookers. The two Crow
brothers are making motions in every direction with their
closed hands, swiftly passing a piece of bone from one
hand to the other. The others sing, "e,e,e,eh,e,e,e,ah",
keeping time by beating with sticks on washbasins and boiler
tops. The singers and players swing their bodies contin-
uously from the hips. One of the Indians from the oppositi-on
is throwing a hex on the two boys. Another is watching
the boys' hands very closely. This is SILK HAT, the Crow
whom Coups had given the silk hat. He is wearing the hat.

                    KURZ

Mein Gott! Now we'll never get to sleep tonight.

                    ANNIE

Oh, Rudolph. Is it some kind of ritual they're doing?

                    KURZ

That? No, it's just a game. Indians are great gamblers.

                    ANNIE

Gambling! I love to gamble.

                    KURZ

No, Annie, come. I'll make a nice fire.

                    ANNIE

Rudolph, please. Let's just watch. Just for a few moments.
Please.

Silk Hat strikes his chest with his right hand and simultaneously cries out a word. The boys freeze. The singing
and dancing stop.

25. CONTINUED

                    ANNIE

How exciting! What's happened?

                    KURZ

He's guessed which hand the bone is in.

                    ANNIE

I know that game: "Button, button, who's got the button?"
One of the boys opens his right hand. It holds the bone.
Silk Hat and his fellow players whoop for joy and gather
in their stakes. Looks For His Horses' friends pass a
pipe to Silk Hat. The two teams smoke together.

                    ANNIE

Those boys were magnificent jugglers. Too bad they lost.
Several players leave, and others join in. A ritual of
laying stakes begins. One player throws down a set of
eagle tail feathers. One from the other side throws down
a skinning knife in an embroidered rawhide sheath. All
this is done with a great deal of haggling and boasting
until there is a great heap of stuff and they are ready
to begin the game.

                    KURZ

You should see Looks For His Horses play. He's a master
of the game. Renowned all over the territory. He's quite
wealthy for a seventeen year old orphan.

                    ANNIE

Oh, poor thing. He's an orphan?
Kurz glances over to the euchre game.

                    KURZ

It looks like our friend Mr. Cooper has lost his shirt.
Annie turns to look. Coups is naked except for his breechcloth. He takes a long swig of liquor. Someone hands him
a coyote skin.

                    A TRAPPER

Hyar ye be, Coups. On the peraira.
Coups puts it on his head, draped down his back. He lets
out a coyote howl.

                    ANNIE

Never mind about him. Ask your friend if he'll play for us.
Kurz steps over to Looks For His Horses, who is standing
imperiously, watching the game, wrapped in his buffalo
robe. Annie watches them talk. There is another howl from
Coups. Annie glances over. Coups is on all fours, crawling
around the campfire, drunkenly howling, and nuzzling the
other players. Coups spots Annie, and begins crawling
toward her. A mulatto trapper, named JIM BECKWOURTH, trails
behind Coups.

25.   CONTINUED

                        BECKWOURTH

Me and the boys was thinkin on pullin for Californy.
Take a look at that ocean. Heer tell they got summer
year round. Fruits jest pop off'n the trees and into yer
mouth. Trap us a passel of sinyoritas. Mebbeso freeze
onto a cavyard o' horseflesh, bring 'em back through
South Pass and trade 'em to the greenhorns on the wagon
trains in the spring.

Coups stops at Annie's feet, looks up at her, and howls
at her. Seeing Annie, Beckwourth jumps to his feet,
embarrassed.

                        BECKWOURTH

'Scuse me, marm. (indicating Coups) Hyar's a pore coon
what's lost his possibles.

Beckwourth exits. Kurz comes back from talking with Looks
For His Horses. Coups sits on his haunches, looking up
at Annie. Annie tries to ignore him.

                        ANNIE

What did he say?

                        KURZ

He says he doesn't play any more. Now that he has had
his vision, he has what he wants.

                        ANNIE

I wish I could play.

                        KURZ

Why don't you.

                        ANNIE

I have nothing to bet.

                        COUPS

Ye kin bet yore ass!

Watson James, Stump and Gouge Eye enter in the background.

                        ANNIE

You can bet your own arse.

                        COUPS

Marm, I' do that sartain as muh gun has hindsight!

                        ANNIE

Mr. Cooper, you've lost everything.

                        COUPS

Marm, muh stick has a barrel as'll shoot the cow, the
other side as'll skin 'em slick, and both sides make the
buffler come. This niggur'll bet ye skin to skin.

25. CONTINUED

                    ANNIE

Whatever do you mean, sir?

                    COUPS

Why, marm, all this niggur's got left is his pore ol' hide.
He'll bet his'n agin your'n. If ye wins, ye gets Coups
Cooper, the mountains' own to do yore biddin.

                    ANNIE

For how long?

                    COUPS

As long as ye like, honey.

                    ANNIE

And what if I lose?
He lets out a howl of delight.

                    KURZ

Annie, you're carrying this too far.

                    ANNIE

It's my own affair what I do, Rudolph.

                    KURZ

You mean you're actually going to....?

                    STUMP

What'll it be, Missy?

                    COUPS

Yore velvet ass agin mine, honey..

                    ANNIE

Who'll give me a button.

                    KURZ

Annie!

There are excited murmurs in the crowd. Watson James
comes forward and hands Annie a gold nugget.

                    WATSON JAMES

You're a very daring woman, Miss Ainley. And I sincerely
hope that you put this oaf in his place. (to the crowd)
I'll cover all bets against Miss Ainley.

                    FOURTH TRAPPER

Not agin Coups Cooper? That niggur's heered the owl hoot
a time or two. Hyar's a pack of plews as says so.

Watty takes out a pad and begins to write down the bets.
Coups is doing warm up exercises by the fire. The drummers
and singers are gathering around.

25.   CONTINUED

> KURZ

Annie! You mustn't do this.

> JIM BECKWOURTH

I'll lay to muh epishamore!

> SECOND TRAPPER

Two pounds o' Galena pills!

> FIFTH TRAPPER

Four point Hudson's Bay blanket...with porkypine quills.

> STUMP
> (to Annie)

Beggin' yer pardon, Missy. (To Watson James) A pound of sugar and a pound of coffee on Cooper.

> GOUGE EYE

I'll take that'un, hoss.

> THIRD TRAPPER

Hyar's muh best scalpin' knife on the Limey punkin.

Silk Hat drops a pile of winnings in front of Watson James. The Indians begin beating on their washboards and boiler tops, chanting and swaying. The French American musicians strike up a riff. Annie steps out into the circle of the firelight. The ground by the fire is covered with fur bets. Coups is crouched facing Annie across the fire, bouncing on the balls of his feet, his eyes screwed intently on the nugget in her hand. Annie closes her hands. She performs an English street game called, "Button, Button, Who's Got The Button". The game involves a little dance, the recitation of a nonsense verse and improvised hand movements. She does it like a child but with sex. She dances around the circle. Coups follows Annie around the circle and Silk Hat dances behind him throwing hexes at her. The music swells.

> GOUGE EYE
> (shouting encouragement)

Freeze onto him, Annie!

> JIM BECKWOURTH

Skin them eyeballs slick, Coups! She's a cunnen crittur!

Looks For His Horses works his way around the circle to Kurz. Looks For His Horses says, "Iron Eyes, do many white men have those black spots on their skin?"

> KURZ

Those spots? They look like they were painted on.

Looks For His Horses says, "That's the white man I saw in my vision."

25. CONTINUED

> KURZ

You saw Coups Cooper in your vision? how odd.

Coups shouts, lunges and grabs Annie's right wrist. The music stops. Annie opens her hand. It is empty. Whhops and hollars from the assembled.

> STUMP

Cuss me fer a Kioway!

> GOUGE EYE

Great Jehosaphat, Pocahontis and John Smith!

> WATSON JAMES
> (holding up pad)

I'll collect from you gentlemen in the morning.

Coups throws himself at Annie's feet.

> COUPS

Hyar's yer nigger honey, I'm yourn.

Looks For His Horses runs to the fire and rescues a burning log from it. He whirls the log in the air, spinning it until it catches fire. He points the burning log at Coups' face. Coups snaps out of his stupor.

> COUPS

Look who's hyar but the coyoye's feed, fat and sassy.

Looks For His Horses rubs a bit of dirt between his hands, and blows dust at Coups. Coups puts his finger in his mouth and smacks his lips.

> COUPS

That thar finger...Umh, my. Heaps good!

Looks throws his buffalo robe at Annie's feet and makes signs to Kurz.

> KURZ

Oh, no, this is too much.

> ANNIE

What does he want, Rudolph?

> KURZ

He wants to gamble for Coups.

> ANNIE
> (smiling)

Ha, ha!

Looks makes signs to Kurz.

> KURZ

What shall he bet?

Annie picks up the buffalo robe and pulls it around her shoulders.

25. CONTINUED

                    ANNIE

This will do.

                    STUMP

Haw! Tie one onto that, Coups!

                    COUPS

Now, honey. Jest one leetle ol' second, hyar...

                    ANNIE

Be quiet, you lout. You said I could do what I liked with
you.

                    COUPS

But honey....

                    ANNIE

And don't call me that.

She hands the nugget to Looks For His Horses.

                    WATSON JAMES

Gentlemen, I'm covering all bets again oh Miss Ainley.

                    KURZ

I'd like to wager on that. A portrait of you, Mr. James,
against that smoking jacket of Sir Harry's.

                    WATSON JAMES

Done.

All the Indians begin to bet heavily on the side of Looks
For His Horses. Watson James writes furiously in his notebook. Gouge Eye covers side bets on Annie. Looks For His
Horses signals for silence. He throws himself on the ground
by the fire. He rakes out all the ashes in front of him,
and conceals the nugget there. He moves his fist among the
ashes in imitation of a coyote, pawing at a rabbit hole and
rolling over in the dust. He yips and yowls, throws ashes
all over himself, and paws and groans like one possessed.
His mimicry is unequalled. Annie watches, entranced. Several
times she begins to point, but only to hesitate and change
her mind.

                    COUPS

Waugh! This niggur's putrefied. What's the boy's name, hoss?

                    KURZ

Looks For His Horses.

                    ANNIE

Stop!

Looks For His Horses freezes. He holds out his closed
hands to Annie. She still can't decide.

                    ANNIE

That one, no, no, that one. Just a minute.

25. CONTINUED

                    GOUGE EYE

Left hand, Annie!

                    FIFTH TRAPPER

Right hand, marm, right hand!

Others in the crowd ad lib advice. Annie covers her
eyes, spins in a circle, stops and points. Right hand.
Looks opens his right hand, it is empty. More whoops and
hollars from the assembled. Someone hands Coups a jug
of whisky. He takes a deep swallow. He is absolutely
wretched there on the ground, staring up at Annie and
Looks For His Horses. The Indian boy takes Coups' coyote
skin and brandishes it proudly.

                    COUPS
                (to Watson James)

Wal, Watty, leastways I brung you down with me!

Gouge Eye goes up to Looks For His Horses and speaks in
signs and English.

                    GOUGE EYE

What'll ye take to sell him back, hoss?

Looks refuses outright.

                    STUMP

Nary mind, Coups. Yore bound ter trap plenty squaw in
Absarokee country.

                    WATSON JAMES

Look at yourself, Cooper. Look at what you've become!
A piece of chattel. You look like an Indian, you dress
like an Indian, you smell like an Indian...You know what
they say: "Lie down with dogs and wake up with fleas!"
You're a white man, sir!

                    JIM BECKWOURTH

Us'n's niggurs, don't ye reckon, Watty?

General laughter.

                    WATSON JAMES

You men have lived out on the edge of the known world.
But it's about to be invaded. Your cherished frontier
will be no more.

Coups starts to get up.

                    COUPS

Thar's always an edge, I'm thinkin'.

                    FIFTH TRAPPER

Might to could go it alone.

25. CONTINUED

                          FOURTH TRAPPER

These mountains'll never be part of the known world.

                          WATSON JAMES

I don't understand you gentlemen. You have been given
the opportunity to join in the building of a new era
in the west. What will you do now, that your livelihood
is gone? Who among you have more than a hundred dollars
to his name? How many acres do you own? When was the
last time your feet were warm? Where is your home? Tut,
tut, gentlemen. Your services are required by a young
and ambitious nation, just beginning to flex her muscles.
Step into the mainstream of history. Lead your people to
their Manifest Destiny!

                          COUPS

No! Damn the white settlements, I say! This chile hates
an American what harn't seed Injuns skulped, nor doesn't
know a Yute from a Shian mok'sin. Sometimes he thinks of
makin' tracks for white settlement, but when he gets to
Bent's big fort on the Arkansa, or this hyar place, and sees
the bushways, an the fellers from the States, how they
rolls thar eyes at an Injun yell, worse nor if a village
of Comanches war on 'em, and pick up a beaver trap, to
ask what it is -- jist show whar the niggurs had thar
brungin' up. 'Sides, it's hard to fetch breath amongst
them big bands of corncrackers down to Missoura, and
t'ain't natural to leave buffler meat and feed on hog.

                          GOUGE EYE

But whar's the dollars, hoss?

                          COUPS

Thar's no cachin whar a niggur feels, leastwise, when
lies is tumblin' outen ol' Watty's mouth like boudins
outen a buffler's meatbag. Why, beavers' bound to rise !
Human nature can't go on sellin' beaver a dollar a plew.
No, no, that aren't agoin to shine much longer, I know.
Them was the times when this chile first come to the moun-
tains: six dollars a plew - ol' 'un or kitten. Waugh!
But it's bound to rise, I says again. And hyar s a coon
knows where to lay his hands on a dozen pack right handy!
Damn the white diggins anyhow!

He beckons to Looks For His Horses.

                          COUPS

Looks Fer Yer Hosses! Are ye bound for Absarokee camp?
This hoss is thar by sundown. The cavyard's out pickin grass,
half froze to travel!

He starts away with Looks.

                          WATSON JAMES

Mr. Cooper.

25. CONTINUED

Coups turns to face him.

                    WATSON JAMES

If you are going to live with the savages, you will share
their fate. No handful of men have the right to withhold
from the great body of mankind a valuable portion of the
Earth's surface without using it. Tomorrow morning a pack
train will leave the fort. At the Little Piney, one party
will turn East, toward St. Louis, and the other will head
into the Yellowstone and across to Oregon. If you change
your mind by then, you're still welcome to join us. No
hard feelings, I hope?

Coups glares at Watson James. There is a pause. Coups
lets out a bloodcurdling war whoop. Looks For His Horses
lifts the coyote skin over his head and lets out his own
war cry. (Every Indian and every trapper had his own
particular war whoop.) All of the other trappers erupt
into their war cries. Some do Indian dance steps, some
shoot off their rifles. Annie dashes for Kurz' apartments
in fright. A trapper slaps Watson James on the back.
Watson stumbles forward. Another trapper catches him
and throws him back at the first trapper. All of this is
quite jovial. Coups and Looks For His Horses walk away.
We see Kurz trot after them to open the gate.

26. EXT. DAY. GATE OF THE FORT

Kurz unlatches the gate and swings it open for Coups and
Looks For His Horses.

                    COUPS

Listen, guvner, does ye figure these hyar mountains'll
be raisin Kentucky Chickens for the balance of days?

                    KURZ

As long as buffalo are found in such large herds it will
be impossible to cultivate fields. It's that simple.
They'll have to exterminate them before they can establish
husbandry in these parts.

Coups is coming down from his long day's drunk. He looks
miserable. He dunks his head in a large barrel of water
by the gate. He shakes off the water and shivers.

                    COUPS

Shoot, guvner, they wiped out the buffler in Pennsylvania,
and Kentucky, and Ohio, and all down through thar. They
could do it. Shore they could. But they ain't rub out
the Injuns!

Kurz turns to Looks For His Horses. He speaks in English
and signs.

                    KURZ

Looks For His Horses. Tell your uncle Four Bears that I
wish to finish his portrait. Ask him to come and see me in
two sun

26. CONTINUED

Looks For His Horses says, "But you will not paint my vision.'
He indicates Coups. "Here is the white man from my vision.
I will have him sit for you."

                    KURZ

I have changed my mind. I will paint your vision.

Looks' face lights up. He says, "But you will leave
tomorrow."

                    KURZ

No, I will not be leaving with the pack train. I have
decided to stay on here.

                    COUPS

Alone in the mountains in the winter, hoss? Aren't every
niggur what kin manage it.

                    KURZ

The Crows look up to me. I will do alright. (to Looks)
Tell the people that I will paint any portrait at a price.
(to Coups) I think I can make quite a bit of money here.

Coups glances up at Kurz' upstairs window.

27. EXT. DAY. KURZ' UPSTAIRS WINDOW

We catch a glimpse of Annie as she backs away from the
window.

                    COUPS

What about Velvet Ass Annie, thar, guv?

28. EXT. DAY. GATE OF THE FORT

We see them from Annie's point of view in the upstairs
window.

                    KURZ

Velvet Ass Annie! Ha ha. Dot's a good one. She doesn't
care for me. She thinks me a fool. She'll go back to
St. Louis, I suppose. You don't have to worry about her.

Looks For His Horses says goodbye to Kurz.

                    KURZ

All right, Schatzie. See you next week.

Looks turns, motions to Coups, and walks away toward the
herd of grazing horses. The Dolores family can be seen
in the background, rigging a travois onto their horse.
Coups starts after Looks. He stops.

                    COUPS

Sya, guvner, what does ye figure that boy aims to do with
this hoss?

                    KURZ

It's very strange. Did you know that he saw you in his
vision?

28. CONTINUED

                        KURZ

You mean you actually were there?

                        COUPS

Sartain, guvner. This niggur see'd him up thar whoopin'
and a-hollerin'. Figgured we'd give the boy somethin'
to brag about in the lodges.

                        KURZ

Is that where the spots came from?

                        COUPS

How does ye figger this beaver ought to tell the boy it war
all a joke?

                        KURZ

Stay in the vision. You needn't worry. He thinks you're
big medicine. Just like me. You don't want to be involved
in this Company business. It's a bad business. Stay in
the vision. He'll take care of you.

Looks calls out to Coups. Coups starts off.

                        COUPS

Wal, guvner, might see you some time, some place.

                        KURZ

Oh, definitely. Looks For His Horses is going to bring
you to sit for me. For his vision painting.

                        COUPS

Take care of Velvet Ass Annie!

Kurz laughs. He swings the gate shut.

29. EXT. DAY. ON THE PRAIRIE

Looks For his Horses and Coups are riding along with the
Dolores family. Coups is riding double behind Looks and
wearing Looks' shirt. Joe Dolores is sitting on his horse,
his wife and family are packed on the travois behind.
Looks is talking animatedly. Joe Dolores is translating.

                        JOE DOLORES

She say de Absarokee country good country. Grande Spirit,
she put him in essackly bes place. She say joo go sout,
joo got desierto, very bad, very hot, no good water, joo
get fiebre. Joo go norte, very cold, no good. No can
have de caballo. Only dogs. What good country wid no
caballo? Joo go west, where de ocean? Dey eat feesh.
Bad teeth. No good same like de buff. Joo go east dey live
in house, drink muddy water. No Absarokee dog drink dat
water. She say Absarokee country in essackly bes place.
Carajo! I tell joo Coups, joo got good deal. Joo yust watch
me. I got good deal. Beeg fat woman. Joo get one too.
She got a leetle bit smokey smell, but joo get to like ett

                                              (cont.)

29. CONTINUED

                    JOE DOLORES
                     (cont.)

in a leetle beet. Joo yust seet by fire, she cook joo food,
she cut joo wood, she pack de water. Ju get nize Injun
girl. Joo beat her, she like joo more.

30. EXT. DAY. BY THE RIVER

Crossing the river, they pass a large oak tree. As they
approach ravens and vultures fly out of the tree. The
riders pass beneath it, and looking up, see several Absaroka
bodies suspended in the branches of the trees. The bodies
are in various states of decay. There are bones lying on
the ground beneath the tree. Looks For His Horses gives
the tree a wide berth. Bits of bone and putrefied flesh
lie on the ground. A mouse scurries off with a piece of
flesh.

                    JOE DOLORES

See, Coups. Pueblo of de dead peoples. See dat dere?
Fresh dead. Very bad. Mal de ojo.

He crosses himself.

                    JOE DOLORES

See? Looks For His Horses say truth. Stay in Absarokee
land, no bad happen. Joo go, bad happen.

He rides up to Looks For His Horses and pats him on the
back. Looks For His Horses beams with pride.

                    JOE DOLORES

Good country. Beeootiful country. Absarokee country
beeootiful country.

31. EXT. DAY. THE OUTSKIRTS OF THE CROW CAMP

It is sunset. The three riders approach the Crow camp.
There are twenty tipis camped in a wide circle by the
river. A hundred horses are grazing on the prairie.
Outside the camp there are twenty dogs nosing around a
great pile of bones and buffalo fat. They run out to
bark at the riders. There is meat everywhere - hanging
on wooden platforms, drying in the sun, being smoked
over small fires. Most of the village seems to be congregated by the river, beside a small sweatlodge -- a
framework of willow branches, covered with buffalo robes.
One of Kurz' eagle pennants hangs from a pole outside
the sweatlodge.

The flap of the lodge opens, and great billows of steam
escape. Two Indians, one naked and one dressed in
breechcloth, come out, the first supporting the second.
The second man is covered with small pox, and walking
unsteadily. Following them is the medicine man, dressed
in an elaborate costume made of a painted amd fringed
coyote skin. He is on all fours.

31. CONTINUED

Four Bears motions the helper away. The man leaves, and
the ailing Indian falls to the ground. Medicine drums
begin. Four Bears begins singing. He whines like a coyote
mother that has pups and trots like a coyote around a
man's body, four times. He turns his back on the man,
sits down on his haunches like a coyote, and howls four
times, lifting the coyote skin head over his own head
each time. The ailing man begins to lift himself up. Four
Bears trots around him again and again, whining, urging
him to get up. The man staggers to his feet. Four Bears
nudges him gently toward the water. (Four Bears' imitation
of a coyote is more than an imitation; he has become a
coyote for this occasion.) We watch the whole procedure
from the point of view of the three men approaching. Now
they are getting close. All of the people are standing in
absolute silence, watching the ritual, with their hands
covering their mouths. Looks For His Horses covers his
mouth. Joe Dolores crosses himself. Coups hangs back a
bit from the others.

Four Bears, trotting and whining, coaxes the sick man into
the freezing water until he is chest deep. Four Bears
follows him into the river. He paws the water, splashing
it over the man's head. He noses the water with the wolf
skin, running the nose of the skin over the man's sores.
A change seems to be coming over the sick man: he seems to
be getting stronger.

Just then, the three men ride up to the crowd of people.
Four Bears, who has his back to them, stops what he is
doing. The drums stop. The medicine man looks around.
He pulls off his coyote skin. The sick man swoons.
Members of his family rescue him from the river. Everyone starts talking at once. Four Bears storms up to Looks
For His Horses. He points to Coups. "Is this the man
from your vision?" "Yes." (All of this in Crow, without translation.) He upbraids Looks For His Horses for
bringing Coups to the ceremony. He turns to the family
of the sick man and gives them instructions. The man's
mother begins to cry. She takes a knife and slashes her
forehead, her arms, and her legs. She wails. They carry
the man away.

Other men have gathered around the three riders. Looks For
His Horses has dismounted and is arguing with two others.
A couple of men are looking Coups over. One of them says
something to him, but Coups doesn't understand. There is
a menacing air about all of this. Joe Dolores crosses
himself.

COUPS

What air they sayin' hoss?

Four Bears begins arguing angrily with Looks For His Horses.

JOE DOLORES

De Four Bears, she think the veeshun of Look For Horses?
She no good. Bad medicine. <u>Carajo!</u> She think you bad
medicine!

31. CONTINUED

Another man takes Looks For His Horses' side against Four
Bears. Part of this man's face is covered with a strip
of buckskin, from which several scalps dangle. He is called
Covers His Face. The Indians suddenly turn away and head
for their respective lodges. Looks For His Horses turns
to Joe Dolores, says something in Crow. He looks at Coups,
grabs a handful of dust from a place on the ground where
Coups' shadow lies, blows it away, and walks off. Covers
His Face comes, up to Coups, points to Coups' pipe hanging
around his neck, and in sign language offers to trade for
it. Coups refuses.

JOE DOLORES

Right now, Crow camp very unhappy. Fort close. Small pox
kill many peoples. Medicine no work. Wolf medicine no
work. Meester Kurz pitcher medicine no work. But, manana,
joo see, Four Bears he find good medicine. Ebrybody happy
again. Hunt de buff. Dance all night. Come, eat puppy.

Covers his face speaks up again. He makes Coups a better
offer for his pipe. Coups refuses again. The man offers
more. Coups signs that he wouldn't trade all of the man's
horses for his pipe. The man signs something that Coups
doesn't understand, and walks away. Joe Dolores laughs.

COUPS

What's that?

JOE DOLORES

She say joo better watch out, 'cause she gonna steal that
pipe.

COUPS

Thar goes an Injun, what a niggur kin trust. He's an
hones thief. Wharas Mister Watson James, he's jist low
down.

32. INT. NIGHT. JOE DOLORES' TIPI

Coups is lying on his back on a buffalo robe, feet toward
the fire. It is quite dark in the tipi. Somewhere in the
darkness on the other side of the tipi, the hulk of Joe
Dolores is in bed, singing softly to himself.

COUPS

Been many a cold winter since this beaver et puppy so
tender. 'Preciate yore hospitality. Got a nice family
hyar, Joe. Real fine. You folks is jest like family.

Near Joe, Mrs. Dolores can be seen, naked, slapping bear
grease on her breasts, under her arms, over her rolls of
fat. She looks coquettish. She gives a shy smile, and
climbs into bed with Joe. Joe continues singing. The
fire is very low. Joe and Mrs. Dolores, under their robe,
are just a dark shape, moving around in the darkness, as
they make love.

Joe is a trapper. There are skins of every kind of animal
piled and hanging everywhere. Also a variety of traps.

32. CONTINUED

Next door, there is the sound of an old woman coughing.
Far off in the camp, drums beating, singing, Indian love
calls, frogs, a puppy yipping in pain, two women shouting
at each other. Coups lies with his eyes open, staring
out through the top of the tipi hole.

33. <u>INT. DAY. JOE DOLORES' TIPI</u>

Coups lies asleep along the side of the Dolores tipi. He
is lying on his side facing inward. There is a great deal
of noise and commotion, both inside and outside the tipi.
Coups opens his eyes. Joe and Mrs. Dolores are having a
fight, screaming and occasionally slugging one another.
Their five year old kid is kicking Joe Dolores in the
shins. Coups closes his eyes again.

The skirt of the tipi behind Coups' head is lifted up,
and two teenage girls slip their heads inside. One of
the girls has a knife. They are giggling. The girl with
the knife reaches out and cuts a lock of Coups' hair off.
Coups whirls around. The girls scramble back out of the
tipi. Coups rolls out under the tipi skirt. He sees the
two Crow nymphets stop at a distance and look back at him.
They giggle and run off.

The village is a noisy, chaotic scene. Women are running
around, carrying wood, yelling at naked children. Several
men lie indolently in front of a tipi, smoking a pipe and
talking. There is a platform where huge strips of meat
are curing in the sun. There are three women laboriously
scraping a buffalo skin stretched out on the ground. There
are the sounds of drums and wailing. Just nearby, three
women are sealing off the skirts of a newly erected tipi,
with stakes and brush. One of them is the mother of the
man who died. She has scars on her forehead, arms and
legs. Her hair is cropped short. She sees Coups. She
screams and throws a hex at him.

                    COUPS

Waugh!

At this moment, Joe Dolores emerges from his tipi.

                    JOE DOLORES

Ay, Coups, carajo! Where joo go?

                    COUPS

What's all this fofurraw?

He jerks his thumb at the three women putting up the tipi.

                    JOE DOLORES

Joo remember de muchacho dat die yesterday?

He points to the tipi.

33. CONTINUED

                    JOE DOLORES

Dey put him...

He starts to walk away.

                    JOE DOLORES

Me go set de traps. Ebryday I puts de trap, leave, when I
come backs no carcasse. Ah! But it's jammay que de wolf
drag de carcasse away from de trap. Most be de cayoute.
Dis niggua gonna go boom! An' dat cayoute she gonna
remember hees madrecita!

Joe Dolores is out of earshot by now. Coups finds himself
alone.

An Indian wearing a stained and decrepit remnant of a full
dress military costume passes him. He holds a woman's
parasol over his head. The man, Wi Jun Jon, calls out.

                    WI JUN JON

Andy Jackson

                    COUPS

Watson James

Coups starts walking through camp, toward the river. He'
passes a man in his fifties, Black Moccasin, with extremely
long white hair, sitting outside the tipi at his toilette.
He holds a mirror in his right hand. His wife is busily
greasing his hair. She is much younger, in her early
thirties, and quite attractive. The couple stares at
Coups.

                    COUPS

How do, marm? How do chief? Pleased to meet you.

Their dogs start barking at him. Perhaps ten or fifteen
dogs join in barking and snapping at his heels. A woman
passes, driving four dogs, who are harnessed in travois,
dragging loads of wood and buffalo chips. The dogs try
to get into the action with Coups, but the woman keeps
them in line by constantly shouting and hitting them with
a long switch.

A twelve year old boy is sneaking behind Coups, carrying
a candy striped "coups stick". He makes a dash for Coups,
and strikes him on the leg with the stick. Coups whirls
around. The boy takes off at top speed, his face in an
expression of absolute terror. He turns back in the direction
he was going. Looks For His Horses blocks his way, holding
the reins to two horses in his hands. He hands Coups the
reins to one of the horses.

                    COUPS

Fer this chile? Say, that's mighty white of you, ol' coon.
Mighty white.

Looks For His Horses grabs a handful of dust from Coups'
shadow and blows it at him again. He turns and leads Coups

33. CONTINUED

through camp, toward a large tipi where Kurz' eagle pennant
now hangs.

34. EXT. DAY.   OUTSIDE FOUR BEARS' TIPI

Several women and children are outside Four Bears' tipi,
amid rolls of tanned animal skins, s trips of sinew, and
bone tools. They are sewing. Looks For His Horses throws
a blanket down on the ground beside the woman. He indicates
Coups, speaking to her in Crow. She grabs Coups' ankle,
and sets his foot down on a piece of tanned deerhide. She
begins to measure him for a pair of moccassins.

Suddenly a group of riders gallops into the camp, led by
Four Bears. Four Bears looks very angry. Beside him is
Crooked Nose and Teeth, the crier. All of the camp is
galvanized by their arrival. Crooked Nose and Teeth
dismounts and leads his horse around the camp, calling
out news and instructions. All of the activities of the
camp change at once. Young men and boys run and ride out
to the cavayard, to drive the horses into camp. Older men
duck into their tipis to don special garments, and begin
to gather at the far end of camp for a council. Women
gather their dogs and children. Others begin dismantling
tipis. Four Bears rides up to his tipi. He gives Coups
a look of hatred, He grabs Kurz' eagle pennant, turns and
rides off.

35. EXT. DAY.   BY THE RIVER

There are several Crow girls and women bathing in the river.
Four Bears rides furiously into the river. The girls
scream and scatter. Four Bears hurls the eagle pennant
into the river, calling incantations against it.

36. EXT. DAY.   THE RIVER

The eagle pennant floats down the river. We follow it
downstream, toward the fort. We can see, in the distance,
the fort, and the pack train, leaving, stretched out across
the plain.

37. EXT. DAY.   OUTSIDE FOUR BEARS' TIPI

Coups makes signs to Looks For His Horses.

                    COUPS

What's goin' on, hoss?

One of Looks' friends from the night before rides up and
begins to talk excitedly to Looks. Looks motions to Coups
to mount his horse. Looks mounts his own, takes the reins
of Coups' horse, and leads him off at a gallop out onto
the prairie.

38. <u>EXT. DAY.   BY A MOUNTAIN LAKE</u>

The two men are in the midst of constructing a sweat lodge.
Willow poles are secured in the ground in an ellipse, bent
inward, and then tied together with rawhide strips to
form a frame.   Then the frame is covered with skins.

39. <u>INT. DAY.   INSIDE THE SWEAT LODGE</u>

There is no light. The flap opens. A bar of sunlight
breaks in. Coups passes in a red hot stone, carried on a
forked stick. Looks For His Horses takes it. We only see
their hands. The flap closes. The stone glows red in the
darkness. Looks For His Horses carries it to a pit and
lays it among twenty other glowing stones. The glow just
illuminates Looks For His Horses sitting beside the pit.
A flash of light comes in for a moment, lighting things
up as Coups crawls in, cutting off abruptly as the flap
closes. Looks For His Horses and Coups sit facing each
other across the pit of hot stones. They are both naked.
Looks For His Horses sings his medicine song. He sprinkles
a pinch of sweet grass on the stones, and then water from
a small wooden cup. The lodge instantly fills with steam,
and Coups gasps with the sudden change in temperature.

Looks For His Horses lights Coups' pipe, blows smoke to
the sky, the earth, and the four directions, then passes
it to Coups. Coups salutes Looks For His Horses with the
pipe.

                         COUPS

Hyar's to yuh, chile.

He puffs on the pipe. The lodge is so filled with steam
that they can hardly see each other. Sweat pours off their
bodies. Looks For His Horses touches his breast. He
begins to sing what he remembers of the song he heard
Coups sing in his vision: "...the sun goes up, the sun
goes down...".

                    LOOKS FOR HIS HORSES

Deezungazah desungdah....

He sings it over and over again. At first, Coups is
puzzled. Then he recognizes it, and begins to sing it for
Looks.

                         COUPS

...the sun goes up, the sun goes down...

Looks For His Horses sings along with him trying to get it,
getting it better and better. He sings it over and over.

The spots on Coups' body begin to wash away in his sweat.
Looks For His Horses begins to cry, still singing. Tears
roll out of his eyes, but he never averts his gaze from
Coups. Slowly, his singing becomes a perfect imitation of
Coups' singing. Coups stops singing. Looks continues,
over and over. Coups is touched, and somewhat embarassed
for the first time. He begins to talk to Looks, in
English, without signs, just talking.

39. CONTINUED

                    COUPS

About ridin' into your dream that time, hoss... It war jist
a joke, chile. Figgered to give ye somethin' to brag about
in the lodges...Thar I war...Eighteen-and-twenty-eight...
ridin' down the road...all muh possibles in muh saddlebags...
dressed up in muh weddin' suit...An' I come to a fork in
the road. And one fork heads for her pappy's place and
the preacher, and the whole kiboodle. And tother fork pulls
for St. Louis. And in St. Louis thar's a Major Henry what's
lookin' for boys to trap beaver in the Rocky Mountains.
(Long pause) ...and this chile jist closed his eyes, and
let the mule decide...(self-mockingly) Hyar's a coon what
always lets a mule decide.

40. EXT. DAY. OUTSIDE THE SWEAT LODGE

Coups emerges from the sweat lodge and, with a whoop, runs
for the lake. Looks, right behind him, does a perfect
imitation of everything that Coups does. He has been prac-
tising all this time, trying to catch every little quirk
of Coups' manner. Now, in a moment of inspiration, he
has caught all, every bit. Coups lets out a shout - his
war whoop - as he jumps in the lake. Looks does an echo-
like imitation and jumps in the lake. As Coups surfaces,
his real echo comes booming back across the lake. As Looks
surfaces, his echo comes back. The echoes die away. There
is a tingling silence. The two men come out of the water.
They wrap themselves in blankets and hunch by the fire.

There is a faint roll of thunder. Way, back in the mountains, they can see vast thunderheads building up. They
watch the storm gathering: vast clouds bumping together,
lightning, turbulent winds, very far off. The camera moves
closer and closer until it is right in the midst of the
storm.

41. EXT. DAY. SITE OF THE CROW CAMP

It is before dawn. The village has moved. What is left
is: the funeral tipi, completely sealed around the bottom
with stakes and brush; wisps of smoke rising from the
embers of thirty fires; much trampled grass and stumps of
sagebrush; hundreds of bones and piles of buffalo fat, now
being ravaged by a pack of coyotes; and a freshly churned
up trail, indicating the direction the village took.

Coups and Looks For His Horses ride across the site of the
encampment and follow the trail.

42. EXT. DAY. OUTSIDE FORT ABSAROKA

Looks For His Horses and Coups follow the trail past the
deserted fort. A solitary horse is tied by Kurz' window.
The mynah bird can be heard inside.

                    MYNAH BIRD

Georg Friederich Teleman.

43. <u>EXT. DAY. PRAIRIE</u>

It is dawn. Looks For His Horses and Coups ride along the
foothills of the mountains. Looks For His Horses points out
a cloud of dust far out on the plains.

                    COUPS

Must be that thar pack train from the fort, headed fer
St. Louis.

Now, Looks For His Horses points to a whisp of smoke coming
from a nearby hill.

                    COUPS

Crows?

He makes the sign for "Crows" - two hands hooked together,
flapping like wings. Looks For His Horses nods.

                    LOOKS FOR HIS HORSES

Absaroka.

They ride up over the hill toward the wisp of smoke.

                    COUPS

Waugh! A raidin' party!

They ride into a scene of furious activity. There are
twenty Crow warriors, each in the midst of performing
his own particular medicine ritual, to insure his success
on the raid. This involves stripping down to the breechcloth, painting one's face and body in a distinctive way,
singing a medicine song to a medicine object - a dead bird,
a particularly interesting rock, a specially made pipe -
perhaps doing a dance, all according to instructions
received in dreams and visions. One brave is earnestly
giving his horse instructions for the battle. In the
middle-distance, the women, children, and horses are
gathered.

Coups follows close behind Looks For His Horses. They pass
Four Bears, who is kneeling on the ground in a trance, his
back tracing the angle of the rising sun. Black Moccasin
is sitting beside Four Bears, eyes closed, singing a medicine
song. Looks For His Horses dismounts by a muddy gray pool
of water. He starts to take off his clothing.

Two warriors approach Coups: Silk Hat and Covers His Face.
Silk Hat has funnelled his hair up through the crown of
his hat so that it spills out over the top like a plant
in a flowerpot. Covers His Face's face is green, except
for the leather patch with the dangling scalps. Looks For
His Horses lifts a handful of clay from the pool, at a place
where Coups' shadow falls. He smears the clay on his face,
arms, and shoulders. Coups is wearing Looks For His Horses'
shirt. Silk Hat points to Coups.

                    SILK HAT

Absaroka.

                    COUPS

Shore. 'sarokee Cooper. That's me.

43. CONTINUED

Covers His Face asks Coups in signs if he will fight today.
Coups speaks in signs and English at the same time.

                         COUPS

This niggur's got friends on that thar pack train an' he'd
hate ter find himself liftin' ha'r off'n an ol' partner.

Looks For His Horses has fashioned wolf's ears over his
own out of the clay. He now takes out his coyote skin,
pulls the head down over his eyes and nose. Silk Hat
embraces Coups.

                    SILK HAT

Absaroka!

Covers His Face embraces Coups.

                  COVERS HIS FACE

Absaroka!

There is a noise, a kind of howl. Everyone looks around.
It is Four Bears, still kneeling, arms outstretched, head
up now toward the rising sun, howling at the sun. All the
warriors gather around him. Four Bears' body is glistening
with sweat. He is trembling. Suddenly all of the tension
in his body slackens, his muscles go limp, and he falls
forward. His head hits the ground, very hard. He falls on
his side. His eyes roll up into the top of his head. His
body convulses, as if shocked, electrically. His tongue
hangs out on the ground, and gulping sounds come from his
throat. Just as suddenly, his fit is over. He seems very
tired, but human once again. he looks up at the other
warriors. He begins to speak to them. His tone is fore-
boding. He is talking about his own death. The warriors
put their hands over their mouths in astonishment, then
look at Coups. Some of the warriors have tears in their
eyes.

The warriors begin crowding around Coups and Looks. Coups
is getting nervous. A warrior strikes him on the back of
the neck with a "coups stick", a feathered stick, painted
green and white, in a barber pole motif. Coups spins around.

                      COUPS

Nobody counts coups on Coups Cooper!

He faces a dozen angry painted faces. Looks For His Horses
draws his knife and interposes himself between Coups and the
other Indians, defending Coups. Four Bears gets very angry.
He interposes himself on the other side, shouting at Looks
For His Horses.

On the far side of the hill there is a yelp. Two Crow scouts
dressed as wolves come running down the side of the hill,
jump on their horses, and gallop toward the assembled warriors,
zig-zagging back and forth. The warriors scatter to mount
their horses.

43. CONTINUED

The Wolves come riding up, circling them, shouting out
information. They are two of Looks For His Horses' friends.
Four Bears grabs Looks For His Horses by the scruff of the
neck and shoves him toward his horse. Looks For His Horses
trembles with rage. He jumps on his horse and gallops off
toward the far hill.

Coups hesitates. He looks around. He is alone. He hears
a shout. He sees Covers His Face holding Coups' pipe.
Covers His Face laughs and rides off. Coups gallops after
Looks For His Horses.

The warriors are riding up the hill. The women and children
are following on foot.

44. EXT. DAY. TOP OF HILL

Looks For His Horses reins up in a grove of trees at the
top of a hill. He is in a rage of resentment. He keeps
kicking and whipping his horse to go ahead, at the same time
holding it back, so that it is constantly jumping forward,
then rearing up and spinning around. Both horse and rider
are gasping for breath. He can see the pack train below
him, quite close. Coups rides up and stops nearby. In
contrast to Looks, he is the model of cool.

The warriors, riding in a single line all abreast, appear
over the top of the nearby hill. All together, singing a
war song, they ride slowly down toward the pack train. The
women and children are gathering on the hilltop. As the Crows
come into view over the top of the hill, chaos strikes the
pack train. The white people try to coax their mules into
a protective circle. There is a great deal of dust and
shouting. One teamster has trouble with a mule, and shoots
it.

Four Bears rides out ahead of his warriors, up to a point
just beyond the range of the pack train's rifles. He
fastens a long strip of bright red cloth around his head,
so that it streams out behind him as he rides. He rides
back and forth, haranguing the whites. He spits at them.
He takes some gray powder from a pouch and shakes it at
them, throwing out little clouds of gray dust.

Then he begins to ride in a wide circle around the pack
train. One by one, the other warriors drop into line behind him. A great high sound goes up from the women on
the hill.

A puff of smoke wafts up from the circle of mules. Then
we hear the sound of the shot. The shot falls short,
kicking up dust at the feet of Four Bears' horse.

The Crows tighten their circle. They hold up their
shields. They are shouting and yelping. More shots
are coming from the circle of mules now. A cloud of
smoke is forming over their heads. The Crow horses are
kicking up billows of dust, which also hangs in the air.

The Crows are now in a much smaller circle, all hanging
down along the sides of their horses, firing arrows
from underneath their horses' necks. Another mule in the

44. CONTINUED.

circle is already dead, with four arrows in its side.
Another mule is rearing out of control.

We see Four Bears break from the circle and charge the
mule enclosure, his shield held before him, his coup
stick raised in the air. A bullet glances off his shield.
He rides directly at Watson James, who is trying desperately to aim his musket.

Behind Watson, we can see Annie, crouching in fear behind
a dead mule.

Four Bears snatches the rifle from Watson's hand, strikes
him across the face with his coup stick, and gallops
off out of range.

The women on the hilltop let out a tremolo cheer. Coups
whoops too, tickled pink.

Silk Hat charges from the circle. Someone shoots him.
He falls to the ground, dead. His horse rears up in front
of one of the mules. The mule rears up with fright. They
both scatter into the circle, causing havoc.

Covers His Face drives in through the opening in the
circle. Everything is clouded with dust and smoke. There
are shouts, shots, whoops, as more warriors ride into
the circle. The voices of the women rise up in a tremolo
cry.

Out of the dust and smoke, two warriors gallop side by
side, carrying the body of Covers His Face between them.
Two more warriors come out, riding double on one horse.
Then, in ones and twos, the others emerge, retreating.

The women on the hill stop singing. The gunshots and
shouts die down. The bodies of the two dead men are
brought up to the women. The warriors regroups down
below. Everything is quiet. The smoke and dust waft
away. There are several dead Indian ponies and several
dead mules in the circle. Two riderless horses run
back and forth across the battlefield.

Slowly, the warriors begin advancing on the pack train
again, keeping very close together, singing first loud
and then low, over and over again. The voices of the
women rise from the hill.

The warriors charge straight for the pack train, jump
over the dead mules, and overrun the enclosure. Looks
For His Horses can contain himself no longer. He looks
at Cooper. He touches his breast.

LOOKS FOR HIS HORSES

(singing)

...the sun goes up, the sun goes down...

He whips his horse and gallops down into the battle.

The Crows are pillaging the pack train. The battle has

44. CONTINUED

broken down to hand to hand combat. We see two warriors
chase three mules across the prairie. Another warrior
rides off with a great bolt of red cloth. Someone
shoots him. He falls from his horse, and the bolt of
cloth rolls open across the prairie.

We see Four Bears charging the Second Trapper. The
Second Trapper kneels and takes careful aim. He fires.
Four Bears keeps coming, unhurt. The trapper tries to
reload, spitting a musket ball into his barrel. Four
Bears raises his war club and smashes the trapper in the
center of his forehead, killing him. Several other Crows
press around the fallen trapper, counting coup.

45. EXT. DAY. ON THE BATTLEFIELD. (CLOSE UPS

Looks For His Horses comes riding out of the dust, carrying
Annie across his horse's back. He sees Coups at the top
of the hill. He waves to him. He sees Coups riding
down toward him. He whips his horse to meet him. Annie
is holding onto the horse's mane and hitting at Looks For
His Horses.

The sun is behind Coups, and he appears as a silhouette:
one can't see his face. At the last moment, as he draws
close to Looks For His Horses, he lifts up a stick and
clubs the boy.

Looks For His Horses grabs Coups' arm. They are both
jerked out of their saddles, and fall to the ground,

Looks For His Horses' pony careers away, with Annie
doubled over on its back. Annie hangs on for dear life.
She struggles and manages to throw a leg over the pony's
back and pull herself into a semi-sitting position. She
clings to the horse with her whole body, burying her head
in its mane. The horse gallops off across the prairie,
in the direction of the fort.

Looks For His Horses charges Coups with his knife. Coups
kicks him, full force, in he stomach. He sees Annie
being carried off. He runs for his horse, gets up on its
back, trying to chase after her. He dashes up a steep,
gravelly slope.

Looks For His Horses pulls his bow from around his neck and
strings an arrow. Coup's horse is having a hard time
getting up the hill -- he keeps losing his footing.
Looks is trying to catch his breath and steady his aim.
He shoots, hitting Coups' horse. Coups falls out of
the saddle, and he and the horse come tumbling down the
hill in a cloud of dust. Coups lays there unconcious.

Looks For His Horses draws his knife, runs to Coups'
body, grabs his hair in one hand, and with the knife
in the other, begins to scalp him, slashing the side of
his head.

45. CONTINUED

Coups wakes up, lunges forward in a rage, and throws
Looks For His Horses to the ground. We hear a shot fired
in the distance. Looks scrambles to his feet. Coups
staggers. Blood is running into his left eye. He tries
to rub it away, groping in front of him with his other
hand. Looks tries to get behind him again, reaching for
his hair, but Cooper makes a blind lunge and traps Looks
For His Horses in a bear hug, lifting him off the ground.
He growls like a bear.

Looks For His Horses sinks his teeth into Coups' ear.
Coups drops him, howling with pain. Looks For His Horses
lashes out at him with his knife. Coups falls backward
on the ground, blinded now by the blood on his face.

Looks goes for Coups. There is a shot. It whips the
boy around, throwing him to the ground. Gouge Eye comes
galloping up. He rides in a circle around Cooper, who is
staggering to his feet in a daze.

                    GOUGE EYE

Come on, ol' coon, come on!

He is reaching out his hand. Looks For His Horses is
getting up. He is holding his side. He lunges toward
them again. Cooper reaches for Gouge Eye's hand, misses,
but grabs on to the horse's tail.

                    GOUGE EYE

Hold on, then, niggur!

He takes off, with Coups trailing behind, dangling by
the horse's tail. He rolls along the ground, then jumps
to his feet. Looks For His Horses is coming up now,
clutching his wound, stumbling toward them. Gouge Eye
circles back. Coups scrambles up behind him on the
horse. Looks For His Horses grabs Coups' leg. Gouge
Eye beats him with the butt of his rifle.

The Indian boy looks up at Coups. Gouge Eye hits him
again. He lets go of Coups' leg and falls to the ground.
Two other Crows are bearing down on them from a distance.

Gouge Eye and Coups head for the mule enclosure. In the
background, the two Crows bend down from their ponies,
pick up Looks For His Horses, and carry him off, back
toward the top of the hill, where the other Crows have
retreated. The sounds of the women have turned to laments.

46. EXT. DAY. PACK TRAIN ENCLOSURE.

The pack train enclosure is in ruins. Many of the mules
are dead, with hundreds of arrows sticking in their sides.
There are broken barrels and goods and furs spilled out
on the ground.

The two trappers ride in. Coups rolls off Gouge Eye's
horse and slumps to the ground. Stump appears.

46. CONTINUED

                    STUMP

Waugh! That niggur's half skulped!

                  GOUGE EYE
                 (to Stump)

Git a hold on him, hoss, and we'll powder him up slick.

Coups moans. Stump bends down and holds Coups tight
under the arms. Gouge Eye sits on his legs, cutting
away the hair around his head wound.

                  GOUGE EYE

Ruction like that makes a niggur feel right peart, don't
it, hoss?

                    STUMP

Wal, some. Ain't had sich a high time since last spring,
with them Shians down by the Niobara. And warn't that
Four Bears somethin' today?

Watson James is coming toward them, fretting and fingering
the welt on his cheek.

                  GOUGE EYE

Waugh! That thar's countin' a mighty coup, eh, Watty?

                  WATSON JAMES

I can't understand it. It's outrageous. Good God! Isn't
that Cooper? I saw him out there. Who's side was he on?

Coups blinks his eyes open.

                    COUPS

Is the topknot gone, boy? Muh head feels queersome, I
tell ye.

Gouge Eye takes the empty pipe sack from Cooper's breast
and stuffs it in his mouth.

                  GOUGE EYE

Take a chaw on this'un, hoss.

                  WATSON JAMES

I just don't understand how a simple business misunder-
standing could provoke such an attack by Four Bears.

                    STUMP

Ye didn't give the niggur what he wanted, Watty. So he
tuk it.

There is a tremolo cry from the Crows on the hill. They
fire off a parting volley of shots, and disappear over
the hill. The Fourth Trapper passes by, holding a scalp
of long white hair, dripping blood. The trapper has a
big smile on his face. Coups mumbles through the pipe

sack in his mouth.

                         COUPS

This niggur knows that scalp.

                    WATSON JAMES

It's ridiculous. Compensation they wanted! For what?
For taking water from the river! For burning wood from
the trees! For the game we ate! What'ever made them
believe it was theirs?

                       GOUGE EYE

Wal, Watty, they thinks o' themselves as sorta like
caretakers o' thar territory. Fer the Great Spirit.

                        STUMP
                      (explaining)

Sorta like Manifold Damnesty.

Stump unplugs his powderhorn and pours the black gunpowder
along Coups' scalp wound. Coups grimaces.

                        STUMP

Hold on, hoss.

Gouge Eye strikes his flint to the gunpowder. It catches
alight. Coups lets out a muffled scream.

                    WA SON JAMES

My God!

Stump smothers the flame with some wet leaves. Gouge Eye
leans back on his heels. Coups spits out the pipe sack.

                        COUPS

Whar's the white woman?

                       GOUGE EYE

Fixin' boudins some Crow tipi, I reckon.

Coups staggers to his feet. He looks at Watson James.

                        COUPS

They tuk her? ...Stand me to a hoss, guvner?

                    WATSON JAMES

You're asking me for a horse? Look around you. Half
of my mounts are dead or stolen. How are we going to
get these furs to St. Louis? And our party to Oregon? A
man has been killed. Our passenger has been carried off --
no doubt to suffer unspeakable horrors at the hands of
those savages. I have half a mind to follow those Indians
and teach them a lesson.

                        STUMP

We gots to go after her, Watty.

46. CONTINUED

Other trappers and engagées gather around.

                    WATSON JAMES

If it were only possible, gentlemen.

                    FOURTH TRAPPER

Send a party out, Watty. Hyar's a coon as keers to see
that face again.

Others volunteer.

                    WATSON JAMES

Just a moment, gentlemen. 'I'm still in command
here, and I must consider the welfare of the whole party,
the interests of the company, and the pragmatic questions
of how things get done. How do we know we won't be
attacked again?

                    GOUGE EYE

Yore leavin' that purty little gal to them Injuns, Watty?

                    WA SON JAMES

For all we know, she might be dead. Look, gentlemen...

                    STUMP

Looky hyar, Watty, send these boys back to St. Louis with
what they kin take. We'll cache the rest, and usn's as is
headed for Oregon kin folly the track o' them Absarokees,
lift us some ha'r, and make tracks for the Yellystone.

                    · WATSON JAMES

But, Mr. Stump, you yourself said that if we don't get
through those passes before the October snows...

Coups holds out his finger to Watson James.

                    COUPS

Pull muh finger, Watty.

                    WATSON JAMES

Please, Mr. Cooper.

                    COUPS

Pull muh finger!

Watson pulls Coups' finger. Coups farts. The crowd breaks
up in laughter. There are "waughs", "hooraws", whoops
of all kinds, and several gunshots.

                    COUPS

Hyar's a mountain man what's on his own mud hook! Waugh!
This beaver's bound to track and trap that limey gal.

Stump hands him his Green River knife.

46. CONTINUED

                    STUMP

I reckon Coups Cooper and ol' Green River'll pass to
do the deed.

Gouge Eye throws Coups a rifle.

                    GOUGE EYE

Take ol' bullthrower, hoss, an' give li'l Miss Annie a
squeeze fer ol' Gouge Eye Ned McLaughlin.

A trapper hands Coups a powderhorn, and another throws
him a bag of musket balls.

                    FIRST TRAPPER

Some Dupont...

                    FOURTH TRAPPER

...an' G'lena pills...

Another trapper throws him a buffalo robe.

                    SECOND TRAPPER

Hyar's a apishamore this beaver traded off'n ol' Bill Williams

Jim Beckwourth hands him a large chunk of buffalo jerky.

                    JIM BECKWOURTH

They's starvin' times up thar in the mountains now, ol'
coon. Best pack some jerky. Take a chaw on it when yore
wolfish, and think of ol' Jim Beckwourth what give it
to ye.

Coups starts to walk away. He turns to Watson James.

                    COUPS

Say, guvner, are ye still sellin' 'bacca at a plug a plew?

Stump throws him a plug from a broken sack on the ground.

                    COUPS
                    (to Watson James)

I owes ye a plew.
                    (to the trappers)

Wal, boys, when the Missoura starts a-breakin' up come
spring, ye'll find Coups Cooper packin' a white squaw on
the Bayou Salade.

                    GOUGE EYE

Watch out for yore scalp, boy.

                    FIRST TRAPPER

Keep yore moksins greased.

                    STUMP

Might see ye, some time, some place.

46. CONTINUED

Coups walks off, stumbling, weak from his wound. Some
of the trappers watch him walk away, others set about
putting the pack train back together.

EXT. DAY. BESIDE COUPS' DEAD HORSE.

Coups looks around, trying to get his bearings. He walks
to the spot where he and Looks For His Horses clashed. He
examines the signs. There is a confusion of tracks, but
he picks out a set and begins to follow them. They lead
in the direction of the fort.

48. EXT. DAY. IN SOME BRUSH NEAR THE FORT.

Kurz is sighting down his rifle at a moving target. He
takes a deep breath and holds it. He pans his rifle back
and forth, trying to catch up with his target. He is
having difficulty keeping his left eye closed. He fires
the gun and jerks back with the recoil.

We see the sho kick up some dirt about ten yards away
from a scampering jackrabbit. The rabbit disappears in
the brush.

Kurz turns and walks back toward the fort. He looks
the perfect European hunting gentleman, completely enclosed in an elegant cape, wearing his Werther hat,
leaning into the autumn wind.

49. EXT. DAY. OUTSIDE THE FORT.

The fort is deserted. The gate flaps open and shut in
the wind. As Kurz reaches the gate, lost in thoughts,
Annie comes riding up, exhausted, dirty, disheveled, and
somewhat hysterical.

                    KURZ

Annie!

                    ANNIE

Oh, Kurz, we were attacked!

                    KURZ

Attacked? Mein Gott. I knew something would happen.
Here, let me help you down.

As he reaches up, his cape flies open in the wind. He
is wearing only soiled longjohns underneath. He also hasn't
shaved in two days, and his stubble gives a comic effect,
superimposed over his neatly sculpted moustache and beard.
Annie can't suppress a laugh as he helps her down.

                    ANNIE

I've been riding all day and night.

She rubs her velvet ass.

49. CONTINUED

                    ANNIE

Oh, me bum.

She absently hands Kurz the horse's reins and walks over
to the window of his apartment. Kurz follows on her heels,
tying the horse to the window post.

                    KURZ

Was it Four Bears?

                    ANNIE

Ohhh, it's much too long a story, Rudolph. Right now,
I must have some food. Have you any of those delicious
candy kisses left?

50. INT. DAY. KURZ' UPSTAIRS ROOM.

Annie climbs in the window.

                    ANNIE

What's that pit for?

Kurz, agitated and embarrassed, climbs in after Annie. He
ties the horse to the window post. There is an open pit
in the middle of the dirt floor, where Kurz' chair used
to go. Strewn around the room are the things that were
buried there: parfleches filled with beautiful, Indian
clothing, many of Sir Harry's possessions - tinned foods,
wine, a red silk smoking jacket, and food staples such
as flour, coffee and sugar.

                    KURZ

Well, I had a few things buried in there.

Annie fingers the clothes.

                    ANNIE

Heavens, how beautiful, but these are Harry's things.

Kurz squats by the fireplace. There are still some glowing
embers from the last fire. He has only a bit of kindling
left on the floor beside him. He strews it on the fire.

                    KURZ

I'm running out of wood.

He turns to see Annie, with her skirt bunched above her
waist, holding a pair of ornamented leggings over her legs,
to see how they look.

                    KURZ

Could you just put those clothes back in the parfleche?

                    ANNIE

Whose clothes are they?

She picks up a piece of dried meat from the mantel and takes
a bite. Kurz picks up his chair and smashes it against the
the pieces in the fire.

49. CONTINUED

                    KURZ

They're no one's. Why don't you make some coffee?

He starts to hand her the coffee pot. His cape and hunter's
sack slip off his shoulders as he stands up. He tries to
be cool. Annie suppresses a giggle. She takes the pot
and dips some water from a large keg by the door.

                    ANNIE

Did you steal that you naughty boy?

Kurz turns red. But he tries to be suave. Annie adds some
coffee to the water.

                    KURZ

Of course, I stole them, my dear. Now, put them away,
they are my ticket to Panamá.

Annie wraps her skirt around the handle of the coffee pot
and tries to set it in the fire.

                    KURZ

You see, I took only the best ones. These bourgeois have
no taste. They pay the same price whether....

Annie's skirt catches fire. She drops the coffee pot which
spills all over Kurz' cape. Kurz beats out the fire with
his hands and the cape. [illegible] ' vision of it.
Kurz beats out.

                    ANNIE
              (suddenly hysterical)

What is all this petty talk? The Crows attacked us! I
was kidnapped! I escaped!

                    KURZ

Was anyone killed?

                    ANNIE

I don't know. They were still fighting when I escaped.

                    KURZ

Mein Gott! They'll come looking for you here! Oh, well,
don't worry, my paintings will save us.

                    ANNIE

No, it's better that we leave right now. We have enough
clothes here certainly. Perhaps we can catch the pack
train. We'll leave right away. Yes.

                    KURZ

My paintings.

                    ANNIE

We'll have to leave them behind, I'm afraid. That way, they
won't come after us.

                    KURZ

I won't run away. I'm a friend of the Crows, n'est-ce pas?

49. CONTINUED

                         ANNIE
But me! That friend of yours, Looks For His Horses?
He's the one who abducted me.

                         KURZ
Looks For His Horses?

He laughs now. Annie picks up Kurz' hunting bag, and
rifles through it.

                         ANNIE
Were you out hunting just now?

                         KURZ
Yes.

                         ANNIE
But there's nothing here.

                         KURZ
I was unlucky.

Annie takes a petulant bite from the dried meat.

                         KURZ
Don't eat all of that meat. I had planned for it to
last me for a while.

                         ANNIE
Kurz, we can't stay here! I'm falling asleep, but I
know that if I fall asleep, I'll wake up a captive.

                         KURZ
Listen Velvet Ass Annie! If we ride to St. Louis, when we
get there you'll leave with your newest beau, and I'll
never see you again. If we stay here through the winter,
and I'm the only man around, you'll fall in love with me,
but we'll starve to death. No, that's not right. What
happens if we stay here through the winter and you don't
fall in love with me, and we starve to death?

                         ANNIE
Despicable!

She starts to climb the ladder.

                         KURZ
Where are you going?

                         ANNIE
I'm going to sleep. I suppose that you'll try to rape
me in my sleep.

She disappears into the upstairs room. Kurz starts up
the ladder after her.

50. <u>INT. DAY. KURZ' UPSTAIRS ROOM</u>

Annie is on the bed with her head buried under a pillow.

ANNIE

I'll go tomorrow morning. I suppose my fate is falling prey to those Indians or starving here with you.

There is a shout from outside the fort. Kurz looks out of his window. Four Bears is outside, mounted on a beautiful Appaloosa pony. Both the Indian and the pony are wearing long feather headdresses. Four Bears is wearing exquisitely decorated buckskin, and the horse is painted all over with magical symbols. Four Bears' face is painted bright scarlet.

Kurz leans out of the window and talks to him in sign language.

KURZ

Hauw! Four Bears! How happy I am to see you still alive. Did many die?....Oh, Covers His Face?...Brave lad...Silk Hat?...White Hair? What a shame...What's that? Tobacco? ...Oh, too bad...Oh, and the daughter too?...Such a pity. She was a pretty little thing.

He turns to speak to Annie.

KURZ

See that family picture over there? The father, Tobacco, and the little girl on the right, they died of small pox.

Four Bears shouts something. The expression on Kurz' face changes to one of horror. He rushes to slam the shutter. Three arrows in rapid succession hit the shutter as he closes it. Annie screams, and dashes for the far corner of the room. Now, only the sun shining through the cracks in the logs illuminates the room. Kurz breaks out into a sweat. Four Bears keeps shouting.

ANNIE

What is it? What's happening? What did he say?

Kurz goes to the window and pee through the cracks. On the wall beside him is a picture of Covers His Face,

KURZ

The ones I painted died with their eyes open because I painted them that way. And they will never rest through eternity. Can you imagine! He says my paintings have robbed them of an honorable death, and caused his brothers to die. Christ, he looks angry...He says that he doesn't want to die with his face rotten, so that even the wolves will shrink in horror at seeing him...The <u>wolves</u>!

Annie lets out a little moan.

ANNIE

Oh, how awful.

50. CONTINUED

                    KURZ

Gott...He wants me to come out and kill him...Mein Gott...
And then I can close his eyes..Gott in Himmel, das ist...

He begins babbling in German, pacing up and down.

                    ANNIE

That poor man, you must go out and do it for him, Kurz.

                    KURZ

Whaaat!

                    ANNIE

Oh, you must.

Suddenly, Four Bears' voice stops. Kurz rushes to look
through the cracks. Annie goes too.

Four Bears is still there, sitting on his pony. He has
opened up his medicine bundle, which contains bat's wings
and the beaks, feet, and tails of several birds. It also
contains several little pouches. He opens one. It is fille d
with a bright green pigment. He covers the palm side of
his left hand completely with the green paint. Then he
places the hand over his mouth and removes it, leaving
its imprint on his face. As he does this, he looks directly
at Kurz, as though he could see him through the log wall.
He pulls his long hair around to the front and wipes his
hands on it. He carefully folds his medicine bundle, and p
puts it away. He closes his eyes. He turns his horse and
gallops a short diastance away

                    KURZ

Whew, he's leaving.

Eyes closed, Four Bears slips down along the side of his
pony, hangs down under its neck, and drops himself under
its hooves. The pony tramples him, in panic, and runs off
a short way.

                    ANNIE

Are his eyes still closed? I can't bear to look.

Four Bears lifts himself up, staggering. He calls to the
horse. He hears the horse running up, and again, throws hi m-
self under its hooves. The pony runs away again.

After a while, Four Bears tries to rise again. This time
he can only get part way up. He calls the pony, but the
pony won't come. He turns around to face in the direction
of the fort. His eyes are still closed. He calls to Kurz
to come and kill him now. But there is no reply.

Four Be   takes an arrow from his quiver, plunges it
down his throat, and dies.

Annie cries. Outside, two women appear from the bushes,
wailing. They wrap Four Bears' body in a buffalo robe and
carry him off. From another direction, we can hear the
sound of approaching hoofbeats. Kurz and Annie look at
each other.

                    ANNIE

50. CONTINUED

                              ANNIE
Now the rest of them are coming. And they'll balme us for
his death. We must hide!

                              KURZ
                           (frantic)
Where?

                              ANNIE
Downstairs.......in the trunks.

They run downstairs.

51. INT. DAY KURZ' DOWNSTAIRS ROOM

Kurz and Annie hide in separate trunks. They remain silent
for a moment. The rider reaches the fort.

                              KURZ
It's only one rider.

                              ANNIE
Please, Kurz, don't speak!

Someone knocks on the window. After a moment, we hear the
gate flapping in the wind, and Looks For His Horses walks
in through the Dutch door. His wounds have been bound with
leaves and rawhide.

Looks For His Horses says, "Iron Eyes!"

Kurz opens the trunk a crack and peers out. He opens the
trunk and gets out. He is embarrassed and doesn't know
what to say.

Looks For His Horses says, "Where is the woman? I see my
horse outside."

                              KURZ
Annie and I were playing a game......

                              ANNIE
                           (from the trunk)
You dirty coward. You'll do anything to save your skin.

Looks For His Horses opens the trunk. Annie is curled up
half-buried among an array of Indian clothing. She shrinks
back in fear. Looks For His Horses turns to Kurz. He says,
"I'll buy this woman from you. How much do you want?"

Kurz laughs. Annie gets out of the trunk.

                              KURZ
That's hilarious. He wants to buy you. You want to buy
Velvet Ass Annie? That's her name.

He does the sign for"soft ass", and laughs. Annie looks at
her torn dress. She looks at the Indian clothes in the trunk.

                              KURZ
Do you hear that, Annie? Looks For His Horses here wishes
to buy you.

He laughs even harder. Annie glares at him. Looks For His
Horses looks from Kurz to Annie, and back to Kurz,
perplexed and a bit angry.

51. CONT.

                    ANNIE
My, my, he's the cheeky one. Does he propose to haggle
over me like a piece of meat?

                    KURZ
Well you know what the mountain men say, "Meat's meat."

Looks For His Horses asks again what Kurz will take for her.

                    KURZ
She is not mine to sell, Schatzie. She is one of those
people who do not belong to anyone.

Looks For His Horses asks where here father is.

                    KURZ
She has no father.

He asks about an uncle or a brother.

                    KURZ
She has no brother, either.... No, no, uncle. No, no one.
(mockingly) No, she is all alone in this world, poor thing.
A poor outcast orphan, just like you.

He smiles shyly at Annie. Looks For His Horses looks
sympathetic. He asks from whom he may buy, then.

                    KURZ
....From whom can you buy her? Why herself, I suppose.

                    ANNIE
                  (fuming)
Does he think me a commen strumpet?

                    KURZ
No one would ever call you common, Annie. (laughs) No,
he wants to marry you.

Annie looks sharply at Looks For His Horses. He draws himself up into his robw, trying to maintain a dignified postture
in these negotiations. He begins to make a speech. Kurz
translates to Annie.

                    KURZ
He says he has had a vision which makes him qualified to
marry. His medicine animal is the coyote. This has been
true since he was an infant, and his uncle le him overnight in a coyote den to play with a litter of pups. Hmmm.
I didn't know that. That's very interesting. He says he
understands their language, and spoke to one in his vision...

Annie is pouting, glancing back and forth from the floor
to Looks For His Horses. She is pulling at the buttons of
her dress.

                    KURZ
What's wrong, my dear? Don't you fancy him? He's quite a
handsome lad don't you think?

He opens Loooks For His Horses robe.

                    KURZ
Look at those muscles! A perfect body, really. Don't you
agree? A veritable Adonis, I would say. And you can take it
from me; I'm an expert on the subject. And you certainly
won't starve with him; he's an excellent hunter.

51. CONT.

He turns to Annie.

                    KURZ
What are you doing, for God's sake?

She is tearing off her dress.

                    KURZ
Annie! Don't be shameless!

Annie steps out of her clothes, naked. She lifts her eyes
to Looks For His Horses. For a moment, she is shy and vulner-
able. Then, she takes three steps toward him, and wraps her
arms around his neck. She presses her body against his.
She kisses him. He just stands there, abashed. Kurz' mouth
drops open. He backs away.

                    KURZ
Mein Gott! You carry this too far.

Annie rubs herself against Looks For His Horses. He encloses
her in his robe. She looks into his eyes.

                    ANNIE
Do you know how the French like to kiss, darling? It's
very exciting.

The tip of her tongue darts out of her mouth and touches
his lips. He jumps as if electrified.

                    ANNIE
Ask him, Rudolph.

Kurz turns away in disgust.

                    ANNIE
Don't you know how to do it, darling? Here I'll show you.

She kisses him again, and forces her tongue deep into his
mouth. Poor Looks For His Horses is quite overwhelmed.

                    KURZ
Stop it, Annie! That's quite enough.

Without a word, Annie drops her arms and disengages herself from Looks For His Horses' embrace. A little moan
escapes his lips as she pulls free. She goes to the trunk
and begins to select an outfit for herself from the Indian
clothing inside.

Kurz sighs and tries to smile. He rubs his hands together.

                    KURZ
Well, now that that's over with.....

Looks For His Horses says to Kurz, "What shall I give for her,
Iron Eyes?" Annie puts on a pair of ornamented leggings.
Looks For His Horses makes an offer.

                    KURZ
Look Schatzie.....

Annie steps into a buckskin skirt. She has her back to the
tow men.

                    ANNIE
What did he say, Rudolph?

                    KURZ
Let me try to straighten this out for you Annie

51. CONT.

                    ANNIE
What did he say?

                    KURZ
He offers three good horses and a ceremonial buffalo robe
for you.....

                    ANNIE
Is that a good offer?

                    KURZ
               (incredulous)
What?

                    ANNIE
I mean, what is the going rate for wives around here?
You know that sort of thing, Rudolph. I don't.

She is trying to decide between a bright silk chemise and
an extravagantly beaded buckskin shirt.

                    KURZ
Look, Annie don't you think that you've had enough fun
with this boy?

                    ANNIE
Is it a good offer?

                    KURZ
Yes, it's extremely generous. But Annie......

                    ANNIE
Then I shall accept.

Annie chooses the buckskin shirt and slips into it.

                    KURZ
Ha!

                    ANNIE
It should be quite an adventure. And since you can't
support me......

She looks at Kurz with defiance.

Kurz hands Looks For His Horses a buffalo robe. Painted
on it is Kurz' impression of Looks For His Horses' vision.

                    KURZ
My wedding present, Schatzie.

The boy looks at it, astonished.

                    KURZ
You see, it's your medicine dream - your vision. You see?
There's the coyote. And there's Coups Cooper....And the hawk..

Looks For His Horses shoves it back at Kurz. He speaks
curtly and turns towards the door. Kurz face falls. Annie
turns around, finished dressing.

                    ANNIE
There, do I look like a good Crow squaw? What's wrong,
Rudolph? What's happened?

                    KURZ
He has refused my wedding present. My painting of his vision.

51.   CONTINUED

                         ANNIE

But why?

                         KURZ

He rejects the vision. He says that Four Bears was right.
He realizes now that his vision was not something he should
seek, but something he should fear.

Looks For His Horses has left the room, and is mounted on
his horse, outside. Annie looks once around the room.
                         ANNIE

Well. I guess I have everything.

She kisses Kurz on the cheek.

                         ANNIE

I've had <u>such</u> a good time, Rudolph. And I'm <u>very</u> fond of
you.

Kurz follows her outside.

52.   EXT. DAY.   OUTSIDE KURZ' APARTMENT

Looks For His Horses has brought her horse. She mounts
it. She looks back at Kurz.
                         ANNIE

Oh, you look so forlorn.

Looks For His Horses makes a sign and starts to ride away.
Kurz pulls his cape around him and draws himself up.

                         KURZ

I shall manage quite well. You needn't worry.

                         ANNIE

We'll come to visit you. I promise.

She blows him a kiss, and rides away. Kurz follows to the
gate and watches them riding off. He hears Annie in the
distance.

                         ANNIE

Goodbye, Rudolph!

53.   INT. NIGHT.   KURZ' DOWNSTAIRS ROOM

Kurz is burning one of his tables. We can hear the sound
of the gate being battered about by the wind. Kurz pulls
his cape around him and goes outside.

54.   INT. NIGHT.   INSIDE THE FORT

Kurz goes to the gate and closes it with some difficulty.
The wind is blowing fiercely. He flaps his arms across
his chest, and goes back to his room.

55. <u>INT. NIGHT. KURZ' DOWNSTAIRS ROOM</u>

Kurz walks in and closes the door. Wind is blowing through the chinks in the logs. A couple of his sketches are blowing around the floor. He picks them up and shoves them under a pile of clothes.

He rubs his hands together. He takes a bottle of Laudenum from the mantel. All of his furniture has been broken up and lies in a pile by the fireplace. Kurz drinks. He can't keep still. He is shivering. He puts more wood on the fire. It's a pretty big blaze by now.

He picks up Coups' lead pencil and a piece of paper. He tries to sketch the fire, but the wood keeps shifting. He puts more wood on, until it is overflowing from the fireplace. He keeps on sketching. Now he begins to inch closer to the fire, as he gets into the details of the sketch. Closer and closer. His piece of paper catches fire. He tries to shake it out but only fans it more. He drops it on the floor. He watches his drawing of the fire burn up. He no longer cares about saving the drawing; he is fascinated by the fire. He picks up another sketch and holds a corner of it to the flame of the burning picture until it too catches alight. This is one of his sketches of Annie. He holds it and watches it burn. Then he touches it to the corner of his incomplete painting of Four Bears. The oil paint catches very nicely.

By now, other things have caught fire behind him. Without remorse, he watches a stack of sketches blaze up and send burning pieces around the room. One piece lands on the cuff of his trousers. He watches it with great equanimity as it sets his pants on fire. His face is glistening with sweat. Flames are leaping up all around the room.

56. <u>EXT. NIGHT. FORT ABSAROKA</u>

A long shot of the fort, with Kurz' apartment ablaze. We see the upstairs window open. The mynah bird flies out. Kurz' clothes are on fire. He turns back inside and slams the shutter.

57. <u>EXT. DAY. ON THE PRAIRIE</u>

Looks For His Horses and Annie lie asleep together under a buffalo robe by a small campfire. Their ponies are picketed close beside them. Annie wakes with a start.

                    ANNIE

Help! Help!

She looks around. It is just before dawn. There is a heavy frost on the ground. Little patches of mist hang over the prairie. Annie is still half asleep. She doesn't know where she is. She looks at Looks For His Horses. She has a moment of panic. She buries her head beneath the covers.

                    ANNIE

Oh, what's to become of my life?

57. CONTINUED

After a moment, she lifts the edge of the buffalo robe.
Light pours in. She looks at their two naked bodies.
She begins to stroke Looks For His Horses' belly, and
then reaches down to caress his groin. She looks up at
his face. He is still asleep. His pupils are moving
frantically beneath his eyelids, in a deep dream. She
strokes him. He begins to swell and rise. She neads
him until he is erect. Looks For His Horses moans but does
not awaken.

Annie climbs on top of him, takes him inside her, and begins
to rock up and down. Looks For His Horses begins to move,
too, and to moan, but he doesn't open his eyes. He doesn't
seem to want to let go of his dream. He is in two places
at once.

His body tenses. He opens his eyes. He grabs her to him.
He rolls on top of her. He holds her tight against
him and pumps his pelvis frantically. He reaches orgasm
very quickly. He lets out a cry. His body jerks.

> ANNIE

Wait wait wait wait wait.

Looks For His Horses sighs. He rolls over onto his side.
Annie clings to him. He rolls over more, covering his
face with his arms. He is halfway back into his dream.
Annie cries and hits him.

She gets out from under the covers, and crouches naked
by the dying fire. Her body shakes with sobs.

She grabs all of her clothes, but doesn't put them back
on. She unpickets her horse and climbs naked onto its
bare back. She gallops out onto the prairie. She gallops
about aimlessly, back and forth, in no particular direction.

Looks For His Horses opens his eyes and stares blankly at
the sky. A shooting star falls across the sky and
behind some distant mountains. He sits up with a start.

Annie is galloping toward him.

> ANNIE:

My God. It's Rudolph. Look. Look over there.

She points to the eastern horizon. There is a red glow --
the fort afire.

Looks For His Horses pays no attention to Annie. He is
staring at the place where the shooting star fell. She
slaps him.

> ANNIE

Look over there, you stupid savage! Look!

He turns dazedly around and looks where she points. He
covers his mouth with his hand.

> ANNIE

My poor Rudolph. My poor old Kurz. We must go there. We
must see if he still isn't alright.

57. CONTINUED

She begins to dress. He begins to talk excitedly in Crow.
He points to the glow of the burning fort. He points to
the sky, to the place where the shooting star fell. Annie
motions impatiently for him to dress.

> ANNIE

Get dressed! Put your clothes on!

Looks For His Horses dresses quickly. He pulls his robe
around him, and goes to unhobble his horse. When he comes
back, Annie is nearly hysterical.

> ANNIE

Hurry up, please, we must hurry.

Looks For His Horses helps her onto her pony, then slips
on to his own. He begins to ride toward the far mountains.

> ANNIE

No! No!

She rides up to him and tugs at his arm. She shouts at
him with exaggerated gestures and enunciation. She points
to him and then to herself.

> ANNIE

You...me...

She makes a sweeping motion with her hand.

> ANNIE

...go...fort...fort. Kurz...Kurz...

She mimes spectacles over her eyes.

> ANNIE

...Big fire...

Looks For His Horses shakes his head. He points to the
mountains. He reaches for her horse's reins. She jerks
the pony's head away from his reach.

> ANNIE

KEEP YOUR HANDS AWAY FROM ME!

Tears are running down her cheeks. Her pony is rearing
around. She is crying hysterically now, and mumbling to
herself.

Looks For His Horses punches her, grabs the reins of her
horse, and gallops toward the mountains with her in tow.

58. EXT. DAY. FORT ABSAROKA.

Coups is walking, carrying his few belongings, straining
to looks at something. His scalp wound is quite notice-
able, large and clotted with mud and leaves. His face is
drawn.

58. CONTINUED

He comes upon a dead horse, body charred black, ᴮᴹᴬᴴ
ᵡᴴᵡᴹᵡᴬᴵᴹᴮᴴᵡᴹᴵᴬᶜ front legs stiff and hobbled together.
A coyote has been at its entrails and is now hovering
back a little way, snarling at Coups.

We see the charred remains of the fort. Coups walks
through the ruins. He steps over what was the gate and
makes his way into Kurz' quarters. He stands there
for a long time, his eyes busy looking for signs. Nothing
much is left that is recognizable. One room has fallen
in on the other, and everything is very thoroughly burned,
much of it still smoking.

He hears something.

A VOICE

Von Kleist!

He looks around. Kurz' mynah bird is perched on a timber.

MYNAH BIRD

Buxthehude.

Coups makes a grab for the bird, but it flies off into
the ruins. There is an ant making its way over the little
dead fox's tail. The mynah bird snaps it up.

Coups follows two sets of tracks from Kurz' door to the
gate. He sets off again, following the tracks across the
prairie toward the mountains.

59. EXT. DAY. ON THE PRAIRIE.

Annie and Looks For His Horses are riding along, seen from
behind, Annie a little bit to the rear of Looks For His
Horses. She rides up beside him and when he sees her, he
gallops ahead ten or twelve feet. She tries to catch up
with him, but he leaps ahead again.

ANNIE

What's wrong? What have I done now?

Looks For His Horses turns around.

LOOKS FOR HIS HORSES

Squaw..!

He makes the sign for "squaw goes behind". Tears come
to Annie's eyes. Looks For His Horses smiles at her. He
says something in Crow, meant to cheer her up, laughs,
and rides ahead.

Annie looks around to her right and to her left. Nothing
but endless prairie and the mountains close ahead. She
watches her lover's back as he leans low over his pony's
neck, talking to it, caressing it, giving it little nudges
with his toes and heels, coaxing it through some chapparal.

59. CONTINUED

Coups is sitting on a little knoll, chewing on a piece of
jerky, staring down at Looks For His Horses' and Annie's
camp of the night before. A coyote sits in the background,
watching him.

At the camp, there is a small, burnt out fire, and a bed
made of hundreds of little pine boughs planted in the
ground. The bed, such as it is, is all crushed down. In
the dirt by the campfire is the imprint of a woman's bare
foot.

Coups gets up and starts off again. He looks in bad shape.
He throws a piece of jerky at the coyote. The coyote
snaps it up and follows him.

Ext. Day Yellowstone Park. Mammouth Hot Springs
Looks For His Horses and Annie are riding through an aerie
landscape. Bubbling sulphur pools are all around them.
It is starting to snow.

                    ANNIE

Dear God, this must be Hell.

She rides up to Looks For His Horses and takes his arm.

                    ANNIE

Please, can't we go back? This place frightens me.

She pantomimes fear. Looks For His Horses nods his head.
He understands. He makes signs: this is a very magic place;
lots of spirits; he agress; very frightening. He rides
ahead of her again.

60. EXT. DAY. YELLOWSTONE PARK.

Coups is standing in the middle of a snow filled meadow.
He has lost the trail. He looks behind him: even his own
tracks are filling up with snow.

61. INT. NIGHT. MAMMOTH HOT SPRINGS.

Annie and Looks For His Horses are huddled in a brush
shelter that Looks has put together. It is very low and
open on one side. They have a small fire. Gurgling,
spitting and roaring sounds can be heard all around.

Annie is reclining under a buffalo robe. Looks For His
Horses is sitting crosslegged beside her. Annie is holding
his hand, and singing to him -- a "Tiptoe Through the Tulips"
kind of song. She is stroking his hand. His forefinger
is wrapped in a large rawhide bandage. He unwraps it to
show her. The stump of his finger is one large scab.

Annie yelps with fright, not having known about his
mutilated condition. It is a loud yelp. Looks For His
Horses jumps, startled.

                    ANNIE

I'm sorry. I'm terribly sorry. I didn't mean a thing
by it. Please.

61. CONTINUED

She takes his hand and kisses it.

                    ANNIE

Here. Let me kiss it better. Mmm. Mmm. There. Isn't
that better?

A heart shaped gold locket on a chain around her neck falls
from Annie's blouse. Looks For His Horses holds it and
looks at it.

                    ANNIE

That's my baby. Do you want to see? Here.

She takes the locket and opens it. There is a lock of
blonde hair inside.

                    ANNIE

See? That's a lock of his hair...

He looks up at her and asks her a question.

                    ANNIE

They took him away from me. That's what they do in England.
They said they'd find him a good home. But I've heard of
other things they do. Black markets. Flesh merchants.
Hideous stories.

Annie begins to cry. Looks For His Horses is very touched.
He doesn't know what to do. Annie looks at him and cups
his face in her hands.

                    ANNIE

You're very sweet, Looks For His Horses...Do you think
we'll ever have babies together? Wild little Rocky
Mountain babies?...You do care for me, don't you? You
must. Say that you do.

62. INT. DAY. THE SHELTER.

Annie is asleep on buffalo robes. Looks For His Horses
can be heard, singing.

                    LOOKS FOR HIS HORSES
                    (Coups' accent)

The sun goes up, the sun goes down...the sun goes up, the
sun goes down...

Annie opens her eyes. She sees Looks For His Horses near
the entrance of the shelter. He has painted his face,
shoulders, arms, and upper chest with a gray clay. His
ears have been shaped into clay coyote ears. He pulls his
coyote skin over his head. He crawls outside.

Annie pulls the buffalo robe around her, and creeps up to
the entrance. She

63. EXT. DAY. MAMMOTH HOT SPRINGS. (ANNIE'S POV)

She sees Looks For His Horses scrambling away through the
snow, on all fours.

The landscape outside is dominated by an enormous,
terraced formation. Steam and boiling water spurt out
from various holes.

64. EXT. DAY. YELLOWSTONE PARK

A coyote is sniffing something in the snow. He paws
at it, then nuzzles it with his mouth. He pulls something
out: a partially eaten hunk of buffalo jerky.

Suddenly the snow covered ground seems to rise up. It is
Coups, who has been sleeping, buried in the snow beneath a
buffalo robe.

The coyote takes off with the jerky. Coups grabs his gun
and charges after the coyote. It disappears over the top
of a hill. Coups scrambles up the hill. It takes some
time. He crawls to the top. He looks over. He sees a
coyote on the other side, near a river. He lifts his
rifle, aims, and fires.

His target rears up. It is not the coyote. It is Looks
For His Horses. He falls backward, into the icy river, and
is carried away in the current.

65. EXT. DAY. NEAR THE SHELTER

Coups follows Looks For His Horses' trail to the shelter.
The sun is beginning to set. He comes quietly to the
brush shelter. There is no sound coming from inside.

                    COUPS

Velvet Ass Annie, are you there?

There is no reply. Coups leans into the shelter.

                    COUPS

It's Coups Cooper, the mountains' own to help ye, marm.

Annie slashes at Coups with a knife from inside the shelter,
cutting his hand. He grabs her knife hand. She starts
beating him. He crushes her wrist, forcing her to kneel.
She drops the knife.

                    ANNIE

What have you done with my husband?

                    COUPS

Made meat of him. This beaver's hyar to rescue ye, marm.
Yore free.

                    ANNIE

You've killed him, you beast!

65. CONTINUED

She swoons, falling backwards. Coups drops to his knees.
He tries to kiss her. She spits at him. He tries to
kiss her again. She bites him. He straddles her on his
knees.

                         COUPS

Thar's grit in ye, and a ha'r o' the b'ar at that. But
ye been axkin for it, and this niggur's bound to give it
to ye.

His left hand is bleeding from Annie's stab. His head
wound is swollen up. He grabs her two wrists in one hand,
and forces them back over her head. He forces his knees
between her legs. She tries to roll over. She tries
to cross her legs. He rips her buckskin shirt away at
the shoulder seam, exposing her left breast. He touches
it with glee.

                         COUPS

Whooee! This hoss's gettin' sassy.

He tears Annie's skirt off. She is naked from the waist
down, except for the fancy buckskin leggings. He pulls
aside his breeechcloth, exposing an erection. Annie
manages to knock him off balance and runs off in the snow.

Coups comes stumbling after her. He overtakes her and
throws her down in the snow. She tries to whirl around.
He throws himself on top of her. He grabs both of her
legs, spreads them wide, and forces himself into her.
Annie scratches his face and tears at his hair. His wound
begins bleeding again. He humps her desperately.

He flattens himself against her, pressing up against
every possible surface of her body. He squirms and wriggles
trying to get deeper, trying to get inside her. He lets
out little grunts.

Annie digs her nails into Coup's scalp wound. He cries out.
Annie lets go, automatically. Coups keeps crying out,
over and over. This is the first time we have seen him
lose control.

Annie is suddenly moved. She begins to stroke his head
and coo in his ear.

                         ANNIE

Ohh. It's alright. It's alright...

66. INT. DAY. SHELTER

It is another day. Coups comes into the shelter, carrying
his rifle. He has snow all over his clothes, and his hands
and face are chapped bright red.

Annie is asleep, wrapped in a buffalo robe by the fire.
Coups heaps dirt on the fire. He stares at Annie for a
long time. She doesn't move.

66. CONTINUED

Coups lies down on his back on a buffalo robe. Annie says
something under her breath and rolls over. Coups stares
at her again. He watches the smoke drift up from the fire,
and out through the top of the brush shelter. Clouds
are rushing by overhead.

Annie squirms on her stomach lasciviously, curls up, and
presses her hands between her thighs. She begins to
talk in her sleep.

ANNIE

What big ears you have...my lover...the wolf man.

Coups grumbles and rolls over, his back to her. His
eyelids begin to droop. Annie speaks again in her sleep,
this time as though she were talking to a little baby, in
a kind of sing-song voice.

ANNIE

Where's your shooting star? Where did you bury it? Yes.
How will the little babies know where to find it?

Coups is now asleep. His eyes begin to move about rapidly
beneath his eyelids. His shoulder and arm begin to
twitch, like a sleeping dog dreaming of digging.

ANNIE
(in her sleep)

Coyote coyote coyote coyote coyote...You found all the
little baby stones.

Coups growls in his sleep.

ANNIE

Quick, quick! The fire's going out!

She wakes up with a start. She looks around, bleary-
eyed. She builds a new fire.

Coups opens his eyes and looks at her. He jumps up
and heaps dirt on the fire.

COUPS

Thar's Injuns about! This niggur seed sign.

ANNIE

Get out of it, you great oaf!

COUPS

Thar's Injuns, I tell ye! Does ye figger on bein' a
Blackfoot squaw now? Wal, this niggur ain't fixin'
to lose his topknot yet.

ANNIE

Anything would be better than sitting in a freezing hovel
with you!

Coups picks up his gun and starts out of the shelter.

66. CONTINUED

continued

                    ANNIE

Where are you going?

                    COUPS

Scout around. If this beaver don't freeze onto some meat
plenty quick, usn's'll be eatin' our buffler robes.

                    ANNIE

What a disgusting thought.

                    COUPS

Them as carries empty paunch for three days don't savyy
what disgustin' is.

He starts out again.

                    ANNIE

You're going to leave me again? You mustn't leave me here.
I'm frightened!

He throws his hatchet on the ground at her feet.

                    COUPS

Go cut some wood. Keeps the blood runnin'.

He leaves.

                    ANNIE

I know it! The Indians know it too! Only you don't know
it! There are spirits in this place.

She picks up the hatchet and makes little chops in the
ground. She shivers. She pulls the buffalo robe around h
her. She goes outside.

67. EXT. DAY. OUTSIDE THE SHELTER.

It is a bright clear day. Annie lo   around. There are
giant, multicolored fumaroles, wierd sounds, steam vents,
bubbling sound. There are no signs of life. Coups'
tracks lead off into the woods. Annie goes back inside.

68. INT. DAY. THE SHELTER

Annie begins to build a fire.

69. EXT. DAY. YELLOWSTONE PARK.

Coups, on horseback, is following the footprints of a
coyote in the snow. They lead into a forest of lodgepole
pine trees. These are very straight, narrow trees that
grow very close together. The horse can't enter.

Coups dismounts and hobbles his horse. It has got very
cold. There are icicles in Coups' beard, hair, and eye-
brows. He follows the coyote's trail into the woods.
All around him, are loud cracks, like gunshots. These
are the sounds of the branches cracking off the trees in the
cold. Coups disappears into the woods.

69. CON INUED

A figure appears from the brush. It is a fierce looking
Indian brave. He carries a very fancy gold inlaid rifle
that has two barrels. He wears a necklace of human fingers.
He sneaks up to the horse, unhobbles it, leaps onto its
back, and gallops away, back in the direction from which
Coups came. Ahead of him, a column of smoke is rising
above the trees.

70. EXT. DAY. LODGEPOLE FOREST.

Coups is examining some coyote droppings. He hears his
horse whinney and the sound of it galloping away. He
turns and races back through the lodgepole pines.

He comes to the spot where he tethered his horse. The
sign is very clear: his own footprints, his horse's, and
another set of moccasin prints; then the hoofprints
leading back in the direction of the shelter. He can
see the thin column of smoke over the trees.

He stands gasping for breath in the thin, freezing air. He
starts to run again, following the horse's tracks.

71. EXT. DAY. NEAR THE SHELTER

It is much laterr in the day. Coups comes to the edge of
the Mammoth Hot Springs, near the shelter. He is
exhausted almost beyond endurance. He sees the shelter,
a tiny wisp of smoke rising out of it. There are no horses.

No signs of life, and lots of tracks in the snow by the
shelter.

He stumbles toward the shelter. There are footprints of
the Blackfoot brave, Annie's footprints coming out of the
shelter, and finally, the two sets of hoofprints leading
off together.

He goes into the shelter. There are only embers left of
the fire. He puts his hand over the embers to gauge the
amount of time that has passed. He sees something scrawled
in the ground by the fire. It says, "I'm a Blackfoot
squaw now."

He kicks the remains of the fire, sending sparks flying
all over the shelter. He picks up his gun and begins
swinging it wildly in every direction. He destroys the
brush shelter. Little twigs here and there catch alight
from the embers of the dying fire.

72. EXT. DAY. OUTSIDE THE SHELTER.

Coups reels out into the open, shouting, swinging, and
whirling around. He stumbles and falls. One arm falls
in the warm water runoff of the hot springs. He lies
there, gasping for breath. His scalp wound is bleeding
again. There are icicles in his hair.

72. CONTINUED

He opens his eyes. He sees a coyote bitch watching him
from a nearby hill. He springs to his feet. He grabs his
rifle from the snow with his wet hand. The remains of
the shelter are ablaze.

The coyote disappears over the hill. Coups tears after her.

73. EXT. DAY. A SNOW FILLED MEADOW.

Coups is tearing after the coyote. The coyote scampers up
a rise, where the snow has drifted. The top layer of
the snow is frozen, enabling the coyote to scamper across
it easily. Coups' weight breaks the ice, and he is
forced to half run, half wade through the snow.

Blood from his scalp wound drips into his mouth. The
left arm of his buckskin shirt is white, frozen solid.
Coups collapses panting at the tip of the rise.

74. EXT. DAY. RIVERBANK.

He is looking down at the river from a steep bank.

Down below is Looks For His Horses' body. It has been
washed up on shore. It's head is still in the water. It
is frozen solid and white from the neck down.

The coyote is beside the body. She is barking at Coups.
Coups raises his rifle. His hand is frozen to the barrel.
He rips his hand away, tearing off a layer of skin. He
licks the blood from his palm. Blood is dripping on to
the rifle from his head and from his hand.

He raises the rifle again. The coyote is dancing around
the body, yapping now at the corpse, now at Coups. Coups
aims. He can't hold the rifle steady. He expends all
of his will steadying his aim.

He pu   the trigger. The gun clicks. Blood has
frozen onto the flintlock.

He throws the rifle down the embankment at the coyote. She
jus t ducks out of the way. She looks at Coups. She
whines and makes little feints at the body -- like a
dog asking to have a stick thrown.

Coups pulls out his knife. He rolls, slides, and stumbles
down the steep embankment. He lunges at the coyote
with his knife. She easily sidesteps him. He stumbles,
recovers, and lunges again. She stays just out of reach.
He swings at her again and again.

He trips over Looks' body and collapses beside it.

The coyote comes up and nuzzles him. She whines and
snaps at the frozen body.

75 EXT. DAY YELLOWSTONE PARK

Coups and the coyote are sitting side by side in the
shelter of a rock, by the Firehole River.This is the
river that drains the geysers of the Yellowstone. The
banks are stained with bands of color. Strewn around

75. CONT.

Coups and the coyete are Looks For His Horses bones.
The coyete is gnawing on one of the bones. Coups is
singing the song he sang earlier in the film - he doesn't
remember the words. He sings manicly. He seems half
crazed. His body breaks into uncontrolable shivers from
time to time.

> COUPS
> (singing)

La la la la da da da dah, lee doo dee doo dee dah. The
sun comes up, The sun goes down. Dum dee dah dee dum dah..

The coyete begins to howl and whine. Coups sings more lustily,
to the coyote. They sing a mad duet.

The coyete nuzzels and paws Coups. She puts her front
paws on his chest. He tumbles backwards. She climbs on top
of him, nuzzling his throat. They are still singing.

Soups rolls over on top of her. They go rolling down the
side of a hill together, yipping and howling,

They fall into a game of tag, feinting and grabbing at
each other. They chase each other across a field. These
games have a sexual aspect to them.

The coyete chases Coups down a steep slope. Coups sl ps, and
grabs for some brush to cling to. It cuts his hand. He lets
go and tumbles down into a meadow.

Coups and the coyete sit facing one another, both breathing
heavily. Coups licks his finger. Blood drips on the
gr und. The coyete comes close and licks up the blood
from the ground. She sits and stares at Coups' finger, droolin

> COUPS
> (laughs and imitates Stumps voice)

"... Bacca, ef'n it's a plug a plew, some Dupont and
G'lena, an' ol' Green River...." Hee hee.

He pulls out his knife laughing. He looks at the coyete.
He stares deep into her eyes. He sees his own reflection
in her eyes. She licks her chops.

Coups shakes his head, as if to snap himself out of a dream.

> COUPS

So, ye wants to make meat of this beaver, eh?

He laughs. He brandishes his knife and cuts off the top
joint of his bleeding finger. He laughs again. He throws
the piece of finger to the coyete. She catches it in her
mouth and chews on it.

> COUPS

On the peraira

Coups is holding his bleeding hand out to the coyete.
She is about to take it in her mouth. Suddenly, he jumps
on her and cuts he throat. Her guts come pouring out.
He thrusts his hands inside her, and pulls apart her rib
cage. He cuts out her heart. He eats her heart.

He looks around smiling, blood staining his teeth. Above
some distant trees, one can see a wisp of smoke, and then
from far off we can hear gunshots.

<u>76.</u> EXT. DAY YELLOWSTONE PARK TWO OCEONS PASS

Watson James' mapmaking party is camped here, by a small
pond. It is just before dawn. There is a heavy frost on
the ground. There are three campfires. There is a white
tent. A lantern glows inside the tent. Two men are finishing
breakfast by one of the three campfires.

A young engagée comes out of the tent, carrying various
surveying instruments. He crosses to a pack mule on the
far side of camp. The mule is strapped into a specially
elaborate leather harness, studded with brass hooks and
leather straps with brass buckles, each designed to hold
a particular piece of cartographic equipment. Throughout
the following scene, the engagée makes several trips
back and forth from the tent loading the mule.

A figure crosses in front of the lantern in the tent,
throwing a shadow on the canvas. It is a female figure.
Stump, Gouge Eye and Watson James are standing beside the
pond, drinking from two bottles of wine.

Stump has a fresh scalp on his shirt and holds a fancy
two-barrelled rifle. Gouge Eye wears a human finger
necklace. All are rather tipsy.

                    WATSON JAMES

Well, boys, this is truly an historic occasion.

                    GOUGE EYE

Shore enough, Watty, ol' hoss!

                    WATSON JAMES

Imagine, gentlemen, we have discovered the head waters
of the two great river systems which nourish practically
the entire continent.

                    STUMP

Shoot, Wa   Gabe used to talk about this hyar place
more'n twenty y'ar ago.

                    WATSON JAMES

Never mind that. We'll be the first to tell it to the
world. Imagine. One pond touching two oceans.

He raises his bottle.

                    WATSON JAMES

Gentlemen, I give you...the Atlantic Ocean!

Stump takes a long guzzle from his bottle. Gouge Eye
grabs it away from his and takes a drink. Watson James
corks the empty bottle and throws it into the pond at
its eastern outlet. They watch the bottle float away
down t stream.

                    WATSON JAMES

Tell me how it goes again, Gouge Eye, you fine fellow.

The bottle floats farther and farther away.

76. CONTINUED

                        GOUGE EYE

Wal, Watty, ol' coon, pretty soon she'll hit a crick
what drops into the Firehole, down the Firehole to the
Madison tuh the Missoura, through Crow country, up around
past the Mandan and Hidatsa lodges, through the Assiniboin
lodges, past Fort Union, down through Assiniboin, Dakota,
Yankton, Ioway, Oto, past the white settlements tuh
Independence, St. Louis, into the Mississip, New Orleans,
into the Mexican Gulf...

                        WATSON JAMES

And into the Atlantic Ocean...2,000 miles.

                        STUMP

Look hyar, Watty. What price did ye say this hyar shirt
would fetch out thar in St. Louis?

                        WATSON JAMES

Probably a hundred dollars in the right circles.

                        GOUGE EYE

Shoot, thar's enough to keep a Ricaree squaw in fancy
fofurraw for the balance of days!

                        WATSON JAMES

Chicken feed, boys. Mere chicken feed. You have to
think big, gentlemen. The mapmaking idea ia only a small
part of my scheme.

                        STUMP

Shoot, Watty, yore going to have to charge an arm and a
leg for them maps.

                        WATSON JAMES

No, no, no. They'll be as inexpensive a s possible.
Look, when the Spring comes there will be other carto-
graphers out here mapping other trails to Oregon. We
want ours to be the one the immigrants actually travel.
Outposts, gentlemen. Outposts is our game. Little havens
of civilization at strategic points along the trail.

                        GOUGE EYE

Ahhh...

                        WATSON JAMES

We'll sell them supplies, shoe their oxen, repair their
wagon wheels. Maybe we'll even have little gardens so
we can sell them fresh vegetables.

                        STUMP

Yo're some, Watty!

                        GOUGE EYE

Well, he are!

Stump slaps him on the back. In the background, the

76. CONTINUED

engagées have packed the mules and are making last
minute preparations. Several riders and mules have
already started out. Annie steps out of the tent and
crosses to the fire. She stands there in a daze. Two
engagées proceed to dismantle the tent.

Gouge Eye takes the last swig of the last bottle of wine.
The three men are walking toward the western outlet of
the pond. Gouge Eye hands Watson the empty bottle. He
corks it and holds it up.

                    WATSON JAMES

Gentlemen, the Pacific Ocean.

Just then, a coyote-like figure leaps out of the underbrush and attacks Watson James. It is Coups, but he
is unrecognizable. He is naked, except for the coyote's
skin which he wears over his head and shoulders. His body
is painted with gray clay. He leaps upon Watson just as
a coyote would attack: snarling and snapping at his throat.
Watson James' bottle falls into the pond and floats away.

Gouge Eye flings his Arkansas toothpick into the figure's
back, while a second later, Stump puts a musket ball
in his side with the two shot rifle.

                    STUMP

Haw! Plumb center!

The figure falls face forward on the ground. Annie and
the various engagées come running up. Gouge Eye says a
quick word to one of them.

                    GOUGE EYE

Scout around and see ef they's any others.

                    YOUNG ENGAGÉE

Gosh! Did you see that?

Stump and an engagée help Watson James to his feet. He
is a bit shaken up and badly mauled. Annie watches the
scene, impassive.

Gouge Eye plucks the knife from his victim's back. The
coyote skin pulls away with the knife. Coups' hair is
filled with icicles and gray clay. One can't see its
true color. Gouge Eye grabs the victim's hair and traces
a circle with the point of his blade around the tip of
the scalp.

                    YOUNG ENGAGEE

Is that a white man?

                    GOUGE EYE

Meat's meat, boy.

                    STUMP

Steady thar, ol' hoss. Believe that scalp belongs to me.

76. CONTINUED

Gouge Eye turns his head to see Stump pointing t he two
barrelled rifle at him.

GOUGE EYE

Oho! The dog struck gives a yelp!

ENGAGEE

Uh oh, Hell's about to pop.

Gouge Eye points to the knife wound in the victim's back.

GOUGE EYE

Great Jehosaphat, Pocahontis and John Smith! First coup
gets the scalp in these parts boy.

Stump points to the bullet hole.

STUMP

Right thar's the hole what put him under, I'm thinkin'.

Gouge Eye turns his back on Stump. He twists the victim's
hair in the fingers of his left hand, and pops the scalp
off.

GOUGE EYE

Yore talkin' Mexican oats, boy. When ol' Arkansas Toothpick tickles a niggur's hump ribs, that beaver's halfway
to the Misty Beyond afore she sets home!

STUMP

Turn around, hoss, and this beaver'll teach yer meatbag
the feel of a English Galena pill.

Gouge Eye turns around, dripping scalp in one hand, Arkansas
Toothpick in the other, poised to throw.

GOUGE EYE

Shoot, boy, you couldn't teach a settin' hen to cluck.

STUMP

Unfinger that scalplock, hoss. Yore as yeller as mustard,
but ye ain't got the bite.

They begin to circle each othe r.

GOUGE EYE

I'll have yore guts, by God!

Suddenly Coups rises up. He reaches out toward Annie.
She screams. Stump lets him have it with the other barrel
of the rifle. He pitches forward and falls into Annie's
arms.

Stump grabs the scalp from Gouge Eye.

76. CONTINUED

                    STUMP

Ef this chile can't keel his own Injuns, he'd just as
soon go under.

                    WATSON JAMES

It's that Cooper fellow!

                    GOUGE EYE
                (under his breath)

Great Jehosaphat, Pocahontis and John Smith!

Coups looks up at Annie through half lidded eyes.

                    COUPS

                I loves ye a leetle,
                I loves ye a lot,
                Muh love fer ye, honey'd
                Fill all the pots.
                The buckets, the pi'chers,
                The kettles and cans,
                The big wooden washtub,
                And the two dishpans.

He dies. Annie says nothing. Watson James takes one of
her arms. He motions for an engagée to take the other.

                    WATSON JAMES

Please, Miss Ainley. Let me take you away from here.
You've seen too much bloodshed already.

She allows herself to be taken away. Stump looks down
at Coups' body.

                    STUMP

Cuss me fer a Kioway. Know'd that niggur'd go Injun.

                    GOUGE EYE

He war <u>some,</u> or this niggur wouldn't say so.

                    STUMP

<u>Well,</u> he war.

Stump tucks Coups' scalp into his belt and walks away.
In the background, the last of the party mount their
horses and ride off. Flies hover over Coups' body. An
ant walks along his face, then into his mouth.

77. EXT. DAY. TWO OCEAN PASS

Two buzzards circle in the sky. Presently, one of them
lands several yards away. Then the other one. They watch
for a long while, then inch toward the body. They begin
to peck at Coups' eyes, tug at his skin. Soon there are
half a dozen of them, making little rips and tears all
over his body.

Two young coyotes sit and watch the spectacle, waiting
their turn. The sun goes down. The buzzards fly away.

78. <u>EXT. NIGHT.   TWO OCEAN PASS</u>

The coyotes go to work on Coups' body. They tear open
his stomach and devour his entrails. From time to time,
they pause to howl at the moon.

79. <u>EXT. DAY.   TWO OCEAN PASS</u>

It is just before dawn. We follow a long trail of ants to
the corpse. It is covered with ants and worms. There is
very little flesh left now, just the bones remain.

The sun comes up. (TIME LAPSE PHOTOGRAPHY)

**   **   **

MY GIRLFRIEND'S GIRLFRIEND
————————————————————————————

First Draft Screenplay

By

JIM McBRIDE

"In the sixties everybody got interested in everybody
else. Drugs helped a little there. Everybody was
equal suddenly.

"In the seventies everybody started dropping everybody."

                              -- Andy Warhol

1   INT: LIVING ROOM-BEDROOM - NIGHT

      RUDY is groaning into pillow as he grips the sides
      of the bed, trying to pull himself deeper and deeper
      into ANNIE. Annie clutches his back, her face
      contorted, straining to keep up with him. But she
      can't catch him. He heaves one last great sigh and
      sinks down on top of her, his body like a lead
      weight. She still clings to him, bumping up against
      him frantically. Nudging and pulling and climbing
      she works him over on his back, herself atop him,
      never stopping her mad undulations. He tries to
      move with her, help her over the top, but he can't
      match her frenzy. She moves so violently that the
      wooden joints of the bed make rude sounds. There
      is a moment when she seems to almost fly away, and
      then she freezes. Then a long sigh escapes from
      deep down in her throat. Not a sigh of release,
      but a sigh of respite.

                                        CUT TO:

2   INT: LIVING ROOM-BEDROOM - NIGHT

      It is just a couple of moments later. Annie's head
      is nestled in Rudy's armpit, his thigh wedged between
      her legs against her crotch. They lie like this for
      a long moment, not speaking or moving. After a
      moment Rudy kisses the top of Annie's head, disen-
      gages his arm, rolls away from her, takes a cigarette
      from a pack on the table, and lights it. He sits
      on the foot of the bed and begins to twiddle the
      dial of the T.V. As he fiddles, we see snatches of
      late night T.V. tapes and a couple of old movies --
      JOHNNY CARSON, a Spanish soap opera, one or two
      commercials, "Yoga for Health," etc. The credits
      are intercut with this sequence. Rudy goes back
      to bed. He takes a long, deep drag on the cigarette.
      He reaches around to take Annie under his arm again,
      but she coughs, waves away the cigarette smoke, and
      finally turns away, her back to him. Rudy pulls
      pensively on his cigarette and stares at the changing
      pattern of light and shadow on the wall opposite,
      made by the passing of cars on the street outside.
      He regards the T.V. BASCOM HUNT, a not-quite-suave,
      slightly tipsy news reporter, is breaking the story
      about Martha Mitchell claiming to have been kidnapped
      and drugged by Secret Service men. Annie, who to
      this point has not moved, reaches across to the
      bookcase on her side of the bed, pulls down her
      diary and a pen and begins to write.

      "Fucked up hateful and blah di blah ... The barometer
      has changed intensely and that may be the cause.

2   CONTD

Humid hot and muggy and domestic. An enormous
instinct to be alone; to be allowed time and turmoil
with no distractions."

Rudy sighs and turns off the T.V. He gets back in
bed. He kisses the back of Annie's neck and rolls
over with his back to her. He closes his eyes.
Annie writes the last line of her entry:

"MAD mad with hunger tonight. How could that be?
Goodnight. 11:45 P.M."

She tosses the diary at the bookcase, rolls over
Rudy to turn off his bedside light and settles down
to go to sleep.

They each lie on their sides, back to back. For a
few moments they lie like that, separate and isolated,
Annie a little restless. She inches herself closer
until her backside touches his. He snuggles a bit
closer to her. They fall asleep.

                                        CUT TO:

3   INT: LIVING ROOM-BEDROOM - NIGHT TO DAWN

A series of shots of Rudy and Annie asleep in a variety
of postures through the night, always touching. Their
bodies fit together in an assortment of comfortable
ways. In the middle of the night, HUEY, a big black
dog, climbs up on the bed and goes to sleep.

In the early hours of the morning, JESSE, Rudy's and
Annie's four-year-old son, stumbles into the bed,
climbs between Rudy and Annie and goes back to sleep.
Huey gets off the bed.

4   INT: LIVING ROOM-BEDROOM - DAY

Jesse sits between the sleeping forms of Annie and
Rudy on the bed, bouncing around. Rudy opens one eye,
looks at Annie's back.

                         RUDY
              It's your turn.

No answer. Jesse notices that Rudy is awake.

                         JESSE
              Hi, dummy!

Rudy groans.

4   CONTD

                         RUDY
             Don't call me dummy.
                  (to Annie)
             It's your turn.

                         ANNIE
                  (mumbles, not turning)
             I heard you.

Rudy rolls over, turning his back to both of them.

                         JESSE
             Don't go to sleep!

He hits Rudy. Annie raises herself up with great
effort. Jesse crawls into her lap with delight.
He twiddles her tit.

                         JESSE
                  (coyly)
             Can I suck your tit?

She looks at him and then at her tits with great
sadness.

                         ANNIE
             There's nothing there. They're
             all sucked out, poor babies.

She pats them sadly. She lifts herself out of bed,
carrying Jesse. She stops in front of the mirror
to check herself out. She looks at her ass, tightens
and untightens her cheeks. She looks at her stomach,
pats it, pulls at the skin.

                         ANNIE
             Oh, Jesse, what you children
             have done to my youth.

They exit. When they have gone, Rudy rolls over on
his back and stares at the ceiling. He glances out
the window: it is a gloomy day. He looks at a
picture hanging on the opposite wall. It is a
reproduction of Giotto's "Saint Francis Renouncing
His Worldly Possessions." All the elders of the
town are arrayed around the half naked saint. They
look angry and embarrassed. They all stare at him,
but he stares at the sky. Up in the sky, a slender,
white hand beckons to him from the clouds. The
camera cuts to a close-up of the hand in the clouds.

                         CUT TO:

5   INT: KITCHEN - DAY

A young black man is sitting in the kitchen, eating
a bagel. Jesse comes running in, followed by Annie,
who is pulling on a robe, but hasn't quite gotten it
on yet. She jumps when she sees the man.

                    ANNIE
          Who are you?

He smiles and looks her up and down. She pulls the
robe tightly around her.

                    MUGGO
          Call me Muggo. I'm a friend
          of Sluggo's.

                    ANNIE
          Oh.

                    MUGGO
          Really appreciate it.

                    JESSE
          I want apple juice in my bottle.

                    ANNIE
          O.K.

She grabs a Smokey the Bear bottle and fills it with
apple juice.

                    ANNIE
               (to MUGGO)
          Sluggo said it was O.K. for you
          to stay here?

                    MUGGO
          Yeah. Hope it's cool, 'cause
          it's the perfect set-up for me.

                    ANNIE
          You didn't speak to Rudy?

                    MUGGO
          Rudy? I didn't meet no Rudy,
          man.

                    ANNIE
          Cause you see, this isn't
          Sluggo's place. It's my place
          ... and Rudy's place. Sluggo
          just rents a room here.

5   CONTD

                         JESSE
           And my place.

                         MUGGO
           I can dig it. You don't like
           havin' me around, you just say
           the word and I'm gone.

                         JESSE
           Right, Mom?

                         ANNIE
                (to Jesse)
           Right, Jess.
                (to Muggo)
           Well, we'll have to talk to
           Rudy about it.

                         JESSE
           And Kirsten's place.

                         MUGGO
           I can dig it. Sure is a nice
           set-up you got here.

                         JESSE
           And Huey's place. Right, Mom?

                                        CUT TO:

6   INT: LIVING ROOM-BEDROOM - DAY

     Rudy is out of bed, sleepily pulling on a pair of
     pants.

     He pads his way to the bathroom.

7   INT: CORRIDOR - DAY

     The bathroom door is closed. He can hear a shower
     going and someone singing. He knocks on the door.
     No response. He turns and walks away.

8   INT: KITCHEN - DAY

     Annie and Muggo are getting chummy. As Rudy walks
     in, Muggo is patting the dogs.

                         MUGGO
           I love your dogs. What's their
           relationship? If you don't mind
           me getting personal.

8   CONTD

                        ANNIE
              Mother and son.

                        MUGGO
              Do they make it together?

                        ANNIE
              She's been altered. Too many
              babies, poor darling.

Rudy shuffles through the kitchen, still half asleep,
not noticing anybody. He opens the door at the back
of the kitchen and steps through a tiny, cluttered
room (his studio), opens another door and steps into
a little half-bathroom.

9   INT: HALF-BATHROOM - DAY

Through the open other door we see PAT and PERRY
asleep in the next room. Rudy lifts up the toilet
seat top to discover that the toilet is completely
clogged with paper. He drops the seat cover in
disgust and goes back into the kitchen.

10   INT: KITCHEN - DAY

Still oblivious, Rudy shuffles up to the sink, unzips his fly and prepares to do his pee. The sink
is full of dirty dishes.

                        ANNIE
              What are you doing?

                        RUDY
              Pissing in the sink. What does
              it look like?

                        ANNIE
              Are you crazy?

                        RUDY
              What'm I supposed to do? Sluggo
              is in that one, taking one of
              his endless showers, this one
              here is clogged up ...

                        ANNIE
              If Sluggo is in the shower,
              that means the toilet's free.
              Why don't you do it in there?

10   CONTD

                    RUDY
          You want me to take a leak in
          front of that fag? Come on,
          Annie.

He starts clearing a space in the dishes.

                    RUDY
          Here. I'll aim right for the
          drain.

                    ANNIE
          Rudy! We have a guest!

Rudy turns around, dick still in hand, and notices
Muggo for the first time. Muggo smiles. Rudy
tucks himself back in his pants.

                    RUDY
          Who's this?

                    MUGGO
              (reaching out his hand)
          Muggo, man.

Rudy wipes his hand on his pants and reaches out for
Muggo's hand. Muggo grabs his thumb in a "power"
handshake.

                    JESSIE
              (to Annie)
          I want grape nuts cereal.

                    ANNIE
              (to Jesse)
          O.K.

                    JESSE
          With bananas.

                    MUGGO
              (to Rudy)
          Sluggo drug me in.

                    ANNIE
              (to Jesse)
          O.K.

The phone rings. Annie answers it.

                    ANNIE
          Hullo ... Oh, hello! How are
          you? ... What? Don't wanna speak
                    (MORE)

10   CONTD (2)

                    ANNIE (Contd)
          to me, eh? ... Oh, alright.
          You're such a pig. Hold on.

She holds out the phone to Rudy, making a face.

                    ANNIE
          It's Bascom Hunt.
               (whispers)
          He's drunk.

                    RUDY
          At this hour?

Rudy grabs the phone.

                    JESSE
          And milk ... and honey ... O.K.?

                    ANNIE
          O.K., already! Get off my back!

                    RUDY
               (into phone)
          Hullo?

                    BASCOM HUNT
               (phone filter)
          Hi, fella. Didn't wake ya, did I?

                    RUDY
          Uh-uh.

Bascom seems to be sobbing.

                    BASCOM
          You haven't seen Lois have you?

                    RUDY
          Uh-uh. Should I?

                    BASCOM
          I don't know. I thought maybe
          you and she might have something
          going or something.

                    RUDY
          Who? Me and Lois?

Annie perks up her ears.

10   CONTD (3)

                    BASCOM
          I'm sorry. I'm getting so
          paranoid lately. You're not,
          huh? I'm sorry. I suspect
          everybody. That bitch is driving
          me crazy. I've been calling her
          all night.
                    (he sobs)
          She never even went home.

                    RUDY
          But she's not married to you
          anymore. She has her own place,
          her own life ... You can't ...

                    BASCOM
          I know, I know. I'm such a
          selfish bastard. That's how I
          lost her in the first place.
          You got a fine family there
          with Annie and the kid. Don't
          blow it. Take my advice.

                    RUDY
          Don't worry.

                    BASCOM
          Listen. Have you got a minute?
          I gotta talk to somebody.

                    RUDY
          Bascom, I can't talk now. I
          gotta take a piss or I'll burst.

                    BASCOM
          Go ahead. I'll wait.

                    RUDY
          I can't. I gotta go out to
          do it.

                    BASCOM
          Huh? What's the matter? Haven't
          you ever heard of toilets?

                    RUDY
          I can't explain it. I gotta go.

                    BASCOM
          O.K. But can I call you later?

10   CONTD (4)

                         RUDY
            I can't. Not today. I gotta
            finish a song and meet Lois
            for lunch.

                         BASCOM
            You're meeting my wife for lunch?

                         RUDY
            She's my agent, you asshole!
            Besides, it's about a possible
            songwriting gig.

                         BASCOM
            Tell her ... Tell her ...

                         RUDY
            I'll tell her you love her and
            why isn't she home more often.
            O.K.? ... I gotta go.

                         BASCOM
            O.K., but watch me on the news
            tonight. I got a great rape-
            murder-suicide story.

                         RUDY
            O.K. Bye.

He hangs up.

                         ANNIE
            What did he say?

Rudy dashes out of the kitchen.

                         RUDY
            He's got a great rape-murder-
            suicide story. I gotta go.

                         ANNIE
                 (calling after him)
            No! What did he say about you
            and Lois?

                                        CUT TO:

11   INT: FOYER - DAY

Rudy slips his feet into a pair of sneakers, pulls
on a T-shirt, and heads for the door.

11   CONTD

                         RUDY
                       (calling)
                 Come on, you dogs!

The DOGS come tearing out of the kitchen and out the
door just as Rudy opens it.

12   INT: LOBBY - DAY

The dogs, followed by Rudy, come dashing out into the
lobby, just as a LITTLE OLD LADY with a cane comes
through the front door. The dogs knock the little
old lady over.

                    LITTLE OLD LADY
              Fucking dogs! Can't you keep
              them on a leash?
              Careful! I'm old! I'm brittle!

Rudy doesn't take time to answer. He simply lifts
her up, sets her on her feet, and runs out the door.

                                        CUT TO:

13   EXT: WEST END AVE. - DAY

Rudy and the dogs run across West End Ave. amid
honking horns and screeching brakes and starts down
84th Street. Rudy is walking very fast. The dogs
are having a leisurely perusal of the scrawny trees
and garbage cans.

                         RUDY
                 Come on, you creeps.

A WOMAN WITH A BEEHIVE HAIRDO, coming from the
opposite direction with a little PEKINESE on a leash,
sees Huey and KIRSTEN approaching, picks up her little
dog and tries to hurry by. Huey jumps up on his
hind legs to sniff the Peke, and the woman screams
and runs away.

14   EXT: RIVERSIDE PARK AT 84TH ST. - DAY

As they cross Riverside Drive, the dogs dash ahead of
Rudy, after a squirrel. They send up a flurry of
pigeons along the way. Rudy crosses the wide, open
promendade that extends up to 90th St.. In the grass
islands of the promenade, every 20 yards or so, is
a large grate. As Rudy walks by, we hear the sound
of a train and see little puffs of black smoke
marching from grate to grate toward the horizon. Rudy

14   CONTD

trips down some stairs, finds a secluded spot in the
shadow of a huge wall and unzips his fly. He relieves
his bladder with a great sigh of release. The dogs
come trotting up and sniff idly at his pee.

                    RUDY
                 (to himself)
          Who the hell is Muggo?

Suddenly Rudy is startled out of his reverie by a
shout. He sees a high-arched gate that looks into
the underground RR tracks. The train is passing and
the MAN ON THE CABOOSE is shouting at him. Startled,
he turns away, and zips up his fly. He sees a
gaudily dressed BLACK GUY approaching him with a
smile. Rudy pulls up his collar and tries to walk
nonchalantly by. The black guy hands him a card.

                    BUDDHIST
          Hey! Like to invite you to a Buddhist
          meeting.

Rudy passes it up. The Buddhist follows along with
him, still proferring the card.

                    BUDDHIST
          Hey, come on to the meeting.
          You'll meet some foxy chicks, you'll
          rap about Buddhist ... Check it out!

                    RUDY
          No, thanks. I'm a non-believer.

                    BUDDHIST
          Hey. Ya gotta believe.

                                        CUT TO:

15   INT: FOYER - DAY

Rudy and the dogs enter. Annie and Jesse are in
the foyer, just finishing dressing, and preparing
to go out. She is wearing a very sexy little
semi-transparent dress and platform shoes. She
looks great. Rudy whistles at the sight of her.

                    RUDY
          I'll never understand why you
          get so dressed up to go wait
          on tables in a bar.

He fondles her admiringly.

15   CONTD

                        ANNIE
          Vanity, vanity, all vanity,
          darling. Now what's this about
          you having lunch with Lois?

                        RUDY
          I have to play her the Christmas
          song.
                   (he runs his hand
                    up her thigh,
                    still looking her
                    over)

                        RUDY
          ... and a barful of fags at
          that!

                        ANNIE
          Not all of them, darling. Which
          reminds me! Remember me telling
          you about Rod, the bartender?
          Who's bisexual and gorgeous and
          has made it with every single
          person who works at that bar?
          Male _and_ female.

Rudy steps back.

                        RUDY
          Every single person?

                        ANNIE
          Except me, of course.

She puts her arms around Rudy, to reassure him.

                        ANNIE
          I told him I didn't want to
          because of you, but I must say
          I was tempted. You know what
          he said? "Shit, honey, bring
          him along. He's cute. And
          three's the best."

Annie grins up against him lasciviously.

                        ANNIE
          What shall I tell him ? Interested?

                        RUDY
          I'd be more interested if number
          three was a female.

15   CONTD (2)

                    ANNIE
You would? That'd be just fine
with me!

                    RUDY
It would?

                    ANNIE
Of course. Haven't I ever told
you about my thing for the girls?

                    RUDY
Is this something new?

                    ANNIE
Heavens no. I've always felt
I could be a bit more bent.

                    RUDY
You're so groovy.

All of this time, Rudy and Annie have been fondling
each other and increasing the rhythm of their
grinding. They are interrupted by the sound of
footsteps.

Pat appears from the kitchen hallway. She is dressed
only in panties and carries a towel around her neck.
She is very voluptous. She is also half asleep.
She stumbles across the foyer, tripping over Jesse,
who is playing on the floor. She turns down the
hallway to the bathroom. Rudy follows her with his
eyes over Annie's shoulder.

                    ANNIE
The phone company called about the
bill.

                    RUDY
Oh, shit.

                    ANNIE
They're gonna cut off our out-
going service tomorrow.

                    RUDY
Gosh. What would we do without
a phone?

Pat reaches the bathroom, bumps into the door, dis-
covering for the first time that it is closed. She
turns around and comes back into the foyer.

15   CONTD (3)

                    ANNIE
          Pat, I wish you wouldn't walk
          around like that.

                    PAT
          Huh?

She disappears down the hallway to the kitchen. Rudy
turns to Annie.

                    RUDY
          Well, what are we gonna do?

Annie's eyes fill with tears.

                    ANNIE
          And you don't have to be so
          obvious!

                    RUDY
          What did I do?

                    ANNIE
          Oh, Rudy, you do love me, don't
          you, darling?

                    RUDY
          Aw, baby, you know I do.

                    ANNIE
          You won't run off with Lois or
          anybody, will you?

                    RUDY
          Lois? Our relationship is
          strictly business. You know
          that.

                    ANNIE
          Ever since she left Bascom, she's
          been spreading her legs for half
          of New York ...

                    RUDY
          Well, not this half.

                    ANNIE
          ... and I know she's got her
          claws out for you. You fancy
          her too, don't you?

15   CONTD (4)

> RUDY
> Honey, you got me exactly where
> you want me. I'm stuck like
> glue. Don't you know that
> after all these years?

He kisses her.

> ANNIE
> Just as long as I know that ...

In the background we see SLUGGO emerge from the
bathroom in a gaudy silk bathrobe and disappear into
his own room. Annie disengages herself from Rudy
and grabs Jesse's hand.

> ANNIE
> I've got to go, darling ...
> Come on, Jess.

> RUDY
> Can you let me have a fin?

Annie looks in her purse.

> ANNIE
> I've only got a dollar and
> change. You take the dollar.
> I'll be making my tips.

Rudy looks sadly at the dollar bill. Annie kisses
him goodbye.

> ANNIE
> (to Jesse)
> Say goodbye to your father.

> JESSE
> Good-bye dummy-daddy.

> RUDY
> (kisses him)
> See ya, kid. And don't call
> me dummy.

> ANNIE
> You won't forget to pick him up
> at school will you?

> RUDY
> Don't worry. But what about
> the phone?

15   CONTD (5)

                    ANNIE
          I'll give them a check.

                    RUDY
          There's only seven dollars
          in the bank.

                    ANNIE
          You see if you can get some
          rent from Perry. I'll call
          you when I get off work tonight.
          We'll think of something

She opens the door and starts out.

                    ANNIE
          Maybe we can go out if one of
          the lodgers is home.

                    RUDY
          I was gonna watch the playoffs.

She looks disappointed.

                    RUDY
          But you can go out if you want
          to.
                    ANNIE
          I can?
                    RUDY
          Sure. We're liberated, right?
          You can do what you want, right?

                    ANNIE
          Right!
                    RUDY
          But keep your legs crossed!

                    ANNIE (O.C.)
          'Bye, darling!

                    JESSE   (O.C.)
          'Bye, daddy-dummy!

The door closes behind them, leaving a black screen.
Rudy turns to the interior of the apartment. Pat
comes out of the kitchen hallway, still barechested,
crosses the foyer. She stops, turns, gives Rudy a
wink, goes down the hall and enters the bathroom.
The door closes behind her, leaving a black screen.

16   INT: RUDY'S ROOM - DAY

Rudy's room is a tiny little garret behind the
kitchen. The main furniture are a beat-up old
spinnet piano and a swivel chair. On top of the
piano is a microphone on a stand, attached to a
cassette tape recorder. There are wires all over
the place. There are postcards tacked all over the
walls, along with scraps of music notation paper.
There is notation paper all over the place. There
are cassettes all over the place. There are postcards all over the place. There is lots of other
junk all over the place.

Rudy comes in, cigarette dangling from his lips.
He shuffles around, sits down at the piano and
plays a few chords. He starts to sing a few lines
of a song.

A door opens behind Rudy, and a naked Perry steps in.

                    PERRY
          Mornin', hoss.

Rudy squeezes up against the piano to let Perry go
by. Perry crosses the room in one step and exits
into the kitchen. Rudy continues to sing.
The song continues over the following sequences:

17   INT: RED PAINT DAY CARE CENTER - DAY

Annie drops off Jesse. The place is full of screaming
KIDS; several PARENTS are milling around. Her getup
draws icy stares from TWO MOTHERS and an adoring look
from a BACHELOR FATHER. Annie kisses Jesse goodbye
and escapes quickly.

18   EXT: BROADWAY - DAY

Annie buys a Daily News at the newsstand. While
waiting for the light to change, she shuffles through
the paper until she finds the horoscope page. While
crossing the street, she reads her horoscope. She
is an Aquarius. It reads: "This is the day to do
that thing you've been putting off."

She crumples up the paper, drops it in a trash can,
and disappears down into the subway.

19   EXT: CANAL ST. SUBWAY STATION - STEPS - DAY

Annie ascends the stairs. AN OLD BLACK MAN slightly
drunk, is following her, bending over a bit.

20   EXT: CANAL ST. SUBWAY - STEPS - DAY
      BLACK MAN'S P.O.V.

      We see Annie from behind. Her dress is of a thin
      material. Backlit by the bright sunlight, it looks
      transparent. Annie's ass sways invitingly.

      TWO SHOT.

      Just as Annie is about to reach the top step, the
      black man leans forward and kisses her ass. She
      jumps, shocked, and turns around. He smiles shyly
      up at her.

                         BLACK MAN
                I couldn't hep it. It was so
                beautiful. I jes had to kiss it.

      Song ends.

                                        CUT TO:

21   INT: RUDY'S ROOM - DAY

      The door to the kitchen opens and Perry steps in,
      squeezes behind Rudy and out the other door.

                         PERRY
                Sorry, hoss.

      Rudy has lost his train of thought. He tries out
      several chord combinations, finds the right one, and
      begins again.

      The phone rings. Rudy answers it, pissed off.

                         RUDY
                Hello ... Hold on ... PAT!

                         PAT (O.S.)
                What?

                         RUDY
                TELEPHONE!

                         PAT (O.S.)
                O.K.!

      Pat enters from the door behind Rudy. She is still
      wearing the same costume, but this time she is wet,
      and the towel is over her head. Crossing the room,
      she manages to knock something off a shelf and drip
      water all over Rudy's music. She goes out the kitchen
      door and picks up the phone.

21   CONTD

                         PAT
               Hello ... I told you not to call
               me here ... I can't talk....

Rudy tries to go back to his playing, but he can't
take his eyes off the image of Pat moving back and
forth behind the frosted glass that separates the
two rooms.

                         PAT
               ... I'll get it to you. Don't
               worry ... Tomorrow ... I'll call
               you ... Yes, I'm sure. I've
               gotta go.

She hangs up, and comes back into Rudy's room.

                         PAT
               Sorry.

                         RUDY
               It's just that I gotta finish
               this song.

Pat bumps into Perry at the doorway to their room.

                         PERRY
               Who was it?

                         PAT
               Oh, nobody.

                         PERRY
               Who the hell is nobody?

                         RUDY
               Hey, come on, you guys. I'm
               tryin' to get some work done.

                         PERRY
               Don't get riled up, ol' hoss.
               We're leavin'. We're leavin'.

They disappear into their room, where we hear them
arguing through the walls.

22   EXT: BROOME ST. BAR - DAY

A GUY who is loitering outside the bar opens the door
and gives Annie the once-over as she passes through.

23   INT: BROOME ST. BAR - DAY

A typical SoHo bar: wooden tables, menu on black-
boards. The WAITRESSES are all beautiful and the
COOKS and BUSBOYS are all gay. The CUSTOMERS are a
mixed arty crowd with a few TRUCKDRIVERS sprinkled
here and there.

Annie is noticed as she makes her entrance.

Customers ad lib greetings. ONE tries to grab her
but she sidesteps him. She strides along the bar.
Rod, the bartender, walks along parallel to her,
behind the bar.

                    ROD
          Ah, the constant wife! Did
          you ask him?

                    ANNIE
          He said he'd rather you were
          a girl.

                    ROD
          He's a fool. I give better
          head than Linda Lovelace.

At the far end of the bar is a little nook where
Annie deposits her jacket and dons her apron. She
meets GUNILLA there. Gunilla is a blonde bombshell.
She greets Annie, kissing her on both cheeks. She
looks Annie up and down, strokes and squeezes her arm.

                    GUNILLA
          You look fantastic.

                    ANNIE
          Do I? You look pretty luscious
          yourself.

                    GUNILLA
          Come up and see me sometime.

Gunilla gives Annie her book of checks.

                    ANNIE
              (looking around)
          How's the action?

                    GUNILLA
          Picking up, Watch out for fifteen.

Annie looks over Gunilla's shoulder to table 15 and
sees a big, husky guy, a little loaded, who gives

23   CONTD

her a lascivious grin.

                    ANNIE
          He's beautiful.

                    GUNILLA
          If you like men. I've given
          them up.

                    ANNIE
               (delighted)
          You mean you're doing it with
          women?

Gunilla smiles.

                    GUNILLA
          Men are such babies.

The customer at table 15 is signalling to Annie.

                    ANNIE
          I've got to go. But I must
          hear all about it.

                    GUNILLA
          I'm serious. Come and see me.

                    ANNIE
          I will.

Gunilla leaves. Annie crosses to her customer, who
shall hereafter be known as the BUSHMASTER.

                    ANNIE
          Did you want something?

                    BUSHMASTER
          Yeah. You.

                    ANNIE
          Me? Don't be silly. What do
          you want to eat?

                    BUSHMASTER
          I want to eat your pussy.

                    ANNIE
          Come on.

23   CONTD (2)

                    BUSHMASTER
          I'm serious. I want to munch
          your twat.

                    ANNIE
          You wouldn't like it. It's not
          very appetizing.

                    BUSHMASTER
          I know what I like. What do
          you say? No balling. Just eat
          you.

                    ANNIE
          Out of the question. Do you
          want to order anything from the
          bar? I have other customers ...

                    BUSHMASTER
          O.K. Gimme a Martell's.

He grabs her by the wrist.

                    BUSHMASTER
               (under his breath)
          I can make you come and keep on
          coming 'til the cows come home.

                    ANNIE
          Do you always go around leaving
          your fingerprints on a girl's
          wrist?

He lifts her hand to his mouth as if to kiss it.
But he goes farther. He takes her thumb in his
mouth and sucks it pornographically. He smiles.

                    BUSHMASTER
          Put that in your pocket.

As Annie moves away, we hear Rudy's song begin again
on the track.

                                        CUT TO:

24   INT: LOIS' OFFICE - DAY

Rudy is sitting at the piano, noodling the intro
to his song. There is no one else in the office.
There is a desk littered with contracts, sheet
music, an electric calculator, a speaker phone,
scripts, memos, etc. There is a stereo set up,

24   CONTD

surrounded by piles of tapes and 45s. There are
photographs on the wall of Lois with each of her
clients -- a couple of well-known faces, the rest
a motley bunch, all male, and all with their arms
around Lois.

Rudy sings his song.

Toward the end of the song, LOIS enters. She is a
voluptuous-looking girl in her twenties who dresses
to show herself off to obvious advantage. Her
manner is direct, aggressive and sexual. She comes
up behind him. As Rudy finishes:

                    LOIS
          It'll never sell.

Rudy turns to see her. He swivels around on the
piano stool and strokes her behind.

                    LOIS
          Get those legs back under the
          piano where they belong.

                    RUDY
          I just want to finish something
          we started a long time ago.

                    LOIS
          Not that again!

Lois steps away and moves behind her desk. Rudy
follows her.

                    LOIS
          Sit down. We've got to talk
          about your career, which is
          going absolutely nowhere in a
          big hurry. And fast -- I've
          got a session at 2:30.

                    RUDY
          Come on, Lois ...

Rudy kisses the back of her neck.

                    LOIS
          I can't, Rudy. It wouldn't
          be fair to Annie.

                    RUDY
          Lois, these are the nineteen
          seventies! You don't even
          like Annie.

                    LOIS
          I do so like her very much.
          I have a lot of admiration for
          her. She's a real ballsy dame.

                    RUDY
          You're not friends.

                    LOIS
          We're not friends because of
          men. It's men that make women
          turn against each other. If
          you weren't in the picture, I'm
          sure Annie and I would get along
          just great.

                    RUDY
          Only in an all woman world. And
          even there I wouldn't bet on it.
          Anyway, let's get back to
          talking about you and me.

                    LOIS
          Forget it.

                    RUDY
          Name one client you haven't
          screwed besides me.

                    LOIS
          Marty Levin.

                    RUDY
          That doesn't count. He's a
          fag.

                    LOIS
              (shrugs)
          Call me sentimental then.

                    RUDY
          Sentimental? You?

                    LOIS
          I'm sentimental about you and
          Annie. You're practically the
          last couple I know that's still
          together. You have a family,
          a home, you love each other ...
          I wouldn't want to do anything
          to come between you.

24   CONTD (3)

                    RUDY
          What makes you think you could
          ever come between us?

Lois falls silent.

                    RUDY
          I'm sorry.

                    LOIS
          No, you're right. And that's
          the point. I know what happens
          when another woman enters the
          scene. I've done that trip.
          It's always the other woman who
          loses out in the end. Is she
          working at the bar tonight?

                    RUDY
          Annie? Yeah. Why?

                    LOIS
          Maybe I'll go visit her. I'll
          be down that way later on.

Rudy puts his arm around her. They sort of wrestle
with each other.

                    RUDY
          Come on, Lois. I just want to
          play.

                    LOIS
          Then go play with yourself!
          I'm not interested.

The phone rings. Lois presses the intercom.

                    LOIS
          What is it, Bernie?

                    BERNIE (V.O.)
          It's Ron Rosen of Run Records.

                    LOIS
          I'll be right with him.
               (to Rudy, suddenly
                all business)
          Ron Rosen of Run Records.
          You know who that is, right?
          Big.

24   CONTD (4)

                         RUDY
          Yeah, I've heard of him.

                         LOIS
          Well, he's heard of you, too.

                         RUDY
          Oh, yeah?

                         LOIS
          And he likes some of your stuff.

                         RUDY
          What do you mean "some" of my
          stuff?

                         LOIS
          Well, you know, he doesn't
          go for the far out stuff.

                         RUDY
          What far out stuff?

                         LOIS
          Come on, Rudy, let's not get
          into that again.

                         RUDY
          No, I mean it.

                         LOIS
          Well, anyway, he's just been
          bought out by the Thallus of
          Marcandia, who's this Arab
          sheik or something ...

                         RUDY
          Yeah, I know who he is, too.

                         LOIS
          Want to write a song for him?

                         RUDY
          Huh?

                         LOIS
          There's two hundred and fifty
          clams in it.

Rudy pulls his phone bill out of his pocket and
looks at it.

24   CONTD (5)

                    RUDY
          My phone bill is two-sixty-
          seven-forty-three ...

Lois picks up the phone and sinks into a sexy voice.

                    LOIS
          Ron? Como esta, amore mio?
          And thanks for running out on
          me at dawn ...

Rudy sits down in Lois' plush executive swivel chair.

                    LOIS
          Yes, I sat there playing solitaire
          until ten A.M. and then went out
          and spent two hundred dollars in
          the thrift shops, I was so
          distressed.

Rudy tries to get Lois to sit on his lap.

                    LOIS
          The Virgin of Guadeloupe has not
          been working lately ...

Lois sidesteps Rudy and dances around the front of
the desk.

                    LOIS
          Listen, honey, with lovers like
          you around, I'm glad masturbation
          is making a comeback ... O.K.,
          we'll talk about that later.
          Look, tiger, I've got about
          twenty-three more tricks to turn
          before five, so let me take care
          of business and get off. Got
          your pen in your hand? Make out
          a check for ...

She grabs the phone bill from Rudy, scrutinizes it.

                    LOIS
               (mumbles to herself)
          Two-sixty-seven-forty-three plus
          ten percent ...
               (to Ron)
          Make out a check for two-
          ninety-four-seventeen ... Come
          on, Ron, don't cock around. The
                    (MORE)

24   CONTD (6)

                         LOIS (Contd)
                kid's got a phone bill to pay
                ... Don't worry, you pay,
                he'll deliver. He's a pro.

BERNIE, Lois' secretary, sticks his head in the door,
gestures toward the corridor outside and mouths
something. Lois covers the receiver and says.

                         LOIS
                    (to Bernie)
                I'll be right there ...
                    (to Ron)
                Got that, Ron? Have it hand
                delivered to me this afternoon
                and you've got a deal ...
                Listen, honey, I've got to go
                ... What's that?
                    (chuckles)
                Think you're man enough? Well
                call me next week. I'm
                booked solid. Ciao.

She hangs up. She swivels around in her chair to face
Rudy.

                         LOIS
                Now, here's what you have to
                do ...

As she swings around, and before she can protect
herself, Rudy slips his hand deftly between her legs.

                         LOIS
                    (sighs)
                Rudy, fer Christ sake! ...

The intercom buzzes.

                         LOIS
                I'm coming! I'm coming!
                    (to Rudy)
                I've got to go. Call me tomorrow
                and I'll tell you what you have
                to do.

She leaps out of her seat and crosses to the door
before Rudy can get up. Halfway out the door, she
turns to Rudy with a slight tinge of regret.

24   CONTD (7)

                         LOIS
               Shit, Rudy, even if I wanted
               to, I wouldn't have the time.

She leaves.

                                             CUT TO:

25   INT: LIVING ROOM-BEDROOM - NIGHT

Rudy reclines in front of the Knicks game on the T.V.,
his eyes at half mast, mesmerized. He hears noises
at the front door, female giggles, someone tripping
over something. Annie and Lois stumble in, drunk
and disorderly. Rudy gets up. Annie throws herself
into Rudy's arms.

                         ANNIE
               Hello, darling!

She kisses him lasciviously.

                         ANNIE
               Guess what, darling? We're
               going to seduce you!

Rudy is dumbstruck. Annie laughs, kisses him again,
and reaches for his fly. He flinches.

                         ANNIE
               You'll like that, darling,
               won't you? Yes you will. Here
               we've all had the hots for each
               other all this time, and now
               we're all going to do it. And
               it'll be great fun, you'll see!

By now she has her hand inside his fly. She gives
him a squeeze and turns suddenly to Lois. She
kisses Lois passionately, strokes her tit, and
darts out of the room.

                         ANNIE
               You two get acquainted. I'll
               be right back!

Rudy sits down hard. He can't believe it. He
glances up at Lois. She is smiling, three sheets
to the wind. He is in shock. Lois approaches,
sits down on his knees and kisses him. A moan
escapes from Rudy's throat. His eyes dart around

25   CONTD

guiltily, as if to see if anybody is watching. His
hand slips into her blouse, he fondles her breast,
his eyes closed.

Annie comes in. The spectacle of Rudy and Lois
making out quite floors her for a second, and she
freezes in her tracks.

Rudy's eyes open. He sees Annie, and his hand shoots
out of Lois' blouse as if it were on fire. Lois
looks up.

                    ANNIE
                (smiles bravely)
          Don't mind me!

She stumbles up and throws her arms around them both.

                    ANNIE
          Come on, darlings.

She goes for Rudy's belt and starts to unbuckle it.
Rudy leaps to his feet, leaving Lois and Annie to
fall into each other's arms on the bed. Rudy's
pants fall down. He is wearing funny boxer shorts.
The girls laugh. Rudy hobbles out of the room,
semi-hysterical, with his pants around his ankles.

                    LOIS
          Where do you think you're going?

                    RUDY
                (stutters)
          I'm j-j-just to the bathroom.
          I'll be right back ...

26   INT: HALLWAY - NIGHT

Rudy stumbles down the hall to the bathroom,
struggling furiously with his pants. He finally
kicks them off, angrily, against the wall, and all
his change comes flying out of his pocket. He
paces up and down. He pulls on his dick to make it
longer. He summons up the courage to go back.

27   INT: LIVING ROOM-BEDROOM - NIGHT

Rudy draws up outside the room, looking in through
the French doors. Lois and Annie are locked in an
embrace on the bed. Lois is naked and trying to
maneuver Annie out of her dress. Annie is fondling
Lois' ample bosom, and they are kissing. Rudy

27   CONTD

watches them for a long time. Then Lois looks
up, wondering where he's gone, and sees him.

                    LOIS
          What are you? Some kind of pervert?

Rudy steps into the doorway.

                    RUDY
          Let me just watch. Just for a
          minute.

                    ANNIE
          Oh, no you don't.

                    LOIS
          Come on, Frigidaire. You can't
          get out of this one.

Rudy starts to undress. (The girls are by now both
naked.) He feels terribly self-conscious. Both
girls are watching him. He feels like a stripper.

                    RUDY
          Well, go on. Do whatever you
          were doing. I'm coming.

Annie kisses Lois' tit. Lois continues looking at
Rudy. Rudy sheds the last of his clothes, and Lois
pulls him onto the bed.

                    LOIS
          Gee, you got skinny.

                    ANNIE
                (a moment of jealous
                 panic)
          How do you know he got skinny?

                    LOIS
          I've seen him at the beach,
          f'chrissakes.

Rudy sighs and falls back on the pillows. The two
girls snuggle up on either side of him. Rudy looks
at one and then the other. He doesn't know where
to begin, what to do.

                    LOIS
          What's the matter? Can't
          handle it?

27   CONTD (2)

                    RUDY
          I don't know whether I'm the
          sultan or the slave.

Lois kisses him again. Annie sticks her tongue in
his ear and whispers.

                    ANNIE
          Isn't this fun, darling?

He turns from Lois and kisses Annie, deeply. Lois,
after watching them for a moment, bends down and
takes Rudy's cock in her mouth.

                    ANNIE
               (still whispering)
          You can do anything you want. I
          won't be angry.

Rudy fondles her tit and kisses her again. His
left hand strays down to Lois' ass. Lois' mouth
strays from Rudy's cock to Annie's pussy. Annie
tries to stop her.

                    ANNIE
          Oh, no. You don't want to do
          that.

                    LOIS
          Oh, yes I do.

                    ANNIE
          Not to that leathery old puss.

                    LOIS
          Shhh.

Lois begins to suck Annie's leathery old puss.
Annie grimaces and whispers to Rudy. Rudy is trying
to sneak a finger up Lois' snatch.

                    ANNIE
               (whispers)
          I feel so ugly.

                    RUDY
               (whispers)
          No, you're not. You're the most
          beautiful woman in the world.

Rudy bends down to kiss her breasts. He and Lois
are now lying parallel to each other at right angles
to Annie.

27   CONTD (3)

                    ANNIE
                (whispering)
          Look how young and luscious she
          is. Don't you just want to
          squeeze those round juicy
          melons of hers? Go on. You
          can touch them. I won't mind.

She pushes his arm toward Lois. He reaches around
and grabs onto Lois' boob. Lois goes at Annie
more passionately. Annie is beginning to loosen up.
She opens her legs a little, lets her head drop
back and stares up at the ceiling. Rudy, working on
Annie's tits and hanging onto one of Lois' too,
finds himself front to back, cheek by Roger, with
Lois. He begins to undulate against her, and soon
finds himself trying a rear entry. Lois, without
stopping work on Annie, reaches around and tries to
guide Rudy's dick in the right direction. But they
can't seem to make it work. Rudy can't wait any
longer. He turns Lois over on her back and climbs
on top of her. He enters her; they kiss and begin
to fuck. There is a moment where Annie remains,
staring at the ceiling. Then, suddenly she notices
that something has changed. She looks down and
sees Rudy and Lois, coupled on top of her. Panic
strikes her. To her, Rudy and Lois seem locked
together in a private world that excludes her.
Tears well up in her eyes. She cannot bear the
sight of her worst fear come true before her eyes.
She pulls herself out from under them and runs out
of the room.

Lois follows her out with her eyes. Rudy can't
stop, but feels he must say something.

                    RUDY
                (feebly, and still
                fucking)
          Annie! Come back.

                    ANNIE
                (off-screen, crying,
                running away)
          It's all right ... Don't let me
          spoil your fun.

Lois tries to push Rudy off.

                    LOIS
          I better go to her.

27   CONTD (4)

                    RUDY
                (sighs)
          Never mind. I'll go.

He pulls himself away and exits. Lois throws something at the wall.

                    LOIS
          Damn!

She lies back on the bed. She hears Annie sobbing
off screen, and Rudy knocking on the bathroom door.

                    RUDY (O.S.)
          Darling, let me in.

Lois pulls the covers over her head. There is a
moment where nothing happens, except for some
muffled sounds from the bathroom. Then, little
three-year-old Jesse stumbles into the room,
still half asleep. He climbs onto the bed and
under the covers beside Lois.

28   INT: BATHROOM - NIGHT

Rudy is slipping it to Annie, propped up against the
edge of the bathrub. Annie has been crying. Rudy
is wiping away her tears.

                    ANNIE
                (sobbing)
          It's just that you were kissing
          her ...

Suddenly, they hear Jesse cry from the other room.

                    JESSE (O.S.)
          I want my Mommy! I want my
          Mommy!

Annie panics anew and dashes out of the bathroom.
Rudy looks mournfully at himself in the mirror.
He looks down at his erect dick. It wilts.

29   INT: LIVING ROOM-BEDROOM - NIGHT

As Rudy comes into the room, Annie is holding Jesse
on the bed, comforting him and Lois is pulling her
clothes on.

                    RUDY
          Lois. You're not going?

29   CONTD

Jesse is still crying.

                    ANNIE
               (to Jesse)
          It's all right, darling. It's
          Lois. You know Lois. She's
          your pal.

                    JESSE
          But what she's doing in your
          bed?

                    ANNIE
          There, there.

                    JESSE
          That's not her bed. That's
          your bed! And my Daddy's bed!

Annie picks him up.

                    ANNIE
          Back to bed now.

                    JESSE
          I don't wanna go to bed!

She carries him out, still crying. Rudy goes to
embrace Lois, but she pulls herself away and runs out
the front door. Rudy goes after her as far as the
hallway.

                    RUDY
          Lois!

The door slams shut. Rudy turns around. Annie is
coming out of Jesse's room. She glares at Rudy.
Rudy opens his arms to her. She runs into the
bedroom, shuts the door, and falls crying on the
bed.

                    RUDY
          Annie! Darling!

We can still hear Jesse bawling, off camera, from his
bed. The front door opens and in walks Perry and
Pat carrying a couch. They look at Lois running
away, then at Rudy. Rudy runs into the bathroom
and slams the door.

29A   INT: LOIS' OFFICE - DAY

Lois pushes a button on her phone and picks up the
receiver.

                LOIS
Hello.

                RUDY (V.O.)
Hi. It's me.

                LOIS
Hi. Who?

29A   INT: LOIS' OFFICE - DAY

Lois pushes a button on her phone and picks up the
receiver.

29A   CONTD

                    RUDY
          Me, Rudy.

                    LOIS
          Oh, Rudy ...

                    RUDY
          Hi.

                    LOIS
          Hi. What do you wnat?

                    RUDY
          Annie's working late tonight.
          I thought maybe you'd like
          to come over and finish what
          we started last night. I
          have to babysit.

                    LOIS
          Don't even mention last night.
          What a bummer.

                    RUDY
          I wouldn't say that.

                    LOIS
          First I escape from your hutnouse,
          then I get home and -- what do
          I find? -- but my ex-husband,
          the alcoholic.

                    RUDY
          Bascom?

                    LOIS
          I had to fuck him, he was so
          pathetic. So, I don't even
          want to hear the word sex
          mentioned, if you don't mind.

                    RUDY
          But, Lois ...

                    LOIS
          Now, about this song ...

                    RUDY
          By the way, you never mentioned
          what you thought of the new song.

29A   CONTD (2)

                    LOIS
          It's a very nice song, Rudy. And
          nobody will buy it. Put it in
          the drawer next to "Black Christ-
          mas" and start thinking Arab.

                    RUDY
          But, Lois, I don't know anything
          about Arabs.

                    LOIS
          Anybody knows enough to write a
          goddam song about them. You
          know: harems, camels, money ...

                    RUDY
               (sings)
          "See the pyramids along the Nile ... "

                    LOIS
          That's the idea --
               (sings)
          "Midnight at the Oasis ... "

                    RUDY
               (sings)
          "Come to the Casbah ... "

                    LOIS
          You got it. Now do it.

                    RUDY
          Are you serious? What's it
          supposed to be about?

                    LOIS
          Anything. It doesn't matter.
          Ron just needs something to kiss
          ass with when the Thallus comes
          to check out the scene. Write
          anything. The old fart probably
          won't understand a word.

                    RUDY
          I can't do it.

                    LOIS
          Rudy, you have to do it.

                    RUDY
          I can't.

29A   CONTD (3)

                         LOIS
          You have to.

                         RUDY
          Sleep with me and I'll do it.

                         LOIS
          Don't do it and this could be
          your last call. I haven't
          paid that phone bill yet.

                         RUDY
          Aw, Lois.

                                        CUT TO:

3   INT: MENDY'S - DAY

     Mendy's is a small apartment filled with eccentric

29B CONTD

objets <u>trouves</u>. In the center of the room, there is
an oasis of two couches and a couple of chairs
arranged in a sort of circle around a rickety Art
Deco coffee table. There are three men seated
around: RANDY, a fat Brooklynese salesman, with
his sample case; ROSCOE, the crazy artist who does
events, lounging around in his leathers; and RALPH,
an interior decorator. MENDY opens the door to find
Annie on the threshhold.

       MENDY
     (to Annie)
   Ah, the divine courtesan!

He holds a little spoonful of coke to her nostril.
She accepts it with gusto.

       ANNIE
   The what?

       MENDY
   That's my image of you, my dear.
   I can't help it. Have you seen
   my latest acquistion?

He shows her a set of three porcelain figures of black
minstrels.

       ANNIE
   Ooh, aren't they lovely!

Ralph is saying to Randy.

       RALPH
   Did you see Cher last night?

       RANDY
   No, I missed it.

       RALPH
   Chad Everett guest starred.

The doorbell rings. Mendy pushes the buzzer by the
intercom.

       MENDY
   You really would make a divine
   courtesan. I could set you up
   in business any old time.

       ANNIE
   What a lascivious thought. Have
   you got any ups?

29B   CONTD (2)

                    MENDY
          Only those yellow things.

                    ANNIE
          Have you got twenty?

                    MENDY
          But of course.

                    ANNIE
          And I probably won't be able
          to pay you 'til Thursday. I'm
          sorry.

                    MENDY
          Don't apologize. It's a sign
          of weakness.

There is a knock on the door. Mendy opens. A DRAG
QUEEN breezes in. He is dressed in a forties tweed
career girl suit. He is not swishy. More like
Rosalind Russell -- a successful illusion. Mendy
laughs as he sees him.

                    MENDY
               (to Queen)
          The kitchen is that way, my
          dear.

The queen kisses Mendy on both cheeks.

                    QUEEN
          Is it crepes again tonight, cheri?

                    MENDY
          Every night.

The queen slips into a chair facing Annie.
MENDY is sifting cocaine through a strainer
and onto a scale. Ralph hands Roscoe a joint.

                    RALPH
          Here. One toke of this and
          you're stunned on your ash.

                    ROSCOE
               (to Ralph)
          I'm seeing seven of my women
          today, so you can imagine what
          this means to me. Three of
          them, their husbands are in
          Europe. It's unbelievable.
                    (MORE)

29B   CONTD (3)

                    ROSCOE (Contd)
          Nobody has any money anymore.

The queen speaks to Annie as if they knew each other.

                    QUEEN
          Hello.

                    ANNIE
               (uncertain)
          I've forgotten your name.

                    QUEEN
          Chuck.

                    ANNIE
               (embarrassed)
          Oh, I didn't recognize you!

                    RANDY
          Are you a boy or a girl?

                    CHUCK
          If you can't tell the difference,
          it doesn't matter.

                    MENDY
               (to Annie)
          And how is that gorgeous man
          you live with?

                    ANNIE
          Who? Rudy? Oh, he's alright.

                    MENDY
               (to Roscoe)
          She lives with Rudy Frigidaire.

                    ROSCOE
          The songwriter?

                    RANDY
          I've heard of him, haven't I?

Mendy scrapes the weighed amount of cocaine into a
glasseine envelope, using a Tarot card.

                    CHUCK
               (to Randy)
          Did you go to C.W. Post College?

29B   CONTD (4)

                    MENDY
                (to Annie)
        You can tell him for me that any
        time he wants a rim job from an
        aging faggot, I'll be only too
        happy to oblige.

                    ANNIE
        Not Rudy. He's straight as a
        gate.

                    MENDY
        How boring.

                    ANNIE
                (sighs)
        Yes, heterosexuality is a bore,
        isn't it?

                    MENDY
        You really should drop him, you
        know. Monogamy has had it.

                    ANNIE
        And what about love?

                    MENDY
        Love? That went out with the
        sixties, my dear. All that
        emotional stuff. I mean, once
        you look at emotions from a
        certain angle you just can't
        take them seriously anymore.
        Can you?

                    ANNIE
        You mean...?

                    MENDY
        After all, what does it mean?
        It means you always have to have
        somebody else around, there's
        never enough room in bed, and you
        wake up to bad breath in the
        morning.

                    ANNIE
        Mendy, you always have such
        novel insights into things.

                    RANDY
        Oh, he just hangs around Andy
        Warhol and gets them from him.

29B   CONTD (5)

                         MENDY
               That way I don't have to think.
               I always agree with him anyway.

                         RANDY
                    (to Annie)
               Did you ever hear of Gaspara
               Stampa?

                         ANNIE
               No.

                         RANDY
               She was a divine courtesan of
               the Italian Renaissance, and her
               motto was: "All my delights and
               all my sports are these/ To
               live in flame and yet to feel
               no pain."

                         ANNIE
               How divine.
                    (she sighs)
               It's so difficult being a girl.

                         CHUCK
                    (nodding)
               Especially if you're a boy.

                         MENDY
               Are you going to the Phil Glass
               concert?

                         ANNIE
               Yeah. Rudy's agent got us
               tickets.

                                   CUT TO:

30   EXT: WEST SIDE HIGHWAY - DAY

Rudy and Annie, driving along in their pick-up truck.
Suddenly the car swerves out of control. The right
front wheel flies off the car and goes careening
down the highway. Cars screech and swerve to avoid
it. Rudy gets the pick-up under control.

                    ANNIE (V.O.)
                  (gives date)
          The car wheel broke ...

31   EXT: BROADWAY - DAY

Annie pushing Jesse along in the pushchair. It begins
to wobble. She looks down and sees the back wheel
fall off.

                    ANNIE (V.O.)
          The pushchair wheel broke ...

32   EXT: BROADWAY - DAY
       INSERT

CLOSE-UP of the heel of Annie's platform shoe. As
she's walking along, the heel breaks.

                    ANNIE (V.O.)
          ... and my shoe broke. All in
          one day.

33   INT: LIVING ROOM-BEDROOM - NIGHT

Annie is sprawled on the bed, writing in her diary.

                    ANNIE (V.O.)
          ... Am feeling slightly sous les
          temps lately. The old body is
          blowing hot and cold ...

Rudy is zonked out in front of the T.V. Sluggo
wanders in and out, looking for something.

                    ANNIE (V.O.)
          ... unpleasantly and disarmingly
          similar to being pregnant ...

34   INT: KITCHEN - DAY

Annie is nipping the mesoderm from her avocado plant.

                    ANNIE (V.O.)
          ... Rudy miserable. Stinks of
                    (MORE)

34   CONTD

                    ANNIE (V.O. (Contd)
          failure. Or thinks he does.
          Lois put down his new song.
          As usual. He got her to pay
          the phone bill in exchange for
          writing a song for some greasy
          Arab.

Through the door, we (and Annie) can see Rudy tinkering at the piano. He suddenly bursts out banging
madly and singing.

                    RUDY
          Thallus!
          Go back to your palace!

35   INT: LIVING ROOM-BEDROOM - NIGHT

Annie writing.

                    ANNIE (V.O.)
          ... Sad part is that for me
          it's a balancing act. Lustful
          interests; carnal desires;
          sexual obsessions against the
          old lure of fear and need and
          passionlessness. Positively
          pulsating with desire for Lois
          -- We are lovers unactivated.
          I called her Friday, the
          morning after that dreadful
          night.

                                        CUT TO:

36   INT: LIVING ROOM-BEDROOM - DAY

Annie is squatting on the floor, crouched over the
phone.

                    ANNIE
          Hi! It's me! ... Did I wake
          you up? ... I hope you're not
          mad at me. About last night.
          Rudy absolutely hates me this
          morning ... I think ...

She listens for a moment.

                    ANNIE
          Oh, I'm alright. Dying,
          actually ... My coil's got
                    (MORE)

36   CONTD

> ANNIE (Contd)
> displaced again ... I can't find
> the thread ... I dread going
> back to that fucking diaphragm
> ... It's such a drag ... And
> I can never get it over that
> hump.

She clutches her crotch and squeezes her thighs
together as if she were actually feeling the discomfort.

> ANNIE
> Listen, darling, to come right
> to the point, because Rudy's
> going to come in any minute ...
> the thing is ... the thing is
> this: that I'd like to do it
> with you ... you would? I'm
> wetting me nickers just thinking
> about it ... How about Monday?
> ... You can't? Can't you get
> out of it? ... No, I can't get
> out in the evenings. Rudy
> would shit. But I'm free in
> the daytime, 'til six ...
> Thursday? Can't we do it
> sooner than that? ... O.K.
> I'll call you Wednesday morning.
> 'Bye, darling!

CUT TO:

37   INT: LIVING ROOM-BEDROOM - NIGHT

Annie writing in diary.

> ANNIE (V.O.)
> But she had a screening on
> Wednesday, and I had to take
> Jesse to the doctor on Thursday,
> and we were supposed to get
> together on Friday, but I got
> the address wrong and we missed
> each other, and the weekend was
> shot, so it's tomorrow, Monday,
> 10 days later ...

CUT TO:

38   INT: LOIS' PLACE - DAY

Lois opens the door to reveal Annie on the threshhold.

                    ANNIE
               (excessively cheerful)
          Hi!

                    LOIS
               (boyishly hardy)
          Hi, toots!

They embrace awkwardly and break apart shyly. Annie
enters the main room and takes it in. It is all
white and devoid of furniture, except for a white-
sheeted mattress, a white telephone, and a white
lamp. The room's single big window faces out on a
small balcony, which in turn faces a plaza and
another giant modern building identical to the one
they are in.

                    ANNIE
          What a dreadful place this is!

                    LOIS
          Yeah, well, I'm gonna fix it
          up. I just haven't gotten
          around to it yet.

                    ANNIE
          Yes, but I mean it's the whole
          place. Those ghastly guards
          at the door ...

                    LOIS
          Well, you're not a single girl.
          Single girls have to be careful.
          We have to worry about things
          like that. About security.

Since there is nowhere to sit except the mattress,
Lois and Annie jockey around the room, keeping their
distance, like two fighters sizing each other up
around a ring.

                    ANNIE
          I've absolutely decided that I
          don't want to take acid.

                    LOIS
          Want some coffee? Want some
          dope? Want a drink? An up?
          A down?

38   CONTD

                    ANNIE
          Coffee.

Lois disappears into the kitchenette.

                    ANNIE
          How are you? What've you been
          doing?

                    LOIS (O.S.)
          Oh, I'm alright. Working hard.

                    ANNIE
          Did you ever get to fuck what's-
          his-name? That beautiful
          cameraman?

                    LOIS (O.S.)
          Nelson? Sure, ages ago. Didn't
          I tell you?

                    ANNIE
          Well, how was he?

                    LOIS (O.S.)
          Eh. Lots of wick and no wax.

                    ANNIE
          Lots of wick and no wax. What's
          that supposed to mean?

                    LOIS
               (emerging with two
                cups of coffee)
          Listen, honey, I'm beginning
          to think that half the men
          south of Fourteenth Street can't
          get it up ...

                    ANNIE
          Really?

                    LOIS
          ... and the other half are all
          faggots.

She hands Annie her coffee, gives her a quick pat on
the crotch and flounces away. Annie can't help but
blush.

                    LOIS
          That's why I'm turning to women.

38   CONTD (2)

                    ANNIE
          What about Hector?

                    LOIS
          I don't want to talk about him
          that way.
                    (slipping into her
                    Southern belle)
          Ah'm rilly ... Ah'm very attracted
          to him.

                    ANNIE
          How would you compare him to ...
          my Rudy, say?

                    LOIS
                    (flushed)
          Ah don't want to say. Ah
          rilly don't want to discuss it.

                    ANNIE
          Oh, alright.

She takes a swig of coffee. She is hurt.

                    LOIS
          Aw, don't be that way.

She puts her arm around Annie and gives her a squeeze
and a kiss on the cheek.

                    LOIS
          I think we should take it. I'm
          up for it. We might as well take
          it. We decided to.

She opens her hand. There are two little window panes
in it. She pops one into her mouth.

                    LOIS
          Open your mouth and close your
          eyes.

Annie obeys. Lois lays the acid on her tongue. Annie
washes it down with a swig of coffee.

                    ANNIE
          I'm sorry I fucked it up for
          you and Rudy the other night.

                    LOIS
          Oh, I can deal with it. It was
          too complicated anyway.

38   CONTD (3)

                    ANNIE
          It was my all my fault. If I
          hadn't been such a jealous
          bitch.

                    LOIS
          No, it was just too difficult
          because we all had such strong
          feelings.

                    ANNIE
          Oh, you mean you and Rudy.

                    LOIS
          No, I mean all of us.

                    ANNIE
          I know it's him you really want.

                    LOIS
          No.

                    ANNIE
          You want to get to him through me.

                    LOIS
          No, it's you I really want. Really.
          Not him.

                    ANNIE
          Anyway, it doesn't matter.

Annie goes out on the balcony, steps into the sunlight,
lifts her face to the sun, closes her eyes. Little
spasms go through her body, and she begins to breath
heavily.

Lois stands in the doorway, looking at her. Then
she disappears into the room and puts on a Phil Glass
record.

                    ANNIE
          I think I'm coming on.

                    LOIS
          You can't be. It's too soon.
          You're just overexcited.

Annie opens her eyes and looks out at the urban landscape. It wobbles ever so slightly, like the heat
from a car engine that makes the highway wobble on a
hot day. Annie flops down in a chair, puts her legs

38   CONTD (4)

up on the balcony rail, and lifts her skirt up to her
waist. She doesn't wear undies. She opens herself
to the sun.

Lois comes up behind her and begins to massage her
neck and shoulders. Annie sighs and leans her head
back, rubbing it against Lois' boobs. They stay
like that for a while, then Lois comes around the
front of Annie's chair, kneels down and kisses her.
It is a long, romantic, exploratory kiss.

Lois puts her arms around Annie, embraces her, and
gradually moves her hand down along Annie, along her
leg, to her thigh, and finally comes to rest on her
bush.

Annie leaps out of the chair and marches off into
the main room.

                    ANNIE
          This music is driving me nuts.
          Let's go outside, shall we?

                    LOIS
          Coward.

                    ANNIE
          This acid is making me jumpy.
          I need people. The smell of
          the streets. The press of flesh.
          That'll do the trick.

39   EXT: A STREET IN SOHO - DAY

Lois and Annie are parading down the street, hand in
hand. EVERYONE looks at them as they pass. They
both look very sexy, and have a kind of electric,
acid glow. They are basking in the attention they
are getting, flaunting the idea that they are lovers.

AN OLD WOMAN curses them in Italian.

Annie is dressed more the butch, Lois the femme. A
YOUNG CONSTRUCTION WORKER calls out to Lois.

                    CONSTRUCTION WORKER
               (indicating Annie)
          Hey, you go with him?

Lois and Annie clutch and swing their asses defiantly
as they pass him.

39   CONTD

                    ANNIE
               (suddenly paranoid)
          What did he mean, him?

                    LOIS
          Oh, nothing. He's just jealous.

                    ANNIE
          Do I look so butch?

                    LOIS
          No. Come on. This is fun.

                    ANNIE
          I was always afraid I should
          have been a man. I'm so big boned.

40   EXT: ANOTHER STREET IN SOHO - DAY

Annie sort of slumps against Lois.

                    LOIS
          What's wrong?

                    ANNIE
          My legs have suddenly gone all
          rubbery. This acid isn't working
          right. I need some Fernet Branca.

                    LOIS
          Here, let's go into this bar.

They head into a seedy Italian bar.

                    ANNIE
          Don't you feel anything?

                    LOIS
          Do I? I come in my pants every
          time someone looks at us.

                    ANNIE
          I meant the acid.

They enter the bar.

41   INT: SEEDY ITALIAN BAR - DAY

It is dark inside. A sprinkling of BAR TYPES are
congregated at the end of the bar, watching a football game on television.

41   CONTD

Annie and Lois come in, giggling conspiratorially.
Everyone in the bar looks around at them. They stride
up to the bar like two cowboys, leaning each on a
single elbow.

The BARTENDER comes up to take their order.

                    ANNIE
          Fernet Branca?

The bartender nods and looks to Lois.

                    LOIS
          Bourbon.

                    BARTENDER
          With a little ice?

                    LOIS
          Straight up.

                    BARTNEDER
                (annoyed)
          Straight up.

Lois sees the football watchers staring at them. She
leans over and whispers something to Annie. They
both laugh. The bartender sets their drinks in front
of them and stands there glaring. They both put away
their drinks in single gulps and plonk their glasses
down together.

                    LOIS
                (to the bartender)
          Do it again.

A guy calls out from the end of the bar.

                    BARFLY
          Hey, you two like each other?

                    ANNIE AND LOIS
                (flushed with wicked
                  pleasure)
          Yes.

                    BARFLY
          Hey, show us how you do it.

They kiss. The audience cheers. The bartender leans
over the bar, grabs them both by the hair and pulls
them apart.

41   CONTD (2)

                        BARTENDER
Oh, no! None of that in my place!

                        ANNIE
Get your hands off, you creep!

                        LOIS
What's the matter? Can't handle it?

                        BARTENDER
I don't want no fucking dyke shit
in my bar. Get your asses outa
here.

                        LOIS
With pleasure.

                        ANNIE
How much for the rot gut?

                        BARTENDER
I don't want your filthy bull
dyke money. I just wanna see
you outa here, now. I don't
wanna catch your germs.

                        LOIS
Ah, I'll bet you can't even get
it up.

They exit.

42   EXT: CANAL STREET - DAY

Annie and Lois, a little more subdued and a little
more stoned, walk into the stream of PEOPLE
browsing on Canal St. Seen from their P.O.V.,
the crowds of people seem to undulate. Lois
steadies herself against a lamppost.

                        LOIS
Whooh. Everything's spinning.

She makes a concerted effort to control herself.
She shuts her eyes, she clenches her teeth, she
breathes deeply. She gets a grip on herself and
marches ahead, very deliberately, smiling, having
won.

                        ANNIE
What are you doing?

42   CONTD

                         LOIS
              I like to prove to myself that I
              can control it.

                         ANNIE
              What a curious idea.

We see the street scene from Annie's P.O.V. as they
walk along. The tone of things has changed. Faces
seem mean, the streets are filthy and squalid. She
notices ugly things: dogshit, garbage, greasy things,
dingy corners, vulgar junk on sale at the outdoor
stands.

                         ANNIE
              This isn't working. People
              aren't right. I thought that
              people would do it, but they're
              not right. Rudy always tells
              me I shouldn't take acid in the
              city. I need <u>vividness</u>. I
              need <u>green</u>.

                                        CUT TO:

43   EXT: LA GUARDIA PLACE - DAY

First the frame is filled with green grass. Annie runs
into the frame, barefoot, holding her shoes in one
hand. The camera pulls back and tilts up with her,
revealing her on the lawn in front of the Grand Union
supermarket. Annie falls to the ground by a big bush.
She throws herself on her back, arms and legs akimbo,
her head under the bush, the rest of her sticking out.
Lois comes along and lies down beside her, a bit more
sedately, and lays her head on Annie's outstretched
arm.

44   INT: LOIS' BATHROOM - DAY

The bathroom is empty. We hear, off camera, the
sounds of Annie and Lois stumbling into the apartment,
breathless. Annie dashes into the bathroom, and in
a rapid series of deft strokes, lifts her skirt,
sets down on the toilet and pees, heaving a big sigh
as she lets it out. Catching her breath, she moans
with exaggerated pleasure at the release.

                         ANNIE (O.S.)
                   (shouting to Annie)
              Can I take a shower? I feel like
              a lump of spit.

44   CONTD

                          LOIS (O.S.)
             You bet.

Annie turns on the shower and starts to undress. As
she does, she glances around the room, She browses
through Lois' medicine chest, helping herself to a
couple of vitamins, spraying herself with some colcgne,
trying out some deodorant ... She is in a stage of
her acid trip where everything around her drips with
sensuality. She climbs into the shower and lets
the water pour all over her. She opens different
parts of herself to the spray.

Lois steps into the shower.

                        ANNIE
             Oh, darling, you look so beautiful!

Annie, who has been soaping herself with one of those
mitten-like washcloths, now begins to soap Lois.
She touches her hungrily, particularly her tits --
she squeezes them, kneads them, strokes them, weighs
them.

                        ANNIE
             Only twice in my life did I
             have tits like that. When I was
             a mother. And they they were so
             sore, and the rest of me was so
             wasted that I couldn't get any
             pleasure out of them ... Rudy
             used to love suck them and
             squeeze them and make the milk
             squirt out of them ... But it
             hurt so much.

Lois takes Annie's head in her hands and kisses her.

                        LOIS
             Let's not talk about Rudy.

                        ANNIE
             I'm sorry, darling.

They embrace and kiss and rub their soapy bodies
against one another. In their struggling, they slip
and fall in the bathtub, have a moment's panic,
then laugh, then try to embrace again. But they keep
slipping and sliding at the bottom of the tub.

                        LOIS
             Let's get out of here.

CUT TO:

45   INT: LOIS' LIVING ROOM - DAY

The two girls come out of the bathroom, towelling
themselves. Annie steps into a shaft of sunlight
that cuts across the room. She closes her eyes and
swoons. Lois comes up behind her and begins towelling Annie's legs, working her way up to the crotch.

               ANNIE
        (gasps)
      EVERYTHING'S so vivid! I'm
      positively pulsating with desire
      for you.

Lois kisses Annie's thighs and moves toward her bush.
Annie takes her by the shoulders and lifts her to
her feet.

               ANNIE
      Let me do you. I want to do
      it to you. I want to look at
      you, and touch you all over. I
      don't even know what other women
      look like. How they're built.
      Let me, please!

Annie goes over to the mattress and starts dragging
it across the floor.

               ANNIE
      Here, let's take this out on the
      balcony where we can be in the
      sun.

Bemused, Lois helps her drag the mattress out on the
balcony.

               LOIS
      (half-serious)
      Sometimes I think you're just
      using me.

               ANNIE
      (slightly hurt,
       slightly guilty)
      How can you say that? Don't
      you know how I feel about you?
      Here, come and I'll show you.

She pulls Lois down onto the mattress. She kisses
her lips, her earlobes, the soft dent in her neck
below her jaw, finally working her way down to the

45   CONTD

tits. She sucks and kneads and licks Lois' tits.
She tries to tickle the nipple into erection with
her tongue, but it doesn't respond. She looks over
to Lois, who is lying back, staring at the ceiling.

                    ANNIE
              (softly)
          Is this too awful for you, darling?

Lois throws an arm over her eyes.

                    LOIS
          No, go on. It just takes time,
          that's all. Just give me a
          little time.

Annie sits back and looks at Lois' body. She considers
it in all its aspects. She strokes her tentatively
here and there. She gently opens Lois' legs and looks
at her bush.

                    ANNIE
          Ooh, you have such cute, fat
          little lips.

Lois squirms with embarrassment. She tries to close
her legs.

                    LOIS
          Don't say things like that.

Annie pries open her thighs again.

                    ANNIE
          Shhhh.

Annie gets down on her elbows leaning her head just a
few inches from Lois' bush. She gently separates the
pubic hairs to reveal her outer lips, sealed. She
rubs her thumb up and down along the slit. She kisses
the lips gently and then strokes them some more.
Very slowly, they begin to open slightly and reveal a
little of the pink flesh inside.

                    ANNIE
          Oh, my dear. It's a miracle.

She leans forward and begins to lick and kiss and suck
Lois' puss with greater and greater passion. Lois,
finally beginning to loosen up, reaches down and runs
her fingers through Annie's hair. They both sigh
audibly.

45   CONTD (2)

After a few moments of this, Annie sits back to catch
her breath. She plays idly with Lois' pubic hair
with her fingers. She spreads open the lips and
admires the plump configurations of pink flesh.

                    ANNIE
          Yours is so beautiful. Mine looks
          like old shoeleather.

                    LOIS
          Oh, go on. Stop always doing
          yourself in.

Lois lifts herself up a little and puts a hand between
Annie's legs. Annie gently inserts a finger into
Lois' vagina. Lois sighs, closes her eyes, and
leans back against the wall. Annie is transfixed
with the fascination of exploring another woman's
insides. She pulls her finger out for a second,
then looks at it and chuckles. It has a drop of
blood on it. Lois sits up in panic. She looks at
Annie's finger and screams.

                    LOIS
          Oh no! It's not fair!

Annie laughs some more and sniffs her finger.

                    ANNIE
          Don't worry, darling. I don't
          mind. Rudy says he likes the
          taste.

She licks her finger tentatively, savors it, wrinkles
her nose. Lois bursts into tears and runs for the
bathroom.

                    LOIS
          No, no, no, no, no.

Annie continues to laugh. The phone rings. Annie
wanders into the living room to answer it, still
laughing.

                    ANNIE
               (cheerily)
          Hello!

                              CUT TO:

46   EXT: RUDY'S APARTMENT - DAY

Rudy has the receiver to his ear and a look of
consternation on his face. He hears Annie's voice
on the phone.

46   CONTD

                        ANNIE (O.S.)
          Hello ...

                        LOIS (O.S.)
          Who is it?

                        ANNIE (O.S.)
          Dunno ... Sounds like one of
          those faggot breathers.

Rudy hangs up the phone, humiliated.

47   INT: LIVING ROOM-BEDROOM - NIGHT

Annie is curled up on the bed, writing in her diary.
Rudy is zonked out on the couch, watching the eleven
o'clock news.

                        BASCOM
                   (on the T.V.)
          A bizarre saga came to an even
          more bizarre ending today with
          the marriage of Charles Merz and
          Geraldine Longhetti in Manhattan
          District Court. Merz, 53, formerly
          a millionaire commodities broker,
          was sent to jail ten years ago
          for hiring two men to throw lye in
          Miss Longhetti's face to prevent
          her from running off with another
          man. He was released from prison
          last week and immediately initiated
          a search for his former fiancee.
          Private detectives traced her to
          a cold water flat in the Bay Ridge
          area of Brooklyn, nearly blind,
          abandoned by the man who had been
          Mr. Merz' rival ten years earlier,
          and living on welfare. They were
          married by Judge Nicholas Beretta,
          who pronounced sentence on Merz
          ten years ago. The couple will
          honeymoon in Bahrein and then
          settle down into Merz' newly-
          acquired penthouse on Sutton Place.
          When asked what plans she had,
          Mrs. Merz replied, "to get paid
          back" before she was hustled away
          by the groom. Channel 11 News
          would like to wish the newlyweds
          all the luck in the world. They're
          certainly going to need it.

47   CONTD

Rudy looks from the T.V. to Annie, who is engrossed
in her writing. At some point, she feels him staring
at her. She looks up, struck by the reproach in his
eyes and looks back to her diary. Here is what she
has written:

CLOSE-UP - DIARY

"I am looking for a mentor, hopefully a woman:
possibly blonde. The more serious business is the
present state of my feelings about Lois, which are
pressing on infatuation ... "

Without looking up, Rudy asks:

                    RUDY
          How was Mendy's?

Annie looks up.

                    ANNIE
          Oh, alright. The usual gay parade.

She goes back to her diary.

                    RUDY
          Stay long?

                    ANNIE
               (not looking up)
          Sure. Ever have a short visit to
          Mendy's?

She goes back to writing:

" ... It's so adorable to be in love with a woman
and feel her sweet touches and little small thing.
It's probably fairly awful for her and not what
she wants at all ... I had a very strong sense the
other day that she was turned off by the wornness of
my body. It would be so normal. I remember clearly
being shocked by older bodies five years ago."

She looks up to find Rudy staring reproachfully at her.

                    RUDY
          Did you stay there all afternoon?

                    ANNIE
          Where?

                    RUDY
          At Mendy's?

47   CONTD (2)

                    ANNIE
          What the fuck does he know about
          love?

                    RUDY
          Who?

                    ANNIE
          Bascom Hunt. Supercilious asshole.

                    RUDY
               (shouting)
          Why didn't you tell me you were
          with Lois today?!

                    ANNIE
          So it was you who called!

                    RUDY
          You bet your boobies it was me!

                    ANNIE
          Why were you calling her? To
          make a date I bet.

                    RUDY
          Looking for you!

                    ANNIE
          What rot! I'll bet you've been
          sticking it to her ever since
          that night. Maybe even before,
          I'll bet.

                    RUDY
          What?

Just then, the doorbell rings. Huey begins to bark
raucously. Rudy goes for the door.

                    RUDY
               (to Huey)
          Shut up you cur!

He opens the door. Lois bursts in, drunk.

                    LOIS
          Hi, Rudy!

She throws herself into his arms and kisses him.
Just then Annie appears at the end of the hall to
see who's there. She freezes. Lois turns to see
her.

47   CONTD (3)

                         LOIS
              Hi, toots!
                   (giggles)
              I'm twisted to the tits!

As she starts toward Annie to kiss her, we discover
that she has another person in tow. She drags him
through the door.

                         LOIS
              Look what I picked up. He's
              Brazilian or something. Aren't
              you honey?

He is an exceedingly thin, gentle looking fellow,
carrying a saxophone case. While Rudy and GLAUBER
shake hands, Lois stumbles up to Annie and throws
her arms around her.

                         LOIS
              Peter Goldschmidt is waiting for
              me at my place, so we couldn't
              go there, and this one's got
              a wife or something, so we
              couldn't go to his place, so I
              thought I'd bring him over here
              and fuck him in your spare room.
              It's O.K., isn't it?

                         ANNIE
                   (nonplussed)
              Oh, sure, of course.

                         LOIS
              What's the matter? Have you
              been crying?

They proceed out of frame toward the kitchen, as
Rudy and Glauber enter and cross.

                         GLAUBER
              Rudy Frigidaire. I like very
              much your work. Do you know
              Phillip Glass? I play sometimes
              with him.

                         RUDY
              That's where I've seen you! Say,
              you're not Arabian are you? You
              look sort of Arabian.

47   CONTD (4)

                        GLAUBER
          My father's family -- all Arabs.

                        RUDY
          Dynamite! Lissen, I've been
          diddlin' around with this tune.
          You wanna lay down some Arabian
          fills for me?

                        GLAUBER
          Of course. But what is this
          you call diddling?

                                        CUT TO:

48   INT: KITCHEN - NIGHT

Annie opens the fridge and gets out two bags of
Zabars coffee, one labeled Vienna, the other labeled
Katmandu -- and pours a little of each into her
Peugeot electric coffee grinder. Lois is giggling.
She starts to speak.

                        LOIS
          He's cute, ain't he? I saw
          him on the street and I
          suddenly remembered what you
          said about skinny men. You
          know. That they have such
          big ...

Annie turns on the grinder, furiously, drowning out
her voice with the din. She turns off the grinder.
She puts a paper liner inside the top of her
Melitta coffee pot. She pours the ground coffee
into the liner. She keeps her back to Lois. We
hear Rudy and Glauber tinkering with piano and
saxophone in another room all through the scene.

                        LOIS
          You've got a fabulous ass.

                        ANNIE
                (under her breath)
          A lot you care.

Annie crosses to the stove.

                        LOIS
          What?

48   CONTD

Annie picks up the kettle with a bare hand and begins
to pour boiling water over the ground coffee.

                    ANNIE
          Nothing. Ow!

She drops the kettle, scalding herself.

                    LOIS
              (aha!)
          Are you jealous?

Annie sits down in defeat. She cries and shakes her
scalded hand up and down.

                    ANNIE
          It's nothing. I'm just a little
          weepy this evening, that's all.

Perry sticks his head through the door, a big, stoned
smile on his face.

                    PERRY
          Do ah smell coffee?

                                        CUT TO:

49   INT: RUDY'S PIANO ROOM - NIGHT

Glauber is standing in the middle of the room,
wearing a pair of headphones, and playing his saxophone into a little microphone which leads to a little
SONY cassette recorder. He plays a plastic sax. He
is obviously playing accompaniment to what he is
hearing through the phones, but we don't hear it.
We only hear him.

Rudy sits at the piano listening with eyes closed.
Glauber plays with eyes closed. After a little
while, Lois wanders in and tiptoes over to sit beside Rudy. Rudy reaches over and strokes one of her
tits. She slaps his hand away and gets up just as
Annie appears in the doorway. Glauber continues
playing, oblivious. Annie disappears from the doorway. Presently Glauber comes to the end of his
piece. Everybody applauds.

Rudy stops the tape recorder and starts to rewind it.
He gives Glauber the high sign.

                    RUDY
          Aces all the way.

49   CONTD

Lois puts her arm around Glauber.

                    LOIS
          That was beautiful, honey, just
          beautiful ...

                    GLAUBER
          Tank you ver' much.

                    LOIS
          ... but what do you say we get
          down to business? Don't you
          have to be home pretty soon?

                    GLAUBER
          Is true.

Rudy starts to leave.

                    RUDY
          Thanks again.

                    GLAUBER
          I am at the your orders.

                    LOIS
               (to Glauber)
          Put that thing over there and
          you come over here.

Rudy exits.

                              CUT TO:

50   EXT: STREET - NIGHT

Rudy walking dogs. It is late at night and the streets
are deserted. Walking past a brownstone, a pair of
red woman's shoes come flying out of a third floor
window and land with a crash on a car hood, just missing Rudy. Rudy stops and tries to see where they
came from. A moment later, an inebriated middle-
aged woman sticks her head out of the window.

                    WOMAN
          Goodbye, red shoes. Goodbye.
          Goodbye. You served us well.
          Goodbye.

51-53   INT: TOWN HALL - NIGHT

We see the back, shoulders and heads of Lois, Rudy,
and Annie seated in the AUDIENCE, watching PHIL
GLASS and his ENSEMBLE performing.

The music is somewhat like what one imagines the
Heavenly Spheres to sound like. It is rhythmic,
airy, monotonous and continuous, each instrument
supporting the flow, and simultaneously weaving
intricate variations. Cosmic but not corny. Also
erotic. We notice Glauber playing in the ensemble.

We see Annie, Rudy and Lois from the front. Each
is posed in an attitude of concentration and
participation in the music.

Rudy glances at Annie out of the side of his eye
and notices that her eyes are closed. He puts hand
on her thigh. Without opening her eyes, she
squeezes his hand. Then he glances over at Lois.
She is slumped down in her seat, with her arms
crossed over her breasts. Rudy places his other
hand gingerly on Lois thigh. Lois doesn't respond.
After a decent interval, he tries to press it
deeper between her legs and up closer towards her
crotch. She pulls his hand away and throws it
back in his own lap. He puts it back on its
original spot on her thigh.

Lois puts her arm around the back of Rudy's seat.
She reaches around until she can touch Annie's
shoulder. Annie glances sidewise at Rudy. Then she
reaches her arm around the back of Rudy's seat.

(CONTINUED)

51-
53   CONTD

     We see them all from the front: Rudy has one hand
     on each of the girls' thighs, and the two girls
     each have an arm around the back of Rudy's seat.
     All three are staring at the stage, pretending to
     be totally involved in the music.

     We see them from the back, the two girls' hands
     clasped behind Rudy's seat.

54   INT: LIVING ROOM-BEDROOM - DAY

     Annie is packing. She goes from room to room in the
     apartment, looking for things to take with her. She
     has only a suitcase and a satchel and can only take
     selected items. There is no one else in the place.
     She moves about expressionlessly, but the way she
     does what she does betrays her hysteria -- she is
     constantly stuffing something into her suitcase,
     then pulling it out and replacing it with something
     else.

55   INT: LIVING ROOM-BEDROOM - NIGHT

     Rudy bursts in with Jesse and the dogs in tow. He
     dashes to the T.V. and flicks it on. An envelope
     that says "Rudy" is taped to the television screen,
     but Rudy doesn't notice it.

                         JESSE
               Is The Munsters on?

                         RUDY
               No, I keep tellin' ya, kid.
               It's the big game.

     Rudy dashes to the bathroom and turns on the bath
     water. He returns to the foyer.

                         RUDY
                    (to Jesse)
               Get your coat off, I'm gonna
               feed the dogs.

     He rushes off to the kitchen, with the dogs pawing
     after him.

56   INT: KITCHEN - NIGHT

     Rudy flicks on the radio by the stove and turns it
     to MARV ALBERT giving the play by play of the game.
     It is well toward the end of the first quarter.

56   CONTD

He opens two cans of dog food, dumps them into a
big bowl. Then he adds dry food, struggling with
a 25 lb. bag. He mushes them together, adds some
water. The dogs are all over him. He sets the
bowl down in the hall and dashes away. The dogs
attack the food savagely.

57   INT: FOYER - NIGHT

Rudy enters, glancing anxiously at the T.V. Jesse
stops him in the foyer.

                    JESSE
          My tushy hurts.

Rudy bends down and unbuttons Jesse's pants.

                    RUDY
          Here. Go take a shit.

He rushes into the living room. It is only at this
point that he notices the envelope stuck to the
screen, because it is blocking his view. But that's
as far as his attention to it goes. He tears it off
the screen and discards it on the couch. Just in
time to catch WALT FRAZIER in a fantastic layup.

                                        CUT TO:

58   INT: RUDY'S ROOM - DAY

Annie tiptoes into Rudy's room. She glances around,
finally finds a pencil and a sheet of music notation
paper. She leans on top of the piano and begins to
write: "Dearest Rudy..."

She pauses and tries to think just how to put it.
She starts to write again.

                                        CUT TO:

59   INT: LIVING ROOM-BEDROOM - NIGHT

Rudy hears Jesse scream from the bathroom.

                    JESSE (V.O.)
          Ow! Ow, ow!

Rudy hurries to the bathroom.

60   INT: BATHROOM - NIGHT

Jesse is perched on the toilet, pants down. His face

60   CONTD

is bright red, from pushing. The room is filled with
steam.

> RUDY
> (coming in)
> What's the trouble, kid?

> JESSE
> My tushy hurts! Ow! Ow!

Rudy squats down in front of him and begins to massage
his stomach. With his other hand, he turns on a
little transistor radio that sits on a shelf by the
bathtub. He flicks the dial to Marve Albert.

> RUDY
> Relaxez-vous. It'll come. Don't
> try so hard.

> JESSE
> Ow!

Suddenly Jesse notices that the bathtub is overflowing.

> JESSE
> Look, Daddy!

> RUDY
> Holy shit!

He dives at the taps, turns them off, and opens the
drain. His right elbow strays into the water. He
looks down and there is water all over the floor.
Jesse is enjoying it tremendously. Rudy dashes out
of the room.

61   INT: KITCHEN - NIGHT

He dashes in, pulls a mop and a pail out of the
broom closet, and dashes back out. Marv Albert
describes a fantastic battle under the boards.

62   INT: FOYER - NIGHT

Dashing through, he pauses to glance through the
French doors at the game. He sees PHIL CHENIER
steal the ball from Clyde.

> RUDY
> Oh, no!

62   CONTD

                    JESSE
          Daddy, it's getting all over!

Rudy tears himself away and goes back to the bathroom.

63   INT: BATHROOM - NIGHT

Jesse is still on the pot, having a good time.

                    JESSE
          I can't get down. Because
          there's water on the floor.

                    RUDY
          Try not to be so obvious, kid.

He begins to swab the floor and wring the mop into
the bucket. He closes the drain. Half of the water
has gone out of the tub. He pulls Jesse's pants
off, then struggles with his T-shirt, while Jesse
remains seated on the throne.

                    RUDY
          Any luck?

Jesse shakes his head.

                    JESSE
          No.

Rudy looks in the toilet. It is full of shit.

                    RUDY
          Whaddya mean, no?

Jesse looks.

                    JESSE
          I was laughing and I forgot
          to hold it in.

                    RUDY
          See. When you stop worryin'
          about it, it just comes out.
          O.K. Ready ... Steady ...

He lifts Jesse up and plunks him into the bath.

                    JESSE
          Eddie!

63   CONTD

          Rudy starts off.

                              RUDY
                    O.K. Call me when you're ready
                    to get out. I'm gonna go watch
                    the game.

                              JESSE
                    Cold!

          Rudy turns around. Jesse is seated in eight inches
          of water.

                              RUDY
                    Oh. Sorry, kid.

          He turns on the taps, tests the water in his finger.

                              RUDY
                    You know how to turn it off,
                    right?

                              JESSE
                    Yeah.

                              RUDY
                    Well, just make sure you turn
                    it off before it gets too deep.
                    O.K.?

                              JESSE
                         (luxuriating)
                    O.K., Dad.

          Rudy exits.

64   INT: LIVING ROOM-BEDROOM - NIGHT

          Rudy enters and sits down on the couch by the T.V.
          He settles into the game. The Bullets are running
          the ball all over the floor, but the Knicks are
          playing super defense. DE BUSCHERRE is crashing
          away at the offensive boards, and BRADLEY has
          the hot hand. Rudy squirms in the couch. He
          reaches underneath his behind and discovers that
          he has been sitting on the envelope. It bulges.
          He opens it and pulls out a cassette. He looks
          at it with curiosity, then flicks it onto the
          T.V. table, and gets back into the game.

                                             CUT TO:

65   INT: RUDY'S ROOM - DAY

Annie crumples up the paper she's been writing on and
throws it away. A microphone on a little plastic
stand and a little cassette tape recorder set up
on the piano ... Annie pushes the "Rewind" button,
then "stop," then "play." She hears Rudy singing
and playing a single phrase, over and over again,
trying it different ways, not getting it right.
The words of the phrase are:

                      RUDY
              With you,
              Without you,
              Over you,
              Or around you ... (etc.)

She runs it forward until she comes to dead tape.
She pushes the "record" and "play" buttons. She
speaks:

                     ANNIE
              Dearest Rudy ...

She stops the machine, rewinds, and begins again,
this time, trying it in a slightly different tone
of voice.

                     ANNIE
              Dearest Rudy, darling ...

                                   CUT TO:

66   INT: LIVING ROOM-BEDROOM - NIGHT

Rudy intently watching the game.

                     JESSE (V.O.)
                 (shouting)
              Daddy!

Rudy ignores it, too engrossed.

                     JESSE (V.O.)
              DADDY!!!

                     RUDY
              WHADDYA WANT!?

                     JESSE (V.O.)
              I WANNA GET OUT!

                     RUDY
              I'LL BE IN IN A MINUTE!

66   CONTD

> BOB WOLF (V.O.)
> Here's Luke with the bomb ...

> CAL RAMSEY (V.O.)
> Who says Jerry Lucas is finished?

> JESSE (V.O.)
> O.K. I'm ready, Daddy!

Rudy exits, harrassed. We watch the game continue.
We hear the sounds of Rudy getting Jesse out of the
bath. Presently he enters carrying Jesse, swathed
in a towel, and crosses to his spot on the couch.

> JESSE
> But you didn't sing, Rockabye Baby.

He pulls Jesse into his lap.

> RUDY
> Shaddap, willya? Let's watch
> the game.

He pulls Jesse into his lap and their eyes glaze
over and become glued to the tube.

> BOB WOLF (V.O.)
> (Knicks announcer)
> There's the buzzer! That's
> the end of the first half, and
> Cal and I will be back with a
> recap and a special report on
> Willis Reed's knees, right after
> this ...

> RUDY
> Shit.

CUT TO:

67   INT: JESSE'S ROOM - NIGHT

Rudy is tucking Jesse into his crib.

CUT TO:

68   INT: FOYER - DAY

Annie sighs, picks up her bags, takes one last look
around and crosses to the door. We can see the
envelope by the T.V. screen in the background. The
dogs follow, excited. They think they're going for
a walk.

68   CONTD

                         ANNIE
               Stay here, darlings. Stay here.
               Mummy'll see you soon.

She leaves. The dogs sit staring at the closed door.

                                        CUT TO:

69   INT: LIVING ROOM-BEDROOM - NIGHT

Rudy comes back into the room. Somebody is being
awarded something on the basketball court. It is
half-time. Now Rudy notices, as if for the first
time, the cassette. He takes it and exits.

70   INT: RUDY'S ROOM - NIGHT

Rudy enters, puts the cassette in the recorder and
turns it on.

                         ANNIE (V.O.)
               Rudy, darling Rudy ... I don't
               know how to say this. I'm such
               a coward I couldn't do it in
               person. I couldn't bear to
               look in your eyes. And anyway,
               if you were here, you wouldn't
               let me finish ... So, I'm doing
               it this way. Forgive me, my
               darling: I'm leaving you ...

There is a long pause, followed by a click. Rudy
is stunned.

                                        CUT TO:

71   INT: RUDY'S ROOM - DAY

Annie pushes the "stop" button. She paces up and
down, then goes back, pushes "play" and "record."

                         ANNIE
               I don't know exactly where I'll
               be staying yet. I'm going to
               try to find myself a little
               apartment. Maybe a sublet or
               something like that.

She turns it off, then on again.

                         ANNIE
               Darling, none of this really
                         (MORE)

71   CONTD

                    ANNIE (Contd)
          has anything to do with you.
          It's all my fault. I seem
          bent on destroying you and me.
          It's the oddest thing, since
          it's so unadmittable. The
          root is in an enormous instinct
          to be alone; to be allowed time
          and turmoil with no distractions.
          It's so hard to cope with one's
          own life and I feel in a shock of
          confusion when everyone is around.
          It would restore my ego a lot --
          my psyche -- to be alone again.
          Learn to be brave again.

                                        CUT TO:

72   INT: RUDY'S ROOM - NIGHT

Rudy listening, in shock.

                    ANNIE (V.O.)
          I wonder a lot if it's all over,
          our love affair. I feel so
          humiliated ...

                    RUDY
          Humiliated?

                    ANNIE
          ... by the slow winding down of
          our once beautiful and lovely
          relationship.

                    RUDY
          But, Annie! ...

                    ANNIE
          We don't share that private
          pool we used to. It all
          dribbles out in day after day
          of being nice to each other.
          In spraying roaches, cleaning
          guck off the floor.
                    (sighs)
          One can probably only meet up
          with an individual every so
          often, even if they are the
          person you love most. Sorry,
          my darling, and give me a bit
          more time. It's so confusing,
                    (MORE)

72   CONTD

> ANNIE (Contd)
> being wracked with desire for
> women ...

Rudy punches the "stop" button.

> RUDY
> Wracked with desire for women?!

He pats his pockets feverishly feeling for his
cigarettes. He dashes out of the room.

73   INT: LIVING ROOM-BEDROOM - NIGHT

Rudy rushes in and grabs his cigarettes. He glances
at the T.V.

> BOB WOLFE (V.O.)
> Five seconds on the 24 second
> clock! ... Three! ... Two!

Rudy doesn't wait to see if they make it. He goes
back to his room.

74   INT: RUDY'S ROOM - NIGHT

Rudy presses the "play" button.

> ANNIE (V.O.)
> You're so dear to me. It's
> just that sometimes one has to
> rearrange things in a relationship
> when some part of it is cramping
> it too noticeably. Do you
> understand what I mean?

> RUDY
> No.

> ANNIE (V.O.)
> But who knows how long it will
> take or whether I'll ever come
> out of it? How can I ask you
> to wait for me? ... Oh, what's
> the use of worrying? Whether I
> stayed with you or not, we'd
> grind together through this
> poverty and sure as eggs is eggs,
> you'd take off with Lois or the
> next one whenever success rides
> you along on the next crest.
> (MORE)

74   CONTD

                    ANNIE (V.O.)
                    (Contd)
          There are plenty of hot little
          groupies around, looking for a
          free ride.

                    RUDY
          Now wait just a goddam minute!

He punches the off button. When he realizes that he
is powerless to reply, he turns it back on.

                    ANNIE (V.O.)
          I didn't mean that. I'm sorry.
          I just meant there are lots of
          people around who could encourage
          you tremendously much more than
          me. Lois, for instance. Isn't
          it likely that she will be the
          heiress to our relationship?

                    RUDY
          Fat chance.

                    ANNIE (V.O.)
          She'd look after you in all
          those ways that I never do for
          you. And she'd look up to you
          too, just as I do.

                    RUDY
          You're perverted. You're really
          perverted.

                    ANNIE
          Oh, fuck it all. What the hell.
          What's the use? Tighten up and
          move out. I'll stop caring
          altogether. It's too exhausting.
          If I am nothing, then let me be
          nothing.

                                        CUT TO:

75   INT: RUDY'S ROOM - DAY

Tears streaming down Annie's cheeks.

                    ANNIE
          All the present vanities will
          have to go. No more nail varnish
                    (MORE)

75   CONTD

                         ANNIE (Contd)
             etc. Get fat. Eat when I want.
             Fuck exercising. Fuck love.
             Fuck other people. Fuck.

She presses the "stop" button.

                                        CUT TO:

76   INT: RUDY'S ROOM - NIGHT

Rudy listening to dead tape. He pushes the "stop"
button.

77   EXT: RIVERSIDE DRIVE - SUNSET

Annie standing in a phone booth, her two suitcases
parked outside. She is dialing a number.

78   INT: LOIS' OFFICE - BERNIE'S DESK - SUNSET

Bernie, Lois' gay secretary, at his desk outside
Lois' office. The phone rings. He answers it.

                         BERNIE
             Ms. Lang's office.

                         ANNIE
             Hello, is she in? This is Annie.

                         BERNIE
             Annie who? Do we know you?

                         ANNIE
             Of course she knows me.

                         BERNIE
             How does she know you?

                         ANNIE
             Through the man that I lived
             with, you asshole -- Rudy
             Frigidaire.

                         BERNIE
             Oh, that Annie! Why didn't you
             say so? Did you say "lived"?

                         ANNIE
             Yes, now put her on.

73   CONTD

                    BERNIE
          I would. Except that she isn't
          here.

                    ANNIE
          When will she be back?

                    BERNIE
          She's gone for the day. Can I
          have her call you?

                    ANNIE
          I'm not at home.

                    BERNIE
          Well, you could try her at her
          place. In about an hour. Unless
          she goes straight to dinner with
          Johnny Fontaine.

                    ANNIE
          Do you know where they're eating?

                    BERNIE
          He has a piece of a bar down in
          the Village. Ernesto's.

                    ANNIE
          Well, if you speak to her, tell
          her I'm trying to reach her. O.K.?

                              CUT TO:

79   EXT: RIVERSIDE DRIVE - SUNSET

                    ANNIE
          Thanks. 'Bye.

      She hangs up. She dials another number and gets a
      busy signal. She dials another number.

                              CUT TO:

80   INT: GUNILLA'S PLACE - SUNSET

      The phone rings in the empty apartment

81   EXT: RIVERSIDE DRIVE - SUNSET

      Annie looks in her wallet. She finds seven dollars
      and change. She gets on a bus with her two suitcases.

82   INT: LOIS' PLACE - NIGHT

The phone rings in the empty apartment.

83   INT: ERNESTO'S - NIGHT

Annie is at the pay phone outside of the ladies' room at Ernesto's. She hangs up the phone and dials again.

                          CUT TO:

84   INT: LOIS' OFFICE - BERNIE'S DESK - NIGHT

The phone rings in the empty office.

85   INT: ERNESTO'S - NIGHT

Annie hangs up the phone and crosses to a stool at the end of the bar, where her suitcases are parked. The BARTENDER comes over.

                    BARTENDER
The headwaiter asked me to tell
you that Mr. Fontaine has cancelled
his reservation for tonight.

                    ANNIE
      (sighs)
I see. Any idea where they went?

                    BARTENDER
      (shakes head)
Sorry.

                    ANNIE
Let me have another double.

She looks over the faces of the other PEOPLE at the bar, as she takes a gulp of her drink. Her eyes connect with those of a swarthy man in his forties. He smiles at her lustfully. She smiles back, encouragingly.

86   INT: ERNESTO'S - LATER

The swarthy man's name is RASHID. They are talking cosily at the end of the bar. He has a heavy accent.

                    RASHID
You have a boyfriend?

                    ANNIE
      (hesitates)
Uh. Yes.

                    RASHID
And you have liberated relationship?
He not mind when you go with other
men?

                    ANNIE
Oh, I don't go with other men.

                    RASHID
You not?

                    ANNIE
No.

                    RASHID
You not go with me?

                    ANNIE
Of course not. I just have
leetle drink with you.

                    RASHID
Tell me. This boyfriend. You
live with him?

                    ANNIE
Uh. Of course.

                    RASHID
          (indicates suitcases)
Then what you are doing with baggage?

                    ANNIE
          (flustered)
Oh, I'm just going on a trip.

                    RASHID
Where you are going?

                    ANNIE
          (bursts out)
I'm not sure! Stop asking me all
these questions. I have to make
a phone call.

She gets up and goes to the phone.

                              CUT TO:

INSERT: Annie's Address Book: "WENDY 595 2416"

87   INT: ERNESTO'S PAY PHONE - NIGHT

She gets a busy signal.

                                        CUT TO:

88   INT: MENDY'S - NIGHT

Mendy is talking on the phone.

                    MENDY
          Uh-uh. I haven't seen her in
          ages. Two days at least. Why,
          is she missing?

                    RUDY (V.O.)
              (on phone)
          Yeah.

                    MENDY
          Anything I can do? Money? Drugs?
          A rim job?

                    RUDY
          No, thanks. Just tell her to
          call me if you hear from her.

                    MENDY
          O.K.

He hangs up.

                                        CUT TO:

89   INT: ERNESTO'S PAY PHONE - NIGHT

Annie dials a few digits.

                                        CUT TO:

90   INT: LOIS' PLACE - NIGHT

The phone rings in the empty apartment.

91   INT: ERNESTO'S - NIGHT

Annie exits phone booth, dejected. Rashid smiles as
she approaches the bar.

                    RASHID
          You need someplace to stay
          tonight?

Annie sighs and shrugs.

91   CONTD

                ANNIE
    Why not? I'm meant to try every-
    thing, aren't I?

                RASHID
      (eager)
    You come?

                ANNIE
    Yes, come on. Let's get going.
    I'm tired.

                      CUT TO:

92   INT: RASHID'S - NIGHT

It's a seedy room with a hotplate and squashed cockroach
stains on the walls. Annie's suitcases are parked by
the door. She and Rashid are locked in an awkward
embrace on top of the bed. He has his hand up her dress
and is kissing her passionately. Annie breaks away.
She whispers in his ear.

                ANNIE
    Rashid.

                RASHID
      (eagerly)
    Yes.

                ANNIE
    Would you mind brushing your teeth
    before we go to bed?

His face drops. He stammers.

                ANNIE
    I'm sorry. It's just the taste
    of tobacco. It makes me nauseous.
    I'm sorry.

                RASHID
      (irritated)
    Alright, alright. I do it!

                      CUT TO:

93   INT: RASHID'S - LATER

On the bed again. Rashid's pants are open, Annie's
tights are around her ankles and he is trying to undo
the buttons of her sweater. She stops him.

93   CONTD

                         ANNIE
          Leave it on. It's cold in here.

Rashid looks angry. He is sweating profusely. Annie
reaches into his pants and pulls him to her crotch.

                         ANNIE
          Here, come on. Put it in. Come
          on. This is what you wanted, isn't
          it?

Rashid lets her guide him inside of her. He plunges
in and out. He tries to embrace her. She holds him
away.

                         RASHID
          You American women ...

                         ANNIE
          I'm not American. I'm English.
          Come on. Come on. Are you
          coming?

Rashid stops, suddenly. Very deliberately, he disengages from her, tucks in his shirt, buttons his pants
and zips up his fly.

                         ANNIE
          What is it? What's the matter?

                         RASHID
          You have insult me too much. You
          are no longer welcome in my house.
          Please to leave.

                         ANNIE
          Oh, come on. I'm sorry. I didn't
          know you were so sensitive. Come
          on, I'll be nice to you.

                         RASHID
          Please to leave.

                         ANNIE
          But I have nowhere to go!

                         RASHID
          Please to leave.

                                        CUT TO:

94   EXT: STREET - NIGHT

        Annie and her suitcases by a phone booth. Annie
        dialing last digit.

95   INT: LOIS' - NIGHT

        The phone rings. Lois' hand reaches into frame and
        picks up the receiver.

                        LOIS
                Hello.

                        ANNIE
                   (on phone)
                Thank God you're there.

                        LOIS
                Who is this? Annie?

                        ANNIE
                Yes. I've got to see you.

        We see a naked man, RUSS, come out of Lois' bathroom
        with a hard-on.

                        LOIS
                Look, can I call you back?

                        ANNIE
                No, I'm in a phone booth not too
                far from you. Can't I come over?
                I desperately need to see you.

                        LOIS
                Can you make it in about an hour?

96   EXT: PHONE BOOTH - NIGHT

        Annie bursts into tears.

                        ANNIE
                But I haven't anywhere to go! I've
                left Rudy, and I've been calling you
                all day and all night, and I went
                home with an Arab, and it was awful,
                and nothing is open, and I don't
                have any place to go!

97   INT: LOIS' - NIGHT

                        LOIS
                   (amazed)
                Oh, Jesus, Annie. I didn't know.
                I'm sorry. Come right over.

97   CONTD

    Russ embraces Lois from behind as she hangs up the phone.

                    LOIS
          Russ, I'm sorry, but you'll have
          to go.

                    RUSS
          What?

                    LOIS
          A girl friend of mine is coming
          over.

                    RUSS
          Well, the more the merrier, as far
          as I'm concerned.

He squeezes her a bit tighter. She turns to face him.
He strokes her ass.

                    LOIS
          I'm serious. She's in trouble.
          You have to leave.

As she's talking, he tries to fit his dick into her
while they're standing up.

                    RUSS
          O.K., honey. Whatever you say.
          But let's just finish up what we
          came here for.

Lois tries to squirm away from him.

                    LOIS
          We can't. There isn't time. She's
          just around the corner.

                    RUSS
              (holding on)
          Won't take but a minute.

Lois pulls away from him and hands him his clothes.

                    LOIS
          Come on, Russ. Don't make things
          difficult.

Russ looks at her, incredulous, holding his clothes in
one hand and his dick in the other. She pulls a bathrobe over herself.

97   CONTD (2)

                    RUSS
          You think I'm gonna walk out on
          the street with this boner?

                    LOIS
          Will you get dressed?!

                    RUSS
          Not until you get me off.

                    LOIS
          WILL YOU GET THE FUCK OUT OF HERE?!

She lunges at him, pushing him towards the door. He
grabs her hand and bends back her wrist. They struggle
until she drops to her knees. He is very big and very
mad. He stares down at her with hatred.

Lois lets out her breath and stops resisting. She takes
Russ' dick in her hand and begins to stroke it. He
moans and loosens his grip on her hand.

                    LOIS
          Is this what you want?

                    RUSS
               (moans)
          Yes.

He leans his head back, closes his eyes and sways his
hips as the rhythm of her stroking increases. He winces
slightly. He leans a hand on her head.

                    RUSS
          Ow, not so hard.

She pumps harder and harder. Brutally.

                    LOIS
          Shut up. This is what you wanted,
          isn't it?

                    RUSS
          Ow! Jesus, ow!

Russ grabs a handful of Lois' hair and pulls. Lois
grimaces with pain but keeps yanking at his dick as
if she were trying to pull it off.

                    RUSS
          OW! FUCK! JESUS!

97   CONTD (3)

He comes. She lets go of his dick. He lets go of her
hair.

                         LOIS
              Now get out.

She goes into the bathroom and slams the door.

Russ steps into his pants, picks up his shoes and exits.

Lois comes out of the bathroom with a wad of toilet paper
in her hand. She squats down on the floor near where
Russ had been standing. There are dollops of semen all
over the shiny waxed floor. Lois daubs tentatiively at
it with the toilet paper. She lifts it to her nose and
sniffs. Her free hand reaches beneath her robe and finds
her crotch.

A buzzer buzzes, interrupting her reverie. She goes to
the house phone and answers it, still stroking herself.

                         LOIS
              Yes.

98   INT: LOBBY - NIGHT

The IRISH DOORMAN is speaking into the house phone. Anni·
is standing beside him.

                         DOORMAN
                    (suspicious)
              There's an English female person
              here to see you, ma'am. A Miss ...

                         ANNIE
              Annie.

                         DOORMAN
                    (skeptical)
              A Miss Annie, she says.

                         LOIS
              Send her up.

                         DOORMAN
              Alright, ma'am.
                    (to Annie, grudgingly)
              She says ye kin go up.

AT THE ELEVATOR

She meets Russ coming out of the elevator. He is button-
ing up his shirt. His shoelaces are untied. His fly is

98   CONTD

open. He is holding his socks and his underpants in his
right hand. Annie looks at him with a trace of amusement.

                    RUSS
               (mutters)
          Everything they say about you New
          York cunts is true!

                    ANNIE
          But I'm English!

He tries to stuff his underpants into his pocket as he
storms away. The elevator door closes as Annie steps
inside.

99   INT: LOIS' - NIGHT

Lois pulls herself together, takes a deep breath and
opens the door. Annie stands on the threshold, with her
two suitcases, looking wretched. Lois looks her over
for a moment, then bends down and picks up one of her
bags.

                    LOIS
          You poor thing! How long have
          you been waiting for me? Are
          you alright?

                    ANNIE
          I hope I haven't ruined your evening.

                                        CUT TO:

100   INT: TRUCK - NIGHT

Rudy is driving around, looking for a parking spot. Huey
is sitting in the passenger seat beside him. It is two
in the A.M.

Pulling up to a stop light, Rudy punches on the radio.
He pushes the cigarette lighter into the dashboard.

                    GARY STEWART
               (on radio)
          She's actin' single,
          And I'm drinkin' doubles ...

Rudy pushes the button and another station comes on. He
lights up a joint, then absently shakes it out like a
match and chucks it out the window.

100   CONTD

> BOB DYLAN
> (on radio)
> I'm out in the rain,
> Oh, and you are on dry land,
> You made it there somehow ...

In the rear view mirror, Rudy sees a police car pull up
behind him. He punches the radio again and it jumps to
a Latin station. The light has turned to green but Rudy
hasn't noticed. The cop car flashes its headlights.
Rudy jumps, slams the car into first, and stalls out.

> IGNACIO PINERO
> (on radio)
> Yo soy el castigador
> Castigador de mujeres ...
> (I am the punisher
> Punisher of women ...)

He gets the rig started again and into gear, and putters
off around the corner. The police car goes off in
another direction.

101   INT: LOIS' - NIGHT

Annie comes out of the bathroom and crosses to the bed,
a mattress on the floor. The room is dark, lit only by
street lamps outside. Lois is curled up on the far side
of the bed, face turned to the wall. Annie undresses
and slips between the sheets. Lois doesn't move.
Neither does Annie. After a long pause, Annie turns
and kisses Lois timidly on the back of the neck.

> ANNIE
> (whispers)
> Goodnight.

Lois turns her head and they kiss. Lois shifts her body
around and they embrace, face to face, lying on their
sides, kissing deeply. They wriggle against each other,
rubbing breasts, bellies, pussies, getting very excited
and very short of breath very fast. Locked in this
embrace, they begin to struggle against one another.
Each one wants to be on top. The struggle excites them
more. Annie overpowers Lois. She comes. Lois appar-
ently doesn't. They catch their breaths. Neither speaks,
then Annie does.

> ANNIE
> You didn't come, did you?

> LOIS
> Never mind. Half the time I don't
> even know if I've come or not anyway.

101   CONTD

                          ANNIE
          Was I an awful lover? Tell me,
          I want to learn.

                          LOIS
          I had a good time.

                          ANNIE
          I think I may be falling in love
          with you.

INSERT: PHONOGRAPH. A record drops onto the turntable
and the needle touches down. This song plays throughout
the following scene.

                          JOHN HERALD (V.O.)
                       (singing)
          At the end of a long, lonely day
             without you
          When the world seems to fall in
             my face
          I'm alright through the day
          But the day fades away
          And a long, lonely night takes
             its place.

          Another day to wish that you were here
          I dread each lonely night that's filled
             with tears
          Though I've tried and I've tried
          These are tears that I can't hide
          At the end of a long, lonely day.

102   INT: LIVING ROOM-BEDROOM - NIGHT

The room is dark. Rudy is alone beside a beat-up super-
eight projector, watching the image on the opposite
wall over the bed.

He is watching a black and white home movie, taken four
years before, when they were living in the country. It
shows Annie, naked and eight months pregnant, eating
an orange in a rustic backyard, doing childbirth exercises in a meadow, and taking a piss in the woods.
These pictures are a stunning contrast to the image of
the present Annie. Here she is healthy, glowing, like
a ripe fruit. She radiates a kind of robust eroticism.

As the film runs out of the projector, Rudy gets up,
pulls back the curtain and stands staring out the
window, as the song continues.

102   CONTD

                    JOHN HERALD
          At the end of the day
          I go up to my room
          And I watch as the sun fades away
          And the loneliness there
          Brings me grief and despair
          At the end of a long, lonely day.

Rudy watches the passing people, leaning up the hill in
the horizontal orange light.

                    JOHN HERALD
          Another day to sit alone and cry
          It makes no difference if I live
             or die
          With the world locked outside
          I just lay there and cried
          At the end of a long, lonely day.

A tear trickles down Rudy's face. Rudy's hand pulls the
curtain to. Rudy lies across the bed in an attitude of
despair, face buried in forearm. A picture falls off
the wall.

103   INT: LOBBY - RUDY'S PLACE - DAY

ROSEANNE, a motherly, but sexy woman in her forties, is
waiting for the elevator with her little poodle. Rudy,
Jesse and the dogs enter from the street.

                    ROSEANNE
          Hello, Rudy.

                    RUDY
          Hi, Roseanne.

The dogs check out the poodle. Rudy goes to his door,
which is right next to the elevator.

                    ROSEANNE
          Hi, Jesse.

                    JESSE
          No.

He hides behind his father's leg. Rudy gets the door
open. The dogs are beginning to threaten each other.

                    ROSEANNE
          How's Annie?

                    RUDY
          Oh, fine. Just fine.

103   CONTD

                              ROSEANNE
              I haven't seen her around for a
              while.

                              RUDY
              Well, she's been working.

                              JESSE
              Downtown.

                              RUDY
                      (to dogs)
              Cut it out, you creeps!

He hustles them all inside.

104   INT: LIVING ROOM-BEDROOM - NIGHT

Rudy enters to find Sluggo and Muggo seated around the
TV, watching Star Trek. Huey jumps on Rudy's chest and
licks his face. Rudy brushes him aside.

                              JESSE
              Hey, daddy! Commercial!

Rudy flicks on the light switch in the foyer. The bulb
flashes and goes out. Sluggo and Muggo wave to Rudy.
Jesse climbs up on the couch in front of the TV.

                              SLUGGO
                      (to Rudy)
              Why so glum, chum?

Rudy shrugs and starts off in the direction of the
kitchen. Muggo turns to Sluggo.

                              MUGGO
              Hey, he's really down in sewer
              seven, pipe eleven.

                              SLUGGO
              Hey, Rudy, don't forget -- there
              are eight million people in the
              naked city, so, if you're one in
              a million, there are eight others
              just like you.

                              MUGGO
              Maybe right next door.

                              SLUGGO
              Cheer up. Life is great. Dead
              people don't get to watch television.

104   CONTD

Rudy bumps into Perry, coming out of the kitchen.

                         PERRY
               Hey, hoss, when's Annie comin'
               back?

Rudy shrugs, crosses to the refrigerator, opens the
door and stares blankly inside.

                         PERRY
               Hey, where-all did she go, anyways?

                         RUDY
               Oh, she just went away for a while.

                         PERRY
               Hey, it ain't nothin' serious, is
               it, hoss? She is comin' back, ain't
               she? I mean, she ain't even called
               or anything and it's been a couple
               of weeks.

The refrigerator is practically empty. Rudy picks up
an orange and discovers that is has gone moldy.

                         RUDY
               She'll be back. She'll be back.

The phone rings. We can hear Sluggo answer it in the
other room.

                         PERRY
               You need a woman, hoss. Want
               Patty to fix you up with some
               Texas pussy?

                         RUDY
               Aw, I wouldn't even know what to
               do, it's been so long.

Sluggo enters and points a finger at Rudy.

                         SLUGGO
               Telephone.

                         RUDY
               I don't want to talk to anybody.
               Who is it?

                         SLUGGO
               Sounded female.

                         PERRY
               Go on, take it, hoss.

104   CONTD (2)

Sluggo slaps him on the back and holds up his thumb.

                    SLUGGO
          Thumbs up! We're right behind ya.

Rudy picks up the kitchen phone.

                    RUDY
          Hullo.

                    ROSIE (V.O.)
          Rudy! Hi! It's Rosie!

(Rosie is a girl who speaks with exclamation points.)

                    RUDY
          Oh, Rosie.

                    ROSIE
          Hey, how long has it been?

                    RUDY
          Geez, I dunno. Listen, Annie isn't
          here right now.

                    ROSIE
          I know.

                    RUDY
          Do you want me to give her a message?

                    ROSIE
          A message? What for? I know she
          flew the coop.

                    RUDY
          What? Who told you that?

                    ROSIE
          I bumped into Norman. He got it
          from Mendy. Everybody knows about
          it.

                    RUDY
          What the ... ?

                    ROSIE
          So, how are ya?

                    RUDY
              (irritated)
          I don't have her number, if that's
          what you're calling for.

104   CONTD (3)

                    ROSIE
          Nah. I'm calling you! I just
          wanted to see how you were doing!

                    RUDY
          Who, me?

                    ROSIE
          Yeah, you know I always had a thing
          for you!

                    RUDY
          Are you pulling my pud?

                    ROSIE
          Wouldn't mind!

                    RUDY
          Huh?

                    ROSIE
          How about it?

                    RUDY
          Rosie, I don't know what you've
          been told, but Annie's just gone
          away for a little while. She'll
          be back.

                    ROSIE
          Bullshit. They never come back.
          So, what do you say? Wanna boogie?

                    RUDY
          Rosie, I can't take you out. For
          one thing, I haven't got any money ...

                    ROSIE
          We don't have to go anywhere! All
          I want is your body! You don't even
          have to talk to me if you don't
          wanna!

                    RUDY
          But, Rosie ...

                    ROSIE
          Come on. I know you like my body --
          you're always coppin' feels! Not
          that I blame you after six years
          with that dried up prune.

104   CONTD (4)

                    RUDY
          Now wait a minute! I thought you
          were supposed to be Annie's friend.
          I never even liked you.

                    ROSIE
          I am her friend. But let's call a
          spade a spade: that chick is not
          what you'd call built. And I am.
          So waddya say?

                    RUDY
          What can I say?

                    ROSIE
          Say yes.

                    RUDY
          Yes.

                    ROSIE
          Tonight?

                    RUDY
          Yes.

                    ROSIE
          Now?

                    RUDY
          Soon.

                    ROSIE
          I'll be waiting.

                    RUDY
          'Bye.

He hangs up. He goes to the bathroom, unbuckles his
pants. The phone rings again. He stumbles toward it,
holding up his pants.

Sluggo and Muggo come in the door, wave to Rudy in
tandem and disappear into Sluggo's room.

                    RUDY
          Hello.

                    ANNIE (V.O.)
          Hi, it's me.

                    RUDY
          Where are you?

                                        CUT TO:

105   INT: LOIS' - DAY

        Annie is sitting on the floor. The contents of her
        pocketbook are arrayed .around her.

        Lois enters the apartment, waves to Annie and disappears
        into the bathroom.

                         ANNIE
                Oh, at a friend's.

                                            CUT TO:

106   INT: RUDY'S - DAY

                         RUDY
                Well, how the hell can I get in
                touch with you? I've got mail
                for you, messages ...

                         ANNIE
                Never mind that. I'll get them
                later. Can you give me Mendy's
                number?

                         RUDY
                Whaddya want Mendy's number for?

                         ANNIE
                Never mind that. Just give me
                the number, will you?

                         RUDY
                Hang on ...

        He burrows through a pile of junk, finds his address
        book, and finds Mendy's number.

                         RUDY
                Got a pencil?

                         ANNIE
                Yes, of course. Go on ...

                         RUDY
                Four seven two ...

                         ANNIE
                ... one five four three. Right.
                I've got to hang up.

                         RUDY
                Annie, when are ya comin' home?

106   CONTD

                    ANNIE
          I'm not, Rudy.

                    RUDY
          Annie, please, explain it to me.
          What's going on?

                    ANNIE
          I can't. I've gotta go. I'll call
          you later.

                    RUDY
          Annie?

                    ANNIE
          Rudy, I can't talk.

                    RUDY
          What about Jesse?

                    ANNIE
          I'm not leaving you in the lurch
          with him. I promise.

                    RUDY
          I didn't think you would.

                    ANNIE
          Poor litle baby. Can you take care
          of him just a little while longer?
          Just until I get a place. We'll
          share him.

                    RUDY
          O.K.

                    ANNIE
          You know I work on Tuesday, Wednesday
          and Sunday. So I thought I could
          take him Monday, Thursday and Friday
          and every other Saturday.

                    RUDY
          What?

                    ANNIE
          Well, we'll talk about it later.
          I've gotta go? 'Bye, darling.

She hangs up.

107   INT: LOIS' - DAY

As Annie hngs up, Lois comes out of the bathroom, fully
dressed and carrying an overnight bag into which she is
throwing a few things.

                    ANNIE
          What's going on?

                    LOIS
          Oh, I have to go up to Boston with
          one of my acts.

Annie is taken aback.

                    ANNIE
          What about me?

                    LOIS
          Make yourself at home. I'll be
          back in a couple of days.

                    ANNIE
          You mean you're going to leave me
          here, just like that? What'll I
          do?

                    LOIS
          I thought you'd like it. Give you
          a chance to get your head together.
          Take a breath. Think things out.

                    ANNIE
          I don't want to think about anything.

Annie turns away from Lois and looks out the window.
Lois comes up behind her and takes Annie in her arms.
Annie turns and buries her face in Lois' bosom.

                    ANNIE
          Who is this act of yours?

                    LOIS
          It's a client. He's starting off
          his first tour. I have to go and
          hold his hand.

                    ANNIE
          Is that all he gets? Your hand?

                    LOIS
          Aw, Annie ... he's a client.

                    ANNIE
          What does that mean? Do you fuck
          him or don't you fuck him?

107   CONTD

>   LOIS
>   If I give him a tumble, it makes
>   him feel better and he performs
>   better, where's the harm?
>
>   ANNIE
>   I don't have to stay here. There
>   are plenty of places I could stay.
>
>   LOIS
>   Annie, don't be that way. This
>   guy means nothing to me. I
>   promise ...
>
>   ANNIE
>   I'm going to get my own place any-
>   way.
>
>   LOIS
>   Look, I'll tell you what: I'll
>   try to get back a little sooner.
>   Say tomorrow night. And then we
>   can have the whole weekend together.
>   What do you say?
>
>   ANNIE
>   Don't hurry back on my account. I
>   can take care of myself.

Lois glances at her watch.

>   LOIS
>   I've got to dash, darling, or I'll
>   miss my plane. Don't be cross with
>   me.
>
>   ANNIE
>   You sound just like Rudy.

Lois takes Annie by the chin and tilts her head up until
their eyes meet. There are tears in Annie's eyes. Lois
kisses her. Suddenly, they are locked in a passionate
embrace. After an emotional moment, Lois pulls herself
away.

>   LOIS
>   (whispers)
>   Tomorrow.

She crosses to the door, opens it and turns. Their eyes
lock across the room. Annie is wiping the tears from
her cheeks. Lois blows her a kiss and disappears through
the door.

107   CONTD (2)

Annie goes to the kitchen and starts opening cabinets
and drawers. She paces around the room. She picks up
the phone and dials a number.

                                        CUT TO:

108   INT: RUDY'S - NIGHT

Jesse, Sluggo, Muggo, Perry and Pat are all sprawled
on Rudy's bed, watching The Lucy Show. The phone rings.
Sluggo answers.

                    SLUGGO
          Uh ... Jello.

                    ANNIE (V.O.)
          Is Rudy there?

                    SLUGGO
          Uh-uh ... Hey, is this Annie?

                    ANNIE
          Yes. Hello, Muggo.

                    SLUGGO
          It's Sluggo. Hey, Annie! Where
          ya been?

                    MUGGO
              (to Jesse)
          Hey, Jesse, it's your mom!

                    ANNIE
          Where is Rudy? Why isn't he there?

                    JESSE
          Mommy!

He reaches for the phone.

                    SLUGGO
          We're all babysitting. I don't
          know where he went. Here, somebody
          wants to talk to you.

                    ANNIE
              (panicked)
          Jesse? I can't talk to him. Not
          now. Tell him it's not me.

                    JESSE
          I wanna talk.

108   CONTD

                    SLUGGO
          It's not your mom. It's not her.

Jesse bursts out crying.

                    JESSE
          I want my mommy!

                    SLUGGO
          Aw, he's cryin'.

                    ANNIE
          Alright, put him on.

Sluggo offers the phone to Jesse. Jesse is bewildered.

                    SLUGGO
          Here, it is her. It is your mom.
          I was just jokin'. Here. Take it.

Jesse takes the phone.

                    JESSE
          Mommy?

                    ANNIE
          Hello, Jesse. Hello, darling.

                    JESSE
          Mommy? Are you in another place?

                    ANNIE
          Yes, darling, I'm in another place.
          That's right. But I'm going to come
          and see you very soon. I promise.
          Just as soon as I ... just as soon
          as I get back. O.K.?

Something funny happens on The Lucy Show and everybody
laughs. Jesse turns to see it.

                    JESSE
          'Bye, mom.

He hands the phone to Sluggo and bursts into laughter
at the TV. Sluggo picks up the phone.

                    SLUGGO
          Hey, Annie! When ya comin' home?

                    ANNIE
          Where's Rudy? What time will he
          be back?

108   CONTD (2)

                    SLUGGO
          Hold on.
               (to the others)
          Anybody know when Rudy's coming
          back?

                    PERRY
          He said he'd be out for the evening.

                    SLUGGO
               (to Annie)
          He's out for the evening.

                    MUGGO
          He told me to walk the dogs if he
          wasn't here in the morning.

                    SLUGGO
          And he might not be back until
          tomorrow.

                    PAT
          Hey, ask her if she's got any Tampax
          stashed away here.

                    SLUGGO
          Yeah, and hey, Annie ...

He hears the click of the receiver. He looks at Pat,
looks at Muggo, they all shrug, and Sluggo hangs up.

                              CUT TO:

109   INT: ROSIE'S PLACE - NIGHT

Rudy rings the bell. After a moment, ROSIE opens the
door, smiling coquettishly. She is wearing a tantalizing
chemise. Rudy pauses for a moment, then bends to kiss
her. At the last moment, Rosie turns, giving him her
cheek instead of her lips. She flounces into the
apartment. He follows.

110   INT: ROSIE'S APARTMENT - NIGHT

                    ROSIE
          Take your coat off and relax.
          I'm on the phone.

Rudy takes his coat off and looks around. Rosie picks
up the phone.

                    ROSIE
               (into phone)
          Rickey? My date is here, so I
          can't talk. Yeah, you know
          him: Rudy Frigidaire.

110   CONTD

Rudy gesticulates. He doesn't want his name mentioned.

                    ROSIE
          Yeah, you didn't hear they broke
          up?
                (to Rudy)
          Want some beer?

                    RUDY
          Yeah, if you're all out of champagne.

                    ROSIE
          It's in the icebox.

Rudy gets a beer out of the fridge and wanders back into
the main room. Rosie is still on the phone. She beckons
to him. He comes over. She takes his hand, seats him in
an easy chair and plonks herself down on his lap, all the
while continuing her phone conversation.

                    ROSIE
          Yeah, I know. It's getting ridiculous.
          Everybody's breaking up. Liz Taylor
          and Richard Burton ... What? You're
          kidding! Bob and Sarah Dylan broke
          up? I don't believe it.

Rudy's hand begins to stray along Rosie's leg, meeting
no resistance. As the conversation goes on, Rudy becomes
bolder. She opens herself to his most imtimate caresses,
but otherwise pays little attention to him.

                    ROSIE
          Who told you? When did this happen?
          Who gets the kids? Really? Well,
          what happened? ... Oh, I see. You
          mean he was heavy into some kind of
          old-fashioned domestic scene, and she
          got fed up and told him where he
          could get off, huh? Isn't that some-
          thing? So they really broke up? ...
          He's coming to New York? Then you've
          got to get your friend what's-his-
          name to introduce me to him. You
          have to. Please, Rickey!

By now Rudy is hot and bothered. He has Rosie's chemise
up around her neck. He is sucking her breast. He lifts
his head up to kiss her mouth but she turns her cheek at
the last minute. He whispers in her ear.

                    RUDY
          Come on, Rosie.

110   CONTD (2)

                    ROSIE
              (to Rudy)
        Wait a minute. This is important.
              (into phone)
        Rickey? What? Aw, can't you tell
        me now? What? O.K. But call me
        later, will ya? Promise? O.K.
        'Bye.

She gets off Rudy's lap to hang up the phone. Rudy
stands up with her. As she turns from the phone, she
greets him ebulliently.

                    ROSIE
        Rudy! Hi! You look terrible!
        Are you suffering a lot?

Rudy pulls her to him and tries to kiss her.

                    ROSIE
        Don't kiss me. I've got a terrible
        cold.

                    RUDY
        Rosie. Am I mistaken? Or did you
        not invite me down here for a fuck?

                    ROSIE
        O.K., O.K. You don't have to make
        a Federal case out of it. It just
        takes me a while. Want a drink?

He holds up his beer.

                    RUDY
        I've got one.

                    ROSIE
        Well, you want something to eat?

                    RUDY
        I'm not hungry.

                    ROSIE
        How about a joint?

Rudy picks her up and carries her across the room to
the bed.

                    ROSIE
        Hey, Rudy, you're not really gonna
        pull this bullshit he-man stuff on
        me, are ya?

110   CONTD (3)

Rudy dumps her on the bed and turns to leave.

                    RUDY
          I knew there was a reason why I
          never liked you.

Rosie chases after him and catches him at the door.

                    ROSIE
          Hey, Rudy, don't go. I'm sorry.
          Stay. I'll be nice. I promise.

She puts her arms around him and grinds her pelvis
against his. He puts his hands on her behind.

The phone rings. She slips out of his grasp, pats him
on the fly and flounces away. She answers the phone.

                              CUT TO:

111   INT: ROSIE'S - NIGHT

It is a little bit later. Rudy and Rosie are both naked,
in bed. Rosie is still on the phone. Rudy has a look
of exasperation on his face. Rosie is lying on her side,
her back to Rudy as she talks. He tries to slip it to
her from behind.

                    ROSIE
          O.K. Alright. But call me tomorrow,
          O.K.? You won't forget? Promise?
          ... Alright ... And Marty ...

But he has already hung up. She sighs and hangs up just
as Rudy is slipping it in. She wriggles away and turns
toward him in the bed. She is trying to hold him off,
but he is determined. They struggle together for a
couple of moments. Then Rosie goes limp.

                    ROSIE
          I can't do it.

                    RUDY
          What?

                    ROSIE
          I'm fucked up. Really. I know
          that. You don't have to tell me
          that.

                    RUDY
          Oh, Jesus ...

111   CONTD

> ROSIE
> See, it's really all Ricky, my ex-
> husband's fault. He was such a sex
> maniac.

> RUDY
> Little Ricky?

> ROSIE
> Are you kidding? He couldn't keep
> his hands off of me. He used to
> make me fuck him ... four, five
> times a day.

> RUDY
> Four or five times a day?

> ROSIE
> So, no wonder I'm fucked up about
> sex. Right?

> RUDY
> Gee, Rosie, I'm sorry. I didn't
> realize ...

She pats his cheek.

> ROSIE
> You're sweet. But it's my problem.
> I realize that I've got my hangups.
> Really. And that's why it's really
> great that we got together. Because
> I really feel good about you. I
> think I'll be able to open myself up
> to you, eventually.

> RUDY
> Well, gee, uh, Rosie ...

> ROSIE
> I know I can do it, 'cause my shrink
> told me I had great pelvic motion.

> RUDY
> Your psychiatrist likes your pelvic
> motion? How does he know?

> ANNIE
> He has me do it when he lies on top
> of me in Group.

> RUDY
> Wait a minute. How does that go?

111   CONTD (2)

                    ANNIE
          See, in Group, when one person
          does a lot of work, and a lot of
          things come out, they get a reward.
          And the reward is that you get to
          get held and squeezed and stuff
          like that. And all the boys like
          to hold me and think I have a great
          pelvic motion.

                    RUDY
          You do. You have a great pelvic
          motion with your clothes on. It's
          just that when you get into bed ...

                    ROSIE
          Yeah, well, that's now.   But wait
          until you see how it's gonna change.
          I'm getting a lot of support from
          my Group on this. Look, it never
          is that good the first couple of
          times, is it? Right?

                    RUDY
          How many times?

                    ROSIE
          I think you're very good for me
          right now. 'Cause I can really
          relate to you.

                    RUDY
          Well, that's terrific, Rosie, but ...

                    ROSIE
          I'm gonna be real good with you.
          You'll see. The next time I'm
          gonna really take care of business,
          baby. I know I've got it in me.

                    RUDY
          Rosie, it makes me really happy to
          hear that. I'm certainly looking
          forward ...

                    ROSIE
          But the thing that bothers me is
          the idea of all these other chicks
          you're probably dating.

                    RUDY
          What?

111   CONTD (3)

                    ROSIE
          I mean, that's not something that's
          just gonna continue to go on, is it?

                    RUDY
          Look ...

                    ROSIE
          'Cause it makes a girl feel kind of
          cheap, you know. And besides, there's
          all kinds of dangers of disease. My
          doctor says it's a real epidemic.

                                        CUT TO:

112   INT: LOIS' - EVENING

The place is in terrible disarray. The phone is ringing. Lois enters the apartment, just back from her
trip, carrying her little overnight bag. She goes to
answer the phone, but she can't find it. Everything in
the room has been swtiched around. The floor is littered with Lois' clothes, newspapers, magazines, an
I Ching, etc. Lois goes to the telephone outlet and
follows the cord until she finds the phone in the bathroom. Lois answers it.

                    LOIS
          Hello.

The line has gone dead.

113   INT: THE FEMME - NIGHT

The Femme is a lesbian bar in the village. Annie is
just hanging up the phone. She retrieves her dime,
re-deposits it and dials another number. Behind her,
we can see the bar and its all-female clientele. There
is a small group at a table near the phone, at which
we recognize Gunilla. Annie hears the phone ring and
Rudy answer.

                    RUDY (V.O.)
          Hullo.

                    ANNIE
          Hi. It's me.

                    RUDY
          Hi.

                    ANNIE
          How are you, darling?

113   CONTD

                    RUDY
                (cheerfully)
          Not so good. How are you?

                    ANNIE
          Not so good.

                    RUDY
          Good.

                    ANNIE
          Don't be that way.

                    RUDY
          When are you coming home?

                    ANNIE
          Don't keep asking me that.

                    RUDY
          Where are you?

                    ANNIE
          Don't ask me things like that.
          You know it'll just fuck you up.
          Anyway, where were you last night?

                    RUDY
          Huh?

                    ANNIE
          Out with one of those hot little
          bitches you've been sticking it to?

                    RUDY
          Wait a minute, Annie ...

                    ANNIE
                (bursts into tears)
          Who was it? I was trying to get
          you all night. It's humiliating
          to keep calling you and always be
          getting those bloody faggots that
          live there.

                    RUDY
          You're the one that brought them
          here.

                    ANNIE
          Which cunt was it? One of my
          so-called friends, I bet. Rosie?
          Was it her?

113   CONTD (2)

                    RUDY
          Calm down, baby, calm down. It
          was nothing. Believe me. It
          was less than nothing. Annie,
          when am I going to see you?

                    ANNIE
          Soon. As soon as I get myself a
          place. Don't press me, darling.

                    RUDY
          Why are you whispering?

                    ANNIE
          I can't talk. I'm with some
          people.

                    RUDY
          Out dyking it up again, eh?

                    ANNIE
          Rudy, if you're going to behave
          like this every time I call,
          then I just ... I'll just have
          to stop calling you.

                    RUDY
          Why don't you just come home?

                    ANNIE
          Rudy, please!

                    RUDY
          Well, why do you call me, then?

                    ANNIE
          Well, just to see how you are.

                    RUDY
          Well, now you know.

                    ANNIE
          Well, look, maybe I'll call you
          back a little later, when you're
          in a better mood.

                    RUDY
          Call me back when you're ready to
          come home.

He hangs up.

                              CUT TO:

114   INT: LOIS' - NIGHT

Lois is tidying up the apartment. She finds a note
under her pillow. She reads it. It says:

          "Darling: Sorry to leave the
          place in such a horrendous state,
          but I'm off in a dash. Have
          found other temporary lodgings
          'til I get my own place. When
          you left for Boston, I knew it
          could never work out for us --
          you're basically very hetero, and
          I am more inclined to the dyke.
          Anyway, I know it's Rudy you
          really want. You're so alike.
          I'm sure you'd be very happy
          together. Anyway, darling,
          thanks for the dance.

               Love, Annie

          P.S. I borrowed your pink top.
          X X X "

                                        CUT TO:

115   INT: LOIS' OFFICE - DAY

Lois is staring out the window. Rudy enters.

                    RUDY
          How's Annie?

                    LOIS
               (shrugs)
          Don't know. Haven't seen her
          recently.

                    RUDY
          Oh, come off it. I know she's
          been shacking up with you.

                    LOIS
          How did you know that?

                    RUDY
          It wasn't the best kept secret
          in town.

                    LOIS
          Well, she isn't any more. Hasn't
          been for about a week.

                    RUDY
          And you don't know where she is?

Lois shakes her head.

                    LOIS
          I hear she's been sleeping around.
          Hitting the high spots. I don't
          know. She doesn't call me.

Rudy notices a wistfulness in her eye.

                    RUDY
          Were you and she having what you
          might call a love affair?

Lois shrugs.

                    LOIS
          Well, I don't know exactly ...
          something like that.

                    RUDY
          Mmm. Well then, what was it like?

                    LOIS
          I think that we both sort of shied
          away from anything that would be
          too intimate. Although sometimes
          she'd get a funny look in her face.
          Her eyes suddenly became dark pools
          and she looked very sort of intensely.
          It's not that she looked intensely,
          but that her eyes did this strange
          sort of flooding, like the pupil
          enlarges a great deal, with strong
          feeling, as it were. Her eyes kind
          of illumine somehow. And she wanted
          to be warm ... Sorry. I do go on,
          don't I?

                    RUDY
          You really did feel strongly about
          her then, didn't you?

                    LOIS
          See, all the time that we went
          together, which was a very short
          time, it was always that we were
          pretending that there wasn't any-
          thing to it, if you see what I
          mean, that it was like for the
                    (MORE)

115   CONTD (2)

                         LOIS (Contd)
          experience. That we had a con-
          spiracy of some kind. She kept
          saying I was just like you. She
          told me that you and I really
          belong together. That's what she
          said when she walked out.

Lois looks at Rudy. Rudy looks at Lois. They fall
into each other's arms. Lois leans up against Rudy's
chest. Rudy strokes her back. They look at each other.
They kiss. Lois is perched on the corner of the desk.
Rudy is pressed against her. They are swallowing each
other's tongues. Lois is reaching into Rudy's fly and
Rudy has his hand up her skirt, trying to work her
panties off.

The intercom buzzes. Languidly, Lois reaches behind
her and presses the intercom button. She disengages
her lips from Rudy's just long enough to say two
words.

                    LOIS
               (to intercom)
          Not now.

Lois' panties are now dangling from her ankles. Rudy
is fitting himself to her.

                    LOIS
          Trouble is ... I'm still hung
          up on her.

Rudy slips it in. They both catch their breaths.

                    RUDY
          Trouble is ... so am I.

Lois sinks back onto the desk, pulling Rudy astride.
Inadvertently, her back presses the intercom button.

                                   CUT TO:

116   INT: BERNIE'S DESK - DAY

BERNIE is Lois' secretary. His desk is just outside
her (closed) door. Bernie is at his desk talking to
BASCOM HUNT and SHORTY. Bascom is nattily dressed but
drunk. Shorty is Bascom's cameraman. He is locked
into an elaborate brace supporting a large single-system
TV News camera on his slight, unsteady frame.

                    BERNIE
          I'm sorry, Mr. Hunt. She can't
          see you just now.

116   CONTD

                    BASCOM
          But I'm her goddamn husband,
          goddamnit!

                    BERNIE
               (bitchy)
          Correction, Mr. Hunt: were. You
          <u>were</u> her husband ...

He turns to his filing cabinet.

                    BERNIE
          I believe I had the divorce papers
          filed here ... under "Old Business."

                    BASCOM
          Goddamnit, don't quibble! I want...

He freezes in mid-sentence as a long, low, sexual moan
escapes from the intercom, followed by Lois' voice.

                    LOIS (V.O.)
               (filter)
          Fuck me, fuck me, fuck me.

Bascom brushes past Bernie and bursts through the door
and into Lois' office.

                                        CUT TO:

117   INT: LOIS' OFFICE - DAY

Caught in the act, Rudy is completely taken aback,
unable to move. Lois, on the other hand, merely
raises herself up onto her elbows and fixes Bascom
with a pitiless glare.

                    BASCOM
          So! I've caught you at last!
          Roll 'em, Shorty!

                    SHORTY
          Rolling, boss.

                    BASCOM
               (holding mike and
               facing camera)
          Your Honor, Ladies and Gentlemen
          of the Jury, never before in the
          history of our American system of
          justice has a jury, sitting in a
          criminal case, had the opportunity
                    (MORE)

117   CONTD

                    BASCOM (Contd)
          that you are about to have. You
          are about to be actual witnesses
          to the actual crime under your
          consideration. Watch carefully.
          This is not a re-enactment.
               (to Shorty)
          Pan over to the desk, Shorty.

The camera pans over to Rudy and Lois in a tableau of
coitus interruptus. Shorty gives Bascom the high sign.

                    SHORTY
          Great stuff, boss.

Bascom sidles up to the desk. Rudy tries to extricate
himself from Lois' embrace.

                    RUDY
          Now, Bascom, keep your shirt on.

Lois won't let him go. She undulates against him.

                    LOIS
          What's your hurry? Let's give
          'em what they came for.
               (looking at camera)
          Fuck you, Your Honor!

                    BASCOM
          You are evil incarnate ...
               (to Shorty)
          Widen out to a three shot, Shorty.

Bascom reaches out and fondles her breast. She looks
at him with contempt. He addresses the camera.

                    BASCOM
          See this? This used to belong
          to me and me alone. I used to
          sit and marvel at this body, long
          after she was asleep, paying homage
          with eyes and hands and lips.

He looks into her eyes.

                    BASCOM
          And I was grateful. You can't
          say I wasn't grateful. I took
          tender loving care of it, didn't
          I? Didn't I? I stroked it and
          groomed it and fed it and pampered
          it.

117   CONTD (2)

He tugs at his fly and tries to mount her.

                    LOIS
          Get off of me, you sot. Your
          breath is foul.

She pushes him off and he falls to the floor in a clump.

Shorty's camera pans down to Bascom, slumped against a
leg of the desk. Bascom, mike still in hand, addresses
the camera.

                    BASCOM
          She was just a kid from the sticks.
          North Carolina. She worshipped me.
          I was the sun and the moon to her.
          Why should a man, once having had
          that, ever have to give it up?

With a gleam in his eye, he pulls out a switchblade
knife.

                    RUDY
          Bascom! Pull yourself together,
          man!

He takes a step toward Bascom. Bascom flicks open the
knife. Click. Rudy freezes.

                    BASCOM
          See this knife? This was the murder
          weapon in the Rose Gagliardi case.
          Now it's going to have a second life
          ... in the Jealous Newscaster Slayings.

He turns and points the knife at Lois.

                    BASCOM
          I wonder who'll cover the story.

He lifts the knife over his head. He glances back at
the camera.

                    BASCOM
          Your Honor! Not guilty by reason
          of insanity!

He lunges at Lois. Rudy grabs his arm but loses his
footing. Bascom fends him off with a couple of deftly
executed judo moves and sends him flying across the
room. Lois grabs Bascom by the wrist, sticks a foot
into his Adam's apple, smashes him against a wall and

117   CONTD (3)

brutally relieves him of his knife. He sinks to his
knees in front of her. She slaps him about the head.
Suddenly he dives for the knife, a few feet away on the
floor. She steps on his hand with her high-heeled
platform shoes. With his free hand, he trips her up
and she tumbles down on top of him. They continue to
struggle for the knife, rolling over and over in a heap
on the floor.

Rudy, by now, has recovered. He picks up a paperweight
from the desk and dances around the tangle of bodies on
the floor, looking for a sure target.

Bascom cries out in pain. Both of his hands leap to
his temple. The knife drops to the floor. Lois lets
go of him with a gasp.

                    LOIS
          Oh, ducky, did I hurt you?

Bascom staggers to his feet.

                    BASCOM
          No, I'll be okay.

He exits quickly, holding his head. Lois takes a step
after him, but Rudy holds her back. Shorty is on the
phone, dialing furiously.

                    RUDY
          Let him go. You'll only make
          it worse.

                    LOIS
          You think he'll be alright? You
          don't think he'd try anything ...
          you know, foolish? Do you?

Rudy shrugs.

                    SHORTY
               (into phone)
          Chief? This is Shorty. Hold up
          the lead story on the Six O-Clock
          News. I got some dynamite in the
          can and I'm bringin' it in right
          now ... I'll tell ya when I get
          there ... And by the way, Chief,
          Hunt won't be goin' on the air
          tonight. Yeah, you better get a
          replacement.

There is a scream from downstairs. Lois dashes out the
door, followed by Rudy.

118   EXT: GREENWICH VILLAGE STREET - DAY

Lois and Rudy come down the stairs that lead to the street. A few PEOPLE are at the foot of the stairs, comforting an HYSTERICAL WOMAN. There is blood on the sidewalk. Lois cries out.

> LOIS
> What happened?

> WOMAN
> He fell down the stairs. And he
> had a great cut, right here.
> (indicates temple)
> And there was blood everywhere.
> So much blood. It was horrible.
> Oh, it was horrible.

She breaks down. Lois and Rudy run down the street, following drops of blood.

119   INT: LOIS' APARTMENT - DAY

Lois and Rudy enter the apartment. The first thing they see is a great smear of blood on the white wall by the door that leads to the balcony. Lois rushes out on the balcony and looks down. On the pavement below, she can see Bascom's clothes scattered all over the place. But no Bascom.

She hears Rudy shout from inside the apartment.

> RUDY (O.S.)
> Lois! He's in here.

She rushes to Rudy, who is standing outside the bathroom door, knocking and jiggling the knob.

> RUDY
> Come on, Bascom! Open up!

> BASCOM
> (through door)
> Get out of here, Judas! I want
> my wife!

Lois leans her cheek against the door.

> LOIS
> I'm here, ducky.

> BASCOM
> (through door)
> Ducky, I'm sorry I got blood all
> over your nice white apartment.

119   CONTD

                    LOIS
          Never mind, ducky, we'll fix it
          up. Open the door, won't ya, huh?

                    BASCOM
          I don't think I can get up.

                    LOIS
               (to Rudy)
          Oh, Christ. Break it down.

                    RUDY
          Huh?

                    LOIS
          Never mind. I'll do it myself.

She flings her shoulder against the door and bounces
off. Rudy has a try, but also doesn't succeed. They
try it together and the door flies open.

Inside the bathroom, Bascom reclines naked in the tub,
with a large gash in his temple. Blood pumps from his
temple and pours down over the ridges of his face.
There is blood all over his face and the water in the
tub is tinted red. The tiled walls are smeared with
blood. Blood dribbles over the edge of the bathtub
and drips into pools on the floor. Bascom's skin has
a white pallor. He is very weak and has difficulty
speaking.

Lois and Rudy gasp at the sight. Rudy takes a step
towards the tub.

                    RUDY
          Come on, Bascom. Time to get up.

                    BASCOM
          Don't worry about me. Ducky'll
          take care of me.
               (he looks for her)
          Won't you, ducky?

Lois rushes away. Rudy grabs Bascom under the armpits
and tries to lift him out of the tub.

                    RUDY
          Come on, Bascom, you asshole!
          This is serious!

                    BASCOM
          First you want to fuck my wife.
          Now you want to save my life.
          Serious? This isn't serious.
          This is cheap melodrama.

119   CONTD (2)

Rudy struggles with the dead weight of Bascom's bleeding
naked body, getting blood all over his white suit. He
wrests it from the tub after a series of breath-stopping
near catastrophes.

Lois re-enters with some clothes for Bascom.

                    LOIS
          I called the ambulance.

                    BASCOM
          I don't need any ambulance. I
          don't need any hospital. I want
          you to take care of me, ducky.

Tears are streaming down Lois' cheeks. She tries to
get Bascom's arm into a shirtsleeve while Rudy props
him up.

                    LOIS
          I'll take care of you, ducky.

                    BASCOM
               (sighs)
          Not that shirt, ducky. Gimme the
          blue one.

Lois disappears back into the bedroom. Rudy wrestles
Bascom into a chair. Bascom looks drunkenly into
Rudy's eyes.

                    BASCOM
          I reckon I've put on a bloody bad
          show, old man. Sorry to have put
          you through it.

                    RUDY
          Shove it up your asshole, willya,
          Bascom?

He goes down on his knees and tries to get Bascom's
feet into pants.

                    BASCOM
          No, I mean it. You'll see. If
          I pull through this one, I'll make
          it up to you. I promise.

Lois returns with the blue shirt, still crying silently.
She gets Bascom into the shirt with little murmurs of
encouragement, like a mother dressing a child.

119   CONTD (3)

They hear a siren, coming closer. Rudy looks out the
window and sees the ambulance pulling up and the men
jumping out. The front doorbell rings. Lois rushes
across the room to buzz them in. At this moment, both
Lois and Rudy have their backs to Bascom. Bascom
lifts himself out of his chair, straightens up,
swoons, moans and begins to tumble toward the floor.
Lois turns and dives, catching his head in her hands
just inches before it was to hit the floor.

                    LOIS
               (crying)
          Ducky, don't be doing this. I'll
          do anything you want. I'll do any-
          thing you want.

                    BASCOM
          Will you, ducky?

                    LOIS
               (stroking his head)
          Yes, I will.

                    BASCOM
          Then, ducky ... ?

                    LOIS
          Yes, ducky.

                    BASCOM
          Suck my cock. Will you, ducky?

                    RUDY
          Oh, for Christ's sake!

The doorbell rings. Rudy goes off to answer it. He
admits the AMBULANCE CREW and leads them to Bascom.
The PUERTO RICAN ATTENDANT kneels down and takes
Bascom's pulse, while the BLACK DRIVER unfolds the
stretcher.

                    ATTENDANT
          Holy cojones! He's lost a lotta
          blood!

                                        CUT TO:

120   EXT: BUSY WEST SIDE STREET - EVENING

P.O.V. from inside the cab of the ambulance as it
tears down the street, sirens wailing, battling
traffic. Rudy is sitting in the passenger seat. He

120   CONTD

turns his head and looks behind him through the little
window to the rear section. Lois and the attendant
are hovering over Bascom, ministering to him.

121   INT: HOSPITAL EMERGENCY ROOM - NIGHT

A high, wide shot that shows the general chaos of the
emergency room. We see Bascom wheeled in, a distraught
Lois clutching his hand, and a perplexed Rudy, following along. They are piloted through a crush of PEOPLE,
mostly black and Puerto Rican, but which also includes
Shorty, the news cameraman, filming, and ROLF PETERS,
Bascom's harried replacement for the Eleven O'Clock
News. The HOSPITAL ATTENDANTS wheel Bascom through
another door at the far end of the room and prevent the
others from following.

122   INT: EMERGENCY ROOM - NIGHT

Back to eye level. The Puerto Rican ambulance guy is
poised on his way through the door.

                    LOIS
          Will he be alright?

                    AMBULANCE GUY
                 (melodramatically)
          I dunno. He's lost a lotta blood.

Peters, followed by Shorty, comes up and shoves a microphone into Lois' face.

                    LOIS
          When will I know something? You
          can tell me that at least.

                    ATTENDANT
          Oh, it'll be quite a while ...

                    RUDY
          Probably won't know anything 'til
          morning anyway, huh?

                    ATTENDANT
          Oh, no. I got no authority to keep
          him overnight. Either we fix him up
          and he go home tonight, or he go out
          in a sack tru de back door tonight.
          But he's goin' out tonight.

123   INT: EMERGENCY - NIGHT (THROUGH P.O.V. OF SHORTY'S
        CAMERA-TV IMAGE)

                        ROLF PETERS
            Hi, Lois. Sorry about old Bascom,
            but I gotta ask you a couple of
            questions for the old 11 O'Clock News.
            He wouldn't want us to miss a scoop
            like this, would he? Now, tell,
            what the heck happened here anyway?

                        LOIS
                    (sobbing)
            It was all an accident. Just a
            terrible, terrible accident ...

                        ROLF
            But, isn't it true that you stabbed
            him in self-defense when he attacked
            you with a knife upon discovering you
            in a compromising relationship with
            another man?

Rudy covers the shot.

                        RUDY
            Now wait a minute, you creep.

                                    CUT TO:

124   INT: GUNILLA'S PLACE - NIGHT
        CLOSE-UP - ANNIE

        watching this on the tube. Shocked to see Rudy. She
        is at Gunilla's place. Gunilla is also watching.

                        GUNILLA
            Isn't that Rudy?

                        ANNIE
            Ssh!

                        ROLF
                    (on TV, noticing Rudy)
            Ah, this must be the other man!
            How do you do, sir? What is your
            name?

                                    CUT TO:

125   TV IMAGE

                        RUDY
            Never mind that ...

125   CONTD

He starts leading Lois away. Rolf and Shorty pursue
them.

                    ROLF
          If I'm not mistaken, aren't you
          Rudy Frigidaire, the well-known
          uh ...

                    RUDY
          Songwriter? No, I'm not him.

Rudy spies an elevator door closing out of the corner
of his eye. He slips Lois through. The door closes,
leaving the news team out.

Rolf turns to the camera.

                    ROLF
          This is Rolf Peters at Metropolitan
          Hospital. Back to you, Mark.

                                        CUT TO:

126   INT: GUNILLA'S APARTMENT - NIGHT

Annie is distraught.

                    MARK
          We'll have another report on the
          tragic injury of our own Bascom Hunt
          at the end of the program.

Annie turns off TV.

127   INT: SUB-BASEMENT - NIGHT

The elevator doors open onto the sub-basement, a maze
of corridors, lined with pipes, wires and humming
machinery. Rudy pulls Lois around a couple of corners
and behind something picturesque, to hide. They catch
their breaths and listen. Lois lets out a deep sigh
and lays her head on Rudy's chest. Rudy wraps his
arms around her and strokes her back.

Lois sobs quietly. Rudy lets his hand stray down to
her flanks and, meeting no resistance, strokes them.
Gradually, he moves his hand down to the hem of her
skirt, then under it and up again. He tightens his
grip and begins to move, ever so slightly, against
her. She remains limp in his arms. He slips four
fingers under the elastic of her panties and slowly
begins to explore her crotch. Her sobbing becomes
more rhythmical, and she begins moving too, and grip-
ping him tighter. Emboldened, Rudy works her panties

127   CONTD

down around her knees again, fumbles with his fly,
lifts her skirt and slips it to her.

Rudy groans as he enters. Lois looks up, surprised and
outraged.

                    LOIS
          What are you doing?

                    RUDY
          Lois. Please. Shh.

Lois struggles with him.

                    LOIS
          Get that thing out of me!

Rudy puts a hand over her mouth and listens. Lois
stops strugggling for a minute and listens too. They
hear running footsteps, people searching for them. Lois
looks Rudy in the eye defiantly. He looks back into her
eyes, and pushes himself deeper into her. She gasps
but he doesn't take his hand away from her mouth. He
moves more urgently in her and she moves more urgently
against him. They are fucking and fighting, silently,
at the same time.

They make love to a climax, then break apart, leaning
up against pipes, catching their breaths. After an
interval, Rudy looks up at Lois and smiles. She belts
him across the face with her right. Rudy goes down for
the count. Lois storms away. Rudy picks himself up
and calls after her.

                    RUDY
          But, Lois! You did it with Annie!
          Doesn't that count?

                    LOIS
              (over her shoulder)
          You low son of a bitch.

                    RUDY
          But, Lois ... !

                                        CUT TO:

128   INT: EMERGENCY - NIGHT

Lois staggers through the door to the stairway. As she
comes out, she is greeted by Bascom, who has a big
bandage over his temple and still looks a little pale,
but is otherwise in tiptop shape.

                    BASCOM
          There you are, ducky! I've been
          looking all over for you.

She throws herself into his arms.

                    LOIS
          Oh, ducky, are you alright?

                    BASCOM
          Never felt better. Look.

He whistles a tune and tap dances a few steps. She
stops him and starts to lead him away.

                    LOIS
          None of that, now. I'm gonna take
          you home and take care of you.

                    BASCOM
          That's my girl. That's what I like
          to hear.

Rudy emerges from the stairway. Bascom throws his arms
around him.

                    BASCOM
          Rudy! You saved my life!

                    RUDY
              (surprised)
          Bascom! How do you feel?

                    BASCOM
          Like a million bucks!

Rudy looks enquiringly to Lois, but she refuses to meet
his glance.

                    RUDY
          Hey, that's great.

                    BASCOM
          I owe it all to you. You saved
          my life!

                    RUDY
              (nervous)
          Aw, no...

Bascom puts his arm around Lois and pulls her to him.

128   CONTD (2)

                    BASCOM
          You and my little ducky here.

Lois smiles docilely up at him. Bascom caresses her
flanks.

                    BASCOM
                 (serious)
          Hey, man, I owe ya.

                    RUDY
          Aw, c'mon, Bascom.

                    BASCOM
          I'm serious, man. And I'm gonna
          make it up to you. I swear. Bascom
          Hunt takes care of his friends.

                    RUDY
          Shit, Bascom, you don't owe me any-
          thing.

As he talks, Bascom lets his hand slip down below the
hem of Lois' skirt. He strokes the back of her leg
and begins to slip between her thighs.

                    BASCOM
          You don't even have to say anything
          about this afternoon. I forgive ya.
          We'll just forget the whole thing ...

Suddenly a look of horror comes over his face. He looks
down at his hand between Lois' legs. Rudy and Lois
follow his eyes with theirs. Bascom pulls his hand
away from Lois' thigh. It is covered with Rudy's come.

                    BASCOM
                 (screams)
          JUDASSSS!!!!

                    RUDY
          Well, see you around.

He splits. Bascom starts after him. Lois holds him
back. He turns to her.

                    BASCOM
          JEZEBEL! While I was on my death
          bed, you were down in the basement...!

                    LOIS
          He forced me! He raped me! I swear!

129   INT: ANNIE'S - NIGHT

Annie's new apartment is a small, shabby, dark walkup
that faces onto a shaftway. It is two small rooms and
a kitchen that open on to each other. There is no
furniture except for a mattress on the floor, and a
linoleum barstool in the kitchen. Jesse is asleep on
the mattress.

Annie is bleaching her hair in front of a mirror. She
does it with anxious strokes. It stings, and she
winces from time to time.

Waiting for it to take effect, she examines her face
minutely in the mirror. She finds a blackhead and
meticulously pops it. Then she finds more and pops
more. Her face becomes pocked with red blotches. Tears
stream down her cheeks.

130   EXT: 86th STREET AND BROADWAY - DAY

Annie and Jesse emerge from the subway station.

131   EXT: RED PAINT DAY CARE CENTER - DAY

Annie and Jesse go up the steps to the Center.

132   INT: RED PAINT - DAY

Annie drops Jesse into the chaos of screaming children
and beats a hasty retreat.

133   INT: LIVING ROOM-BEDROOM - DAY

Rudy is asleep in a tangle of covers. The place is a
mess. The bed has become the central focus of the
room: the TV set at arm's reach, a side table strewn
with leftover Burger King wrappers and Sarah Lee
Brownies tins, newspapers, headphones, dope paraphernalia. The room is quiet. The dogs are asleep curled
up at the foot of the bed.

We hear the sound of a key in the lock, and the door
opening. The dogs rouse themselves and go to investi-
gate. Rudy opens one eye to see Annie tiptoeing into
the foyer. The dogs are all over her, whimpering. She
is whispering to them.

                    ANNIE
                 (whispering)
          Yes. Hello, darlings. Yes. I'm
          happy to see you, too. Shhh. Don't
          wake Daddy.

133   CONTD

She goes to the hall closet, burrows in among a vast
assortment of junk on a shelf and pulls out a tiny
packet, wrapped in tinfoil.

She tiptoes toward the Living Room-Bedroom. Rudy closes
his eye. She surveys the mess and Rudy in the midst of
it. She reaches down to his bedside table. He opens
his eyes, grabs her arm and pulls her down beside him
on the bed.

              ANNIE
          (surprised)
    Hello, darling.

Rudy kisses her. She kisses him back. He has his hand
under her shirt.

              ANNIE
    I just stopped in to pick something
    up. I didn't mean to wake you ...

He kisses her again. She wraps her arms around him.
His hand goes between her legs. Her hand drifts down
along his back to the crack of his ass. She speaks
without disengaging her lips:

              ANNIE
    Mmmm. No knickers, eh?

He pulls her panties down around her knees. She takes
hold of his dick.

              ANNIE
    Oooh, he's big today, ain't 'e?

They touch, feel, maul, massage each other passionately,
neither wanting to take the time to remove Annie's
clothes.

              ANNIE
    Put it in me now. I've got to have
    it.

He climbs on top of her and puts it to her.

              ANNIE
          (whispers)
    Let's not do it on the bed. I
    hate this bed.

They slip off the bed, onto the floor. They heave at
each other in a kind of savage urgency, ending up partly
under the couch.

133   CONTD (2)

                          ANNIE
            I'd forgotten what it feels like.
            Oh, my dear!

Annie works her lips along the ridge of Rudy's jaw to
his ear. She sticks her tongue in his ear. She whispers in his ear.

                          ANNIE
                     (whispers)
            Don't come inside me. I haven't
            got my diaphragm.

                                        CUT TO:

134   INT: RUDY'S BATHROOM - DAY

Rudy is sitting on the throne, still naked. Annie comes
in, rearranging her clothes. She strikes a pose in front
of Rudy.

                          ANNIE
            Notice anything?

Rudy is bewildered. He looks her over up and down.

                          RUDY
            Is that a new dress or something?

Annie looks hurt. Suddenly, Rudy notices Annie's
bleached hair. He is dumbstruck. His jaw hangs open.

                          ANNIE
            You hate it.

                          RUDY
            No, no, it's great ...

Annie bursts into tears, slumps against him and cries
on his chest.

                          ANNIE
            Oh, Rudy, I wanted to do some-
            thing.

135   INT: FOYER - DAY

Rudy wanders out of the bathroom to find Annie has
packed some odds and ends into a shopping bag. She
comes back out of the living-bedroom with a plant and
a picture.

135   CONTD

                    ANNIE
          This was always my picture. Mendy
          gave it to me.

                    RUDY
          Take it. Take it.

                    ANNIE
          And this poor little baby ...
               (indicating plant)
          ... is dying.

                    RUDY
          All the plants are dying. Every-
          thing. You brought us all here, the
          plants, the animals, the fish, Jesse:
          even the lodgers, you brought us all
          together, and now you leave us all
          to fend for ourselves.

                    ANNIE
          Oh, Rudy, don't be so maudlin.

                    RUDY
          Sorry.
               (pause)
          Having fun with your new life?

                    ANNIE
          Yes, sometimes.

                    RUDY
               (choked up)
          Annie, I'm having a rotten time.

                    ANNIE
          Are you, darling?

                    RUDY
          Yes.

                    ANNIE
          I'm so sorry, darling. I'm so, so
          sorry. You're so dear to me.

                    RUDY
          Yes.

                    ANNIE
          But I must do this or I shall die.
          It's my last chance. I've never
          been on my own. All my life I was
               (MORE)

135   CONTD (2)

                    ANNIE (Contd)
          always with someone, or attached
          to someone. I sponged off of their
          lives. I never even had a job
          before I met you. So, now's my
          last chance to find out.

                    RUDY
          Find out what?

                    ANNIE
          If I'm a person.

                    RUDY
          But I feel like half a person with-
          out you. I feel like one of my vital
          organs has been removed.

                    ANNIE
          Do you, darling? So do I sometimes.

                    RUDY
          Then come back to me, Annie.

                    ANNIE
          I can't.

                    RUDY
          But why not?

                    ANNIE
          I just can't.

                    RUDY
          What is it you want?

                    ANNIE
          I don't know what I want! I just
          know what I don't want.

Annie puts her arms around Rudy's neck.

                    ANNIE
          Darling, I've got to go. I've
          left my new address on the table.

She kisses him.

                    ANNIE
          It's been lovely seeing you, darling.

                    RUDY
          Will I see you again?

135   CONTD (3)

                        ANNIE
          Of course. I can't imagine life
          without you. I guess you can only
          meet up with another person every
          so often, even if they are the person
          you love most.

                        RUDY
          Will you come and stay with me every
          once in a while?

                        ANNIE
          Well, now that I've got my own place,
          you can come and stay with me. I
          hate this house. But I'd love you to
          ask me out for a date.

                        RUDY
          How about tonight?

                        ANNIE
          Not tonight. I've got a ...

Rudy looks pained.

                        ANNIE
          Look, let me call you. As soon as
          I get a phone. 'Bye, darling.
          I've got to dash.

She picks up her shopping bag, gives him a peck and disappears out the door.

                                        CUT TO:

136   EXT: 84th STREET & BROADWAY - TELEPHONE BOOTH - DAY

Rudy talking on the telephone.

                        BERNIE (V.O.)
          Miss Lang's office.

                        RUDY
          It's Rudy, Bernie. Lemme talk to
          Lois.

                        BERNIE
          Hold on.

There is a click, then a pause, then Bernie comes back
on.

136   CONTD

                    BERNIE
          She's not in. May I have her
          call you?

                    RUDY
          Come on, Bernie. Lemme talk to
          her.

                    BERNIE
          She'll have to call you.

                    RUDY
          Bernie! It's me! Rudy!

                    BERNIE
          She won't talk to you, Rudy. I'm
          sorry.

Rudy hangs up.

137   EXT: 84th STREET & BROADWAY - DAY

A very neatly-groomed young man stands on the corner
with a clipboard. He accosts Rudy as he passes with
the dogs, carrying a shopping bag.

                    RONNIE REDUNZO
          Got a minute?

Rudy stops, shifts his package, fumbles in his pocket
and pulls out a pack of matches.

                    REDUNZO
          No, I said have you got a minute?

                    RUDY
          Oh, a minute! What for?

Redunzo consults his clipboard.

                    REDUNZO
          Are you worried about rising costs?

                    RUDY
          You bet.

                    REDUNZO
          Worried about losing your job?

                    RUDY
          I haven't got a job.

                    REDUNZO
          Well, are you just plain worried?

137   CONTD

                    RUDY
          Well, I guess you could say so.

                    REDUNZO
          There is a solution.

                    RUDY
          There is?

                    REDUNZO
          There is a program. People are on
          it. It's called Scientology and
          Dianetics.

                    RUDY
          Oh, I've seen you guys. You're
          right across the street, right?

                    REDUNZO
          Would you like to come up to our
          center? We'll give you a free
          personality profile.

                    RUDY
          What'll it do for me?

                    REDUNZO
          It will teach you how to change.

                    RUDY
          Change to what?

                    REDUNZO
          Hey, all I know is I'm changing
          and it's really great. It's a
          process, man. Where we end up is
          beside the point.

                    RUDY
          Well, when you get there let me
          know how it turned out and maybe
          I'll join you.

138   INT: LOBBY - RUDY'S PLACE - DAY

Roseanne and her poodle are waiting by the elevator.
Rudy and the dogs enter from the vestibule.

                    ROSEANNE
          Hi, Rudy.

                    RUDY
               (coming out of a fog)
          Oh, hi, Roseanne.

138   CONTD

He crosses to his door and fumbles with the key.

                    ROSEANNE
          Where's Annie? I haven't seen her
          in donkey's years.

                    RUDY
          Oh, she's ...

His voice breaks and tears well up in his eyes.

                    RUDY
          ... she doesn't live here anymore.

Roseanne has a pained look on her face.

                    ROSEANNE
          Oh, I'm sorry ... I didn't ...

                    RUDY
          No, no. It's nothing. I'm sorry.
          It's ...

He rushes into the house and slams the door. Unfortu-
nately, he has left Kirsten outside. He opens the
door. She slips in. He glances sheepishly at Roseanne. He closes the door.

139   INT: ANNIE'S - NIGHT

Rudy knocks on the door. It opens with the force of his
fist. Through the open door he sees Annie, talking
frantically on the phone, Jesse standing in a corner
crying, and a quiet 13-YEAR-OLD-GIRL sitting in a
chair, a little dumbfounded.

Annie waves Rudy in. The girl looks up at him.

                    RUDY
          Hi. I'm Rudy.

The girl doesn't reply. Rudy bends down and picks up
Jesse, who continues to cry.

                    RUDY
          What's the story, Jerry?

                    JESSE
               (hits Rudy)
          No!

139   CONTD

                    ANNIE
              (into phone)
     I have to go get it first! Then
     we'll come right over. I promise
     ... Well, when will you be there?
     ... No, how can you call me? I
     won't be anywhere ...

She motions to Rudy that she needs a pencil. Rudy
searches around the table and finally finds her one.

                    ANNIE
     O.K. What's the number ...
              (she writes it on wall)
     ... Right. I'll call you there,
     say, in about an hour.

She hangs up.

                    ANNIE
     Hi.

                    RUDY
     Hi.

They sort of make tentative moves to embrace, but then
don't.

                    RUDY
     Who was that?

                    ANNIE
     Oh, somebody you don't know.
     Have you met Rhoda?

                    RUDY
     Sort of.

They both smile at Rhoda. Rhoda looks down at the
floor.

                    ANNIE
     Well, she's kind of shy.

Jesse has calmed down and is only sniffling.

                    RUDY
              (to Jesse)
     Feel better?

Jesse nods his head.

139   CONTD (2)

                    JESSE
          And **all** you sleeping downtown
          tonight?

Rudy looks hesitantly over to Annie.

                    RUDY
          Well, we'll see ...

Annie comes over.

                    ANNIE
          You can, if you want to.

                    RUDY
          Well, only if you want me to.

                    ANNIE
          I'd like you to, if you'd like
          to.

                    RUDY
          I'd like to if you'd like to have
          me.

                    ANNIE
          I would ...

Her voice drops to a whisper.

                    ANNIE
          But I don't think we can fuck ...
          I think I'm getting me monthlies.

                    RUDY
               (disappointed)
          Oh, that doesn't matter.

Annie puts her arms around the two of them (Jesse and
Rudy.)

                    ANNIE
          So we'll all be together tonight.

                    JESSE
          Yaaay.

Rudy carries Jesse to his bed, plonks him down and
starts to tuck him in.

                    JESSE
          But daddy ...

139   CONTD (3)

                    RUDY
          What?

                    JESSE
          Are you gonna be here in the
          morning when I wake up?

                    RUDY
          What did I just tell ya?

                    JESSE
          You promise?

                    RUDY
          Promise ...

                    ANNIE
               (who has been talking
                to Rhoda)
          Come on, we have to go.

He bends down and kisses Jesse.

                    RUDY
          Off to dreamland.

                    JESSE
          But I don't want to dream.

                    RUDY
          Well, then, off to oblivion.

Annie is already at the door with her coat on.

                    ANNIE
          Quick!

                    JESSE
          What's oblivion?

                    RUDY
          No more talking.

                    JESSE
          Who's gonna sing me a song?

                    RUDY
          I am. Tomorrow. When you get
          up. Now, shut up and go to sleep.

He kisses him again and walks toward the door.

139   CONTD (4)

                    JESSE
          But Mommy didn't kiss me goodnight.

Annie sighs, crosses to Jesse's bed, kisses him.

                    ANNIE
          Goodnight, pumpkin.

She dashes out with Rudy, before Jesse can speak.

140   INT: SUBWAY STATION - NIGHT

Annie and Rudy squeeze through the turnstile on one
token. They do it in a way that suggests it is a
normal procedure for them.

                    RUDY
               You haven't organized a whole
               evening of running around, have
               you?

                    ANNIE
               Just a couple of things I've got
               to do. I thought it would be
               nice. We'll stop at Mendy's and
               get a snort. Then I just have
               one stop to drop something off,
               and then we can go to Mel's party.

                    RUDY
               You don't really want to go to that
               party, do you?

                    ANNIE
               Why not?

                    RUDY
               Well, Lois is going to be there,
               for one. Don't you think it'll
               be kind of awkward?

                    ANNIE
               Oh, don't be such a stiff. Has
               she gone back to Bascom?

The train comes barrelling into the station.

141   EXT: MENDY'S - NIGHT

As Annie and Rudy enter Mendy's building, we see a
couple of empty police cars double parked outside.

142   INT: HALLWAY - MENDY'S - NIGHT

Mendy opens the door a crack with the chain on. Seeing that it's Rudy and Annie, he closes the door,
removes the chain, and opens again.

                    MENDY
               (frantic)
          Thank heavens you're here! Come
          in.

He hurries them in, looks apprehensively up and down
the hallway and closes the door.

143   INT: MENDY'S - DAY

He closes the door and fastens several locks.

                    ANNIE
          What's the matter?

                    MENDY
          Oh, my dear. There are cops all
          over the place.

                    ANNIE
               (panic)
          What?

She starts for the door.

                    MENDY
          Don't go, please! I beg of you!

                    RUDY
          Mendy. What's going on?

                    MENDY
          Mrs. Incza, the old lady from
          upstairs just called me. The
          cops are up there. They got a
          report there was a man with a
          gun on the roof.

                    ANNIE
          A man with a gun!?

                    RUDY
          The one who's been threatening you?

                    MENDY
          Well, I can assure you, my dear,
          that I didn't go have a look.
               (to Annie)
          I've got a sharp stabbing pain,
          right here.

143   CONTD

                    ANNIE
          Angina pectoris.

                    MENDY
          No!

                    RUDY
          Oh, come on.

Mendy is hurrying around the tiny apartment collecting
remnants of his drug collection from a variety of
unlikely places. There is a cluster of baggies, tinfoil, pill bottles, pay envelopes, etc., on the couch.
Mendy reaches under the couch.

                    RUDY
          What are you doing?

                    MENDY
          I'm flushing everything.

                    RUDY & ANNIE
                 (together)
          Mendy, no!

He pulls an oblong cardboard box out from under the
sofa, opens it, pulls out a children's size, gray
enema bag, unscrews the lid, and extracts a trans-
parent plastic bag, chock full of white powder.

                    RUDY
          My God!   Is that all cocaine?

                    MENDY
          You better believe it.

                    ANNIE
          And you're going to flush all of
          that down the toilet?

                    MENDY
          Not before all three of us have
          more cocaine stuffed up our noses
          than you ever imagined three people
          could ...

He reaches behind him into a drawer and pulls out a
teaspoon.

                    RUDY & ANNIE
                 (in unison)
          A teaspoon!

143   CONTD (2)

He dips the teaspoon into the plastic bag, pulls out a
breathtaking amount of coke and proceeds to take
breath. He passes the spoon -- very carefully -- to
Annie. He talks very fast.

> MENDY
> Don't spill any. They mustn't be
> able to find a trace. Mrs. Incza
> said they're going around inter-
> viewing all the tenants.

Annie takes a big hit of the coke.

> RUDY
> But, Mendy, that doesn't mean
> they'll search your apartment.
> They'll probably just ask you
> if you heard anything unusual ...

Annie passes the spoon to Rudy. He bobbles it, giving
both a heart attack, but saves it at the last minute.

> MENDY
> (hysterical)
> But I KNOW I'LL BREAK! I just
> know it. If I have to look them
> in the eyes, I'll go all to pieces
> if I have a drop of the stuff in
> the house ...

Suddenly Mendy moans and falls back on the sofa.

> ANNIE
> Help!

This is just at the moment that Rudy is lifting the
spoon to his nose. In all the excitement, he acci-
dentally breathes out instead of in, blowing a puff
of coke into the air. Quick-thinking Annie cups her
hands under Rudy's chin and manages to capture most
of it. By now it has become apparent that Mendy's
moans are moans of ecstasy, and so there is no further
need for alarm on the part of Rudy and Annie. Annie
licks the white dust from her palms and fingers, while
Rudy proceeds to take a couple of deep snorts. He
replaces the spoon in the bag. Annie suddenly swoons,
with a rapturous cry.

> ANNIE
> Ohhh, heeeeeelp ...

Rudy looks at the two prostrate bodies with dismay.

143   CONTD (3)

                    RUDY
          Hey, come on, you creeps, what's
          happening?

Mendy suddenly sits straight up, eyes still closed.

                    MENDY
          I've got it!

                    RUDY
          What? ... Who ... ?

He, too, passes out. Mendy speaks.

                    MENDY
          You can do it! You can take my
          stash!

He opens his eyes to see the two of them out cold.

                    MENDY
          Wake up, you kumquats! This is my
          lifestyle we're talking about!

Annie comes out of her rush.

                    ANNIE
          What?

                    MENDY
          You've got to take my stash. You
          can get down the fire escape and
          grab a cab on Madison. Here, I'll
          give you the cab fare.

He hands her a ten spot.

Rudy revives.

                    ANNIE
          Oh, Mendy ...

                    RUDY
          Huh?

                    MENDY
              (a bit hysterical)
          It's gotta be you. I can't leave.
          I've got to be here when they get
          here, because if I'm not here,
          they'll get the super to let them
          in with the passkey, and when they
                    (MORE)

143   CONTD (4)

                         MENDY (Contd)
              find all this homosexual literature,
              and all this homosexual art, and
              all this homosexual sensibility!
              See, this way, if I'm here, I can
              just talk to them at the door, and
              I can sound pretty straight when I
              want to. Can't I? They hate
              perverts.

                         RUDY
              Huh?

                         ANNIE
                  (to Rudy)
              We're taking his stash.

                         RUDY
              What?!

There is a loud knock on the door. Everyone freezes.
Another knock.

                         MENDY
                  (trying a deep voice)
              Who is it?

                         ROSENGARTEN
              Officers Rosengarten and Ricovici.
              Wonder if we could talk to you for
              a minute?

Mendy begins madly stuffing his various dopes in a
"Wilson for Governor" shopping bag.

                         MENDY
                  (still deep voice)
              Why, certainly, officers, just
              let me get dressed.

He presses the bag on Rudy and pushes them both to the
window.

                         RUDY
              But, Norman ...

                         MENDY
              Don't argue. You've got to do it.
              Can't you see ... ?

He opens the window and forces them out onto the fire
escape. There is another knock on the door.

143   CONTD (5)

                    ROSENGARTEN
          Mr. Randolph!

                    MENDY
               (deep voice)
          Coming.
               (to Rudy and Annie)
          Go quickly! You'll hear from
          me in a couple of days.

Rudy starts to speak, but Mendy shuts the window and
turns away.

144   EXT: MENDY'S FIRE ESCAPE - NIGHT

They see Mendy check himself out in the mirror, then
proceed to the door. He opens the door just enough
to stick his head out. Rudy stuffs the shopping bag
in his jacket and starts down the fire escape. Annie
comes after him, having difficulty with her platform
shoes.

                    ANNIE
          Isn't this exciting!

145   INT: TAXI - NIGHT

Annie is going through the contents of the shopping
bag, sniffing and tasting different things.

                    RUDY
          What are you doing?

                    ANNIE
               (whispering)
          I'm looking for the Quaaludes for
          Ruby. That's what we went to
          Mendy's for.

                    RUDY
          Who's Ruby?

                    ANNIE
          Ruby Red.

                    RUDY
          The singer?

                    ANNIE
          Ever heard her?

145   CONTD

                    RUDY
          Heard of her.

                    ANNIE
          I'll introduce you. She's fan-
          tastic.

                    RUDY
          Look, Annie, after we take care
          of this little errand, is there
          any chance that I can get you
          alone for a few minutes?

                    ANNIE
          What's the matter with right now?

She puts a reassuring hand on his thigh, while she
continues through the shopping bag with the other.

                    RUDY
          Somehow, I imagined a more romantic
          setting.

                    ANNIE
          Well, I've just got to deliver these
          to Ruby. She'll never speak to me
          again if I don't.

She pulls a finger out of the bag. It's been dipped
in white powder. She holds it up to her nose, takes
a sniff, then holds it up to Rudy's nose.

                    ANNIE
          Take a hit. I think it's MDA.

Rudy snorts. Annie licks the remains off her finger.
She puts down the bag.

                    ANNIE
          It's very sexy stuff.

                    RUDY
          I feel like we haven't talked to
          each other in weeks.

                    ANNIE
          I call you all the time!

                    RUDY
          Yeah, but I mean really talk.
          You're always in a phone booth,
          or at work, or in a hurry, and
          it's always about Jesse's under-
          wear or something.

145   CONTD (2)

Annie puts one arm around Rudy's neck; the other hand
caresses his crotch.

> ANNIE
> Oh, darling, are you feeling
> unloved?

She kisses him on the neck. Rudy sighs.

> RUDY
> I was just wondering what your
> current thoughts were. About
> life and things like that.

Annie shifts herself, sinks to her knees on the floor
of the taxi, facing him.

> ANNIE
> Oh, let's not have another dreary
> conversation. Let's have fun.

She kisses him on the lips and begins to fiddle with
his belt.

> RUDY
> Aw, Anniee

> ANNIE
> Shhh.

She kisses him again; a long one; while her hands
unbuckle his belt, undo his button, unzip his fly
and fish out his dick.

> RUDY
> (shocked)
> Annie!

> ANNIE
> Shhh.

She leans back and looks at his dick, caressing it
with both hands, inspecting it.

> ANNIE
> You know, this is the only dick I
> ever get to see anymore.

> RUDY
> Really?

> ANNIE
> Yeah. I've gone off men.

145   CONTD (3)

                    RUDY
          Uh.

                    ANNIE
          Except you, of course, my darling.

                    RUDY
          Let's tell the driver to take us
          back to your place. I want you.

Rudy removes his dick from her hands and begins to tuck
himself in and zip himself up.

                    ANNIE
          Come on, darling, we're almost
          there.

                    RUDY
          And then straight home. O.K.?

                              CUT TO:

146   EXT: CBGB'S - NIGHT

The cab pulls up outside CBGB's a Soho nitery. Rudy
and Annie get out of the cab. As they start for the
door, Rudy grabs Annie by the elbow.

                    RUDY
          I want to get in, get on with it,
          get it over with, and get out.
          Get it?

                    ANNIE
          Got it.

                    RUDY
          Good.

They enter.

147   INT: CBGB'S - NIGHT

The interior of CBGB's is long, narrow and dark. There
is a stage at the far end. The place is crowded with
the pansexual crowd. They are there to hear Ruby Red.
She and her group are just beginning a number as Annie
and Rudy walk in.

(RUBY RED is an electrifying singer. Her songs deal
with the dark side of things: lust, violence, magic,
excess ... Some people describe her as a cross between
Bob Dylan and Mick Jagger.)

147   CONTD

As she sings, Annie makes her way up toward the side
of the stage, Rudy in her wake. Many of the people
whom they pass or brush up against recognize Annie:
One gives her a smile, one gives her a pat, somebody
points her out to somebody else and whispers something.
They all look at Rudy with curiosity. He feels intimi-
dated.

                    RUDY
              (whispers to Annie)
          They look at me the way Arabs
          look at pork.

                    ANNIE
              (whispers to Rudy)
          Isn't she fabulous?

Rudy nods.

                    ANNIE
              (whispers)
          She's the absolute star of the
          scene down here. I think she
          likes me. So keep your mitts
          off. She's my latest project.

                    RUDY
          Is she just a dyke? Or is she
          bi-sexual too?

                    ANNIE
          Say pan-sexual. Bi- is so racist.

She squeezes his hand.

                    ANNIE
          Come on, darling, relax. I wish
          you'd try it with a man sometime.
          You might like it. And it would
          make things so much easier between
          us.

Ruby Red breaks into an extended, pulsating finale to
her song. The crowd throbs along with her. She
finishes to wild applause. She sees Annie as she
steps off the stage and greets her with an embrace.
She ducks backstage, beckoning Annie to follow.
Annie pulls Rudy after her.

148   INT: CBGB'S BACKSTAGE - NIGHT

Safely inside, Ruby Red turns to Annie.

148   CONTD

                    RUBY
          Did you bring them? I really
          need a down.

She is pouring with sweat. Other people are crowding
in. She notices Rudy. Annie hands her a little bag.

                    ANNIE
          Here it is. And it's dynamite.

                    RUBY
          Who's this?

                    ANNIE
          This is Rudy ... Frigidaire.

                    RUBY
          The songwriter?

                    RUDY
          I thought you were terrific.

                    RUBY
          Oh, yeah?

                    RUDY
          Yeah.

                    RUBY
              (to Annie)
          And what is he to you?

                    ANNIE
          Oh, Rudy? He's ...

                    RUDY
              (cuts in)
          Ex-co-person.

                    RUBY
              (to Annie)
          What are you? A songwriter
          collector?

                    RUDY
          Now, wait a minute!

                    ANNIE
          Don't say anything, Rudy. She's
          very temperamental.

                    RUDY
          I was just ...

148   CONTD (2)

                         RUBY
                    (to Rudy)
               Go back to Tin Pan Alley, will ya,
               buster? I don't remember inviting
               you back here.

                         RUDY
               I'm with her.

                         ANNIE
               Ruby, listen ...

                         RUBY
               Go on. Make like there's an egg
               in your shoe and beat it!

She gives Rudy a shove. Rudy puts up his dukes.

                         RUDY
               Come on! You wanna act like a
               man? Then put up your dukes like
               a man!

                         ANNIE
                    (terribly embarrassed)
               Rudy! Please!
                    (to Ruby)
               Don't pay any attention to him,
               Ruby. He's just geezed to the gow,
               that's all.

A large bull dyke grabs Rudy in a half-Nelson from
behind. Rudy breaks the hold, turns around and
flattens the dyke. Ruby jumps on his back and begins
to pull at his hair. Everybody, dykes, transvestites,
the whole pansexual scene, descends on Rudy. A few
stray straights back him up. There is a heavy brawl
which ends with Rudy being forcibly ejected from CBGB's
by two hefty transvestites.

149   EXT: CBGB'S - NIGHT

They throw Rudy out on the street, dust off their
hands, straighten their skirts, and go back inside.
Rudy picks himself up, checks himself out, looks
around, finds himself alone and barges back into the
club.

150   INT: CBGB'S - NIGHT

Rudy bursts in through the door, pushes his way through
the crowd, grabs Annie away from the throng and out the
door again.

151   EXT: CBGB'S - NIGHT

When they get outside, Annie extricates herself from
Rudy's grip. She is crying.

                    ANNIE
          How could you humiliate me in
          front of all those people?
          They were going to be my friends.
          They liked me.

Rudy grabs Annie and kisses her hard. She pulls away,
doesn't let him kiss her. She walks off. Rudy
follows.

                    RUDY
          What about me? Am I some kind of
          piece of shit to be walked on by
          a bunch of perverts?

                    ANNIE
          How do you expect me to take you
          into my life if you're going to
          constantly pull this macho possess-
          ive bullshit?

Rudy grabs her again. Annie turns. They look at each
other. They embrace. They hold each other tight. They
both have tears in their eyes. Rudy slips his hand
under Annie's skirt.

                    RUDY
          Let's go back to your place. Don't
          you want me any more?

                    ANNIE
          Why does sex always have to be the
          issue?! I'm fed up with sex! Dykes
          are just the same. Everybody's
          always at me about sex. Why can't
          everybody just leave me alone?

Annie sighs, steps out in the street and hails a cab.

                    ANNIE
          Come on. Let's go home.

The cab pulls up. Rudy opens the door. Annie gets
in, but Rudy doesn't follow.

                    ANNIE
          Aren't you coming?

Rudy shakes his head. Tears come to Annie's eyes.

                    ANNIE
          Rudy, can't you just love me
          for what I am?

151   CONTD

                              RUDY
                    What are you?

He closes the taxi door. Rudy reaches an arm through
the window and caresses her cheek.

                              ANNIE
                    Come home with me. We can do
                    it, if it's so important to you.

                              RUDY
                    Naw, I'm gonna go home and jerk
                    off in peace.

He turns and walks away. The cab drives off.

                                        FADE OUT.

FADE IN:

152   INT: LOIS' - SUNDOWN

Lois picks up the phone and dials Annie's number.

153   INT: RUDY'S - NIGHT

Rudy picks up the phone and dials Lois' number.

154   INT: LOIS' - NIGHT

Lois hears a ring at Annie's.

155   INT: ANNIE'S - NIGHT

The phone rings in the empty apartment.

156   INT: RUDY'S - NIGHT

Rudy gets a busy signal. He hangs up.

157   INT: ANNIE'S - NIGHT

We see the door and hear a key fumbling with the lock.
Annie bursts into the apartment.

158   INT: LOIS' - NIGHT

Lois hangs up.

159   INT: ANNIE'S - NIGHT

Annie grabs the phone. She hears the click of Lois
hanging up.

160   INT: LOIS' - NIGHT

Lois starts to dial Rudy's number.

161   INT: RUDY'S - NIGHT

Rudy picks up the phone and starts to dial Annie's
number.

162   INT: ANNIE'S - NIGHT

Annie is changing blouses. She grabs something from
the table and dashes out the door.

163   INT: RUDY'S - NIGHT

Rudy hears the ring in Annie's apartment.

164   INT: HALLWAY OUTSIDE ANNIE'S - NIGHT

Annie hears the phone ringing. She fumbles with her
keys.

165   INT: RUDY'S - NIGHT

Rudy hears the ring at Annie's.

166   INT: LOIS' - NIGHT

Lois hears a busy signal and hangs up.

167   INT: RUDY'S - NIGHT

Rudy hangs up.

168   INT: ANNIE'S - NIGHT

Annie just gets the door open as the phone stops
ringing.

169   INT: LOIS' - NIGHT

Lois walks out onto her little terrace. She stares
at the windows of the big building across the way.

170   INT: ANNIE'S - NIGHT

Annie takes a deep breath and lets it out with a sigh.
She stares across the shaftway into a kitchen, where
a Puerto Rican family are arguing.

171   INT: RUDY'S - NIGHT

Rudy sinks onto the couch and looks at the TV. There
is a wide shot of rolling prairie, with the sun

171   CONTD

setting over the mountains in the background. A title
is supered:

"THE END"

FADE TO BLACK.

<u>THE END</u>

www.ingramcontent.com/pod-product-compliance
Lightning Source LLC
Chambersburg PA
CBHW070850160726
48004CB00003B/1007